PRAISE

"After reading the memoir, you will not want to have lived the author's life, but you will want to have her ability to recall and formulate memories into words. For most of us, memories are only random fragments in the brain. For Iboja Wandall-Holm, they are not." – **Martin Ciel**

"...it is an ethical illumination of experiences where person and time intersect; a reworking of history where past and present are not closed entities, because life experience is used and respect for the human being prevails. This makes the book beautiful, present and necessary." – **Chr. Mailand-Hansen in** *Informationen*

"Her voice is filled with a painful knowledge and yet moving faith in humanity. It is important to listen to, not least at a time when neo-Nazis are trying to whitewash the past and inflame people's xenophobia." – **Vibeke Blaksteen in** *Kristeligt Dagblad*

"...a valuable book, a memoir whose literary qualities make it deserve to be called more than just a story...a beautiful picture of a rich life." – **Annelise Vestergaard in** *Jyllands-posten*

"I have not read such an impressive book in years. In spite of the horrors experienced in the concentration camps, it is written with humour and love of life..." – **Mogens Kofod-Hansen**

"...a significant piece of European cultural history." – **Ib Falkencrone in** *Vendsyssel Tidende*

THE MULBERRY TREE

THE STORY OF A LIFE
BEFORE AND AFTER THE HOLOCAUST

TRANSLATED FROM THE AUTHOR'S SLOVAK
TRANSLATION OF THE DANISH ORIGINAL BY
DAVID SHORT

IBOJA WANDALL-HOLM

ap

ISBN 9789493418301 (ebook)

ISBN 9789493418288 (paperback)

ISBN 9789493418295 (hardcover)

Publisher: Amsterdam Publishers, The Netherlands

info@amsterdampublishers.com

The Mulberry Tree is part of the series Holocaust Survivor Memoirs WWII

Copyright © Iboja Wandall-Holm 2025

Translated from the author's Slovak translation of the Danish original by David Short

Language editor: Dobrota Pucherová

Cover text: Angus Blair

Cover image: The only preserved photo of the five children.

All Rights Reserved. No part of this publication may be reproduced or transmitted in any form or by any means, electronic or mechanical, including photocopy, recording or any other information storage and retrieval system, without prior permission in writing from the publisher.

This book was published with financial support from SLOLIA, the Slovak Literary Centre.

Slovak Literary Centre

CONTENTS

Preface by the author vii

Book 1   1

Book 2   83

Book 3   161

Book 4   233

Notes   299
Interview with the Author   303
Acknowledgements   315
About the Author and Translator   317
Amsterdam Publishers Holocaust Library   321

PREFACE BY THE AUTHOR

I only know my life from memories. These are not photographically recorded events with exact data regarding people still living or dead, liquidated or saved, or places and their names – nor do they come spilling out from the frame that is historical reality. They surface from the catastrophe-ridden cache of my perceptions and experiences, whenever they're caught in some random light or shade.

The war was over, and those of us who were still alive and who would always, to the end of our days, remember the terrible, incomprehensible crimes committed in Europe, had begun making our way back to a life of liberty.

We travelled on foot. We were given lifts on hay wagons and tractors. On motorbikes with Russian soldiers. In cars that only had enough petrol for a short distance. In goods trucks on railway lines that had survived the air raids. Across lunar craters and great heaps of brick rubble. Bombed-out houses had become monuments to generations of builders. A mockery of the straight lines of planners. A decree of mortality written by some old, ill-tempered god. In the remnants of shattered days, people lived on top of fresh tombs in their temporary dwellings. Everywhere staircases that had been trashed, the remains of jagged, incinerated walls, stations razed to the ground, crippled folk without arms or legs. And amongst all the rubble trees were growing, and grass, and out in the meadows cows grazed.

Through an open window in the small German town of Mulda a schmaltzy old jingle spilled out into the open: "*Sag beim Abschied leise Servus...* [Say goodbye quietly as you leave...]." That was when my cloud-beset mind gained a first glimmer of hope, and I saw the words of that sentimental song as the harbinger of a farewell to war, violence, contempt for human life, and to lying as a political weapon.

However, nothing has gone for good and everything that had once been keeps sneaking back into the dreams that accompany my thoughts, my actions and my days. Those dreams bring all my senses to life, laying bear things we all prefer to keep under wraps – things iniquitous, heinous, malodorous, agonizing. They bond shivered, hidden, seemingly disconnected and absurd fragments of a reality that floats like an embryo in the amniotic fluid of a succuba inseminated by the immediate past. They strip away the mask of deceit, self-deception and illusions. They remind me how mankind and history can change colour like a chameleon. Suppressing, forgetting, not stirring.

One of my dreams is a surreal, symbolic image of the days immediately after the war and of what came next. Like all my dreams, it carries me back to the hidden fountainheads of chains of events:

Some town or other bearing the hallmarks of war. A room. A shambles of unidentifiable furniture. A bed. In the bed a dark-haired girl and an unknown man. A black billow of girly hair. Perhaps mine, sometime before the war. The man is missing most of his right arm, cut off some twenty centimetres above the elbow. Clean-cut. Dry. The polished, shiny surface of a split pebble on the seashore. A thin layer of skin, a cross-section of muscle, tendons, bones, a brightly painted picture.

The man may have lost his arm as a soldier, perhaps as a partisan. He turns towards me. Puts his good arm round me and I blend into him and fall blissfully unconscious.

It's dark all round, but I did register the man's twisted, ironic smile. Letting on that he knew things of which I knew nothing.

We're out in the streets of the darkened town. I sense that this stranger wants to help me in a way that would, in normal circumstances, be unacceptable. In this town and in this world integrity will get you nothing.

We're walking towards some large building. Mysterious and without clear contours, it is melting away under the onslaught of darkness.

The mist rolls about its edges, softening its outline. The building is leaning and hanging high above a space where vague shadows ripple. The sheer obelisk of the adjacent tower has been punctured by the empty arc of a gateway.

We're sitting in a car. Besides me and the one-armed man the car holds another man wearing a dark-blue coat of real wool. The soft fabric is indecently gentle and warm in the cold, harsh night amid the ruins of the town.

My unknown saviour is holding a briefcase. I am convinced it contains compromising documents that are to ease negotiations with the new passenger.

The man in the blue coat could be a top trade-unionist, black-marketeer, party official or everything at once. I know the car has a driver, though I can't see him.

The black-marketeer is ignoring me. "What you got there...? Where'd you pick her up?" he asks my chaperone.

"She's lost everything. She's got nobody. She's got nowhere to stay. She's got no money!"

"Hooker...?" the party official asks with a cynical smile.

"No!" I protest. "The Germans shot my parents. And I..."

The man won't let me finish. "There's plenty o' them around... But to hell with it... Here...!" The spiv turns and tosses some golden-brown velvet trousers onto my lap. On the back seat I put them on and catch sight of the red, star-shaped mark on my thigh.

"What's that? You got any more...?"

"Just the one."

In the dark of the roadside the vague outline of an emaciated old man wearing an outsized suit takes shape. He looks like a scarecrow. He raises a hand to get the car to stop. The party official orders the driver to stop, then opens the door. "What do you want?" he barks.

"You know full well what I want," the thin man says.

The party official takes out a well-stuffed leather wallet. From the stack of banknotes he extracts two large ones and one small one.

"And what about her...? Have you forgotten her? She needs money as well!" says my protector.

The plump, wrinkle-free face above the blue collar wavered. A hand projecting from one woollen sleeve tosses the smaller note out into the road to the scarecrow and hands me the two larger ones.

I open the rear door of the car and step out into the darkness, in which two odd little flames are flickering. I'm only vaguely aware of windows, doors, street corners. How shall I cope moneywise? Where am I going to spend the night? Who'll let me have something to eat? I might be alone, but I know I'm just part of the sluggish, undulating darkness in streets that, despite the soft blur, have to be here. Flickering points of light are floating around like the fluorescence in an old mine shaft.

I pause and take a hesitant look round. A figure looms out of the darkness and walks towards me. My familiar stranger greets me with two sound, outstretched arms.

What does he want...? Who is he...? A spectre? A person? A chance way-out from a predicament that has none?

What is he bringing? Hope...? Love...? A life without the horror of forgetting...?

2025: the 103-year-old author with left Lena and Nina right.

BOOK 1

ONCE UPON A TIME

I

I was born in Vrbové, where my parents were on a brief visit. As a child, I imagined that I'd been born in a willow carr.[1] And since I have always been bewitched by the magic of words, to me the royal borough of Podivín, which we moved to from Piešťany, was always a wonderland.[2] It had a river covered in white water lilies, and a little hill from which, through a rotten gate, I once went tumbling down some crumbling steps into an old overgrown garden, ending up face-down in some dense, dark-green grass. I was lying in a thicket, recovering from the shock, and found that I didn't need to cry because I wasn't in any pain. I rolled over onto my back, rested on the flattened grass and, for the first time in my life, saw how soothing and beautiful the sky is when viewed from a horizontal posture.

At Podivín I received my first ball. It was large, red, smooth, it smelled nice and was in one piece. One day, someone's Alsatian ripped it open and let out its air of certainty and warmth. I can see flashes of sunlight in the large wheels of a tall pram next to a bench under the trees. An older woman is sitting on the bench and lying inside the pram is me or my one year younger sister, Lila.

One Sunday morning Lila ran away. On the main street, a stray cow scooped her up with its horns and went lumbering off through the town with her. The cow was followed by the marching band of the local fire brigade to the local park, where, under their conductor's baton, they played on the bandstand for the good folk of Podivín, all dressed in their Sunday best. Lila was eventually saved by a trumpeter, who brought her home unharmed.

Podivín left me with one sombre echo in the form of an image of a sad woman in black. She came by to sell us some silhouettes cut out of black paper, mounted under glass and framed. I imagined, I've no idea why, that she had a ladder inside her which she could pull out and reach up to the ceiling.

During Mum's fourth pregnancy we moved house, to Liptovský Svätý Mikuláš.[3] There my brother Ernest was born, followed in due course by my youngest sister, little Gréta. We acquired a flat in the school courtyard, in a house that backed onto the Hotel Europa. The huge windows of the hotel, on the corner of two main streets, were obscured by white curtains to shield gamblers from the prying eyes of passers-by.

This must have been in April or May. Trees are in flower and the gravel between the short blades of grass beneath my bare feet is pleasantly warm. The sun is shining and I'm sitting on my potty beneath an old chestnut tree, taking in my surroundings.

I can see furniture, unloaded from our removal van, the half-empty crates, wood shavings, pots, pans and other kitchenware. Shelves and boards propped against the house, in a spacious yard surrounded by high walls. Lila is hopping about on her sturdy legs among the young linden trees. Eighteen-month-old Dalma is asleep in a large wicker basket beneath a sunshade.

In the centre of the square space between the school and a

huge building with four pillars, there's a well.[4] A girl in an expansive floral skirt is turning the handle. The cold silvery water streams into her bucket, spills over and splashes in every direction. To the right is a rubbish heap. Beyond a wire fence some chickens are clucking away, pecking at this and that, picking odd bits of weed and scratching away at the ground with their claws. Suddenly a loud bell rings and children come streaming out through a yellow door and run about all over the yard. I am surrounded by four girls of different heights. The tallest one has long fair hair like a princess. They join hands, dance round me and sing: A girl is sitting on her potty, on her potty, on her potty... I would rather get up and leave, but can't. I'm sort of paralysed and my head's drooping almost down to my tummy.

"Stop!" the princess commands and, the children having fallen silent, she says, "I'm Boba. What's your name?"

"Iboja, but they also call me Sima after my granny."[5]

"They call me... call me... call me..." The children are making fun of me.

"Shut up!" the princess orders and the girls all run off.

I'm not aware that I've been speaking in the Moravian Czech that I picked up in Podivín. So I've no idea why they were laughing at me. I am saved by the loud ringing of the bell and the children go streaming back into the school through the wide double door. After it closes behind them, I can once again hear the hens clucking.

Access to our first-floor flat is through a massive doorway. The top part of the door itself has a mosaic of red, yellow, green and blue glass, which casts colourful shadows onto the marble floor of the cavernous hallway. To the left is a large storeroom and a space for coal. To the right, a stone staircase that I only ever went up, never down. I was always carried down by angels. I never told anyone that they floated down with me above the stairs and out through the door and gateway into the yard, where they settled me

5

down, tenderly and with care, beneath the old linden tree overhanging the well.

I've said nothing about the man with black hair and black eyes, who wore a red cape of heavy-duty silk and highly polished black boots with spurs. I used to see him at night in the corner by the bedroom door. He would watch me with eyes like red-hot coals. "My father won't let me go! My button will keep me safe!" In my imagination, the big leather button given to me by a neighbour had magical properties. It felt nice when I clutched it with a special sense that nothing bad could happen to me. The figure in the red cape was a hybrid of the bogeyman with which parents would scare their disobedient children: "If you don't stop, the Gypsies will come and get you!" – and that aria in *The Gypsy Baron* operetta. Mum was in the habit of singing the aria as she washed the dishes or cooked dinner in our vast kitchen with its lining of little blue tiles. The kitchen window gave a full view of the schoolyard.

From the window of our biggest room you could see the inn across street, at the corner, and with it the innkeeper's large garden. The garden contained a table, benches and some red, wooden, four-seater swings. Posh girls and ladies in bright summer dresses and carrying parasols used to promenade along the paths between the flowerbeds and fruit trees.

There were three flats on the first floor. The one next to ours was vacant, with windows covered in dust and smelling like old straw. The only item of furniture in it was an unwieldy, dark-brown, branching coatstand. It irradiated the whole room with its tight-lipped detachment. We used to dance round it and play a game called Black Cook. We were taught it by Erna from Vienna when she came to see us with her father, one of our father's army friends: "*Ist die schwarze Köchin da? Ja, ja, ja... Zwei Mal muss sie rummaschieren, das dritte Mal den Kopf verlieren...* [Is the black cook there? Yes, yes, yes... Twice she has to mess about, the third time she must lose her head.]" Apart from the game, a shadowy image of Erna is etched into my memory because she always carried a large black umbrella, even when it wasn't raining. One day, when instead of "ja, ja, ja" we said "nein, nein, nein", the massive stand toppled over and caught Lila on the head. She suffered concussion and the cut on her head needed stitching. She would lie in bed with a white bandage on her head and all this bred, inside my head, the notion that the coatstand was haunted by the evil spirit of the black cook.

Every accident, major or minor, invariably happened to Lila, because she was a perpetual daydreamer. One cold morning, while she was still in her nightie, she went to warm up by the kitchen stove and leaned against the oven door. Burned into her bottom she had the entire floral wreath that encircled the manufacturer's name and address. Later, on account of her mellifluous eyes and occasional drifting into a pensive silence, Lila was appointed the family philosopher.

The third flat on our floor had just one large room. It was occupied by an old man. He never got out of bed and would keep emitting furious animal noises. He was cared for by his unmarried daughter. Her name was Vilma, which she pronounced Vem-ma. She had substantial light-brown tresses tied wreath-like round her head and her clothes looked like embroidered nightgowns. I was scared of her horrible father and my fears only rose when I saw Vilma showing mother her arms, which were covered in weals and bruises all the way up to her shoulders. Her father would bite, pinch and scratch her. The thought that she needed the help that no one was giving her left me with a guilty conscience. I toyed with the idea that Vilma, having one day been magicked away by the good fairy, would turn into a beautiful young woman. Though I realised at once that that was never going to happen.

The big room reeked of mothballs and urine. I let myself be lured inside solely because of the large trunk stuffed with gaily coloured ribbons, silk scarves, embroidered blouses and dresses carrying a faint odour of better days. The greatest attraction, however, were the boxes of buttons of all sizes, shapes and colours, made of bone, glass, mother-of-pearl, leather and other materials. I loved tinkering with them. The magical leather button, a talisman to protect me from the wiles of the Gypsy Baron, was given to me by Vilma herself.

2

As we grew we learned to speak the local Liptov dialect. The folk living round the yard accepted us as being of their number. We gradually got to know the mountain ranges that surrounded the whole Sub-Tatra Basin. We learned that the peak topped with a white cross was Poludnica, learned which one was called Ďumbier, that the mountain with the twisty top was Kriváň, we got to know the names of faraway mountains and the villages nearby – Vrbica, Palúdzka, Ondrašová, Okoličné, Porúbka, Beňadiková – and we knew that the river flowing beneath the willows was called the Váh.[6] We joined in all the fun and games in the school yard. The big girls made dolls of us. They took us to hospital, operated on our appendices, told us off for all kinds of imaginary misdeeds and used us as bridesmaids at royal weddings. When they discovered that I had a nice clear voice and could even remember the words of songs in films, the content of which was still beyond my understanding, they had me sing. I would sing accompaniments to the plays they put on between the tall pillars and on the broad steps of the synagogue.[7]

All kinds of music, even hits, jingles and broadside ballads had a huge effect on my imagination. The period hit "Oh, Donna Clara", which we had on a transparent gramophone record, coloured my image of the huge synagogue building. The place of worship became a chateau, whose mystique would be revealed only at full moon, and Donna Clara, queen of the apple trees, would dance between the pillars.[8]

In a small flat stuck onto the school building like a bird's nest, lived the caretaker, Mr Hladký, with his wife, their son Mišo, and daughter Anička. Both children had tuberculosis and Mišo spent a lot of time at the sanatorium. Everybody was scared of TB, and the fact that sufferers were credited with a remarkable capacity for love swathed their destiny in a romantic melancholia and endless regret for the happiness stolen from them. They were kept in their red-and-white striped pyjamas in a separate pavilion of the hospital on the far side of the Váh; "normal" people's pyjamas were blue-and-white. Red was the colour of the blood coughed up by the sick, and whenever I happened to find myself close to their pavilion, hidden by trees, I was seized with a doleful sense of futility.

The chickens behind the wire fence surrounding the rubbish heap belonged to the Hladkýs. Anička and I would throw them corn and freshly cut nettles. I loved to listen to them clucking away and to watch the clumsy flight of their rust-coloured wings. All smells sharpened the sense of life as being lived. But most of all I loved the scent of carpenters' fresh and friendly, curly wood shavings.

Anička's cheeks were only red when she was feverish; otherwise she was pale and often suffered stomach pains. She treated them with fistfuls of caraway seeds. She coughed a lot and after every bout she would look anxiously at the handkerchief with which she had covered her mouth. I knew she was scared in case some smudgy, wet, red blotch appeared on the neatly ironed, clean, white fabric. She spent her afternoons sitting on the steps, winding up the gramophone and always playing the same two records: "Ramona, I hear the mission bells above"[9] and "Sonny boy".[10] They were sad enough to bring tears to the eyes. In brief, dizzily bottomless moments the possibility of my own death would come over me.

There were many trees in the schoolyard. In addition to a long line of chestnuts there was the spreading linden, some acacias and a group of linden saplings among which the pupils would play the scissors game. The other, long side of the yard was separated from neighbouring gardens by a wall. Poking above it you could see the branches of fruit trees. At the back of the synagogue there was a grassy patch where, at break time or after school, the children would play "Eeny-meeny-miny-moe" or "Adam was one, he had seven sons", leaving the grass completely trampled.

Next to the wall grew nothing but weeds and burdock. The latter's prickly round seedpods would catch on our clothes and in our hair. We used to pick chamomile flowers and dry them to make herbal tea. We applied plantain leaves to cuts. We used to run all round the synagogue, playing tag or hide-and-seek. Its rear wall struck me as disturbing, even forbidding: its dark doors seemed to me to be hiding a secret. Left half-open, they revealed some stairs leading who knows where, up towards the first floor, and I would always run past them fast in case I disappeared forever.

Our courtyard had two entrance gates. One led to the square with the County Hall on it, the other one, ours, out into Priečna Street. Every Friday, as dusk descended, members of the Reform Jewish congregation, dressed to the nines, would come streaming through both. The multicoloured mosaics of the synagogue windows lit up and beneath the azure blue of the vault the singing of the choir floated up and over the heads of the worshipers. I had no notion of the architecture of this singular building. (I saw it again, many years later, while I was preparing a programme about my life for Danish Radio. The synagogue building had suffered neglect, its walls were shabby, windows broken, and the interior was being used as a general dumping ground. The school and houses in Priečna Street were still standing. Today, it has all been knocked down and replaced with car parks. But Donna Clara is not a day older. She has her Shangri-la in my memory, for all the holes burnt through it and the ashes that endure.)

Boys would come cycling along the rectangle formed between the rear walls of the houses on the main street, past the chestnut trees, ringing their bells and feeling so important. Boy scouts of the Maccabi Hatzair would gather here, hold meetings, sing and plan outings to the mountains and valleys. They were overlooked by an extension of the balcony at the rear of a shoe shop. The owner's freckled, red-haired children would jostle against the guardrail. They would spit at us with shouts of: "Lutheran, great gentleman," and the Lutherans shouted back: "Catholic, Catholic, he's the one to shit a brick."

The abuse they heaped on the Jewish children was rife with vulgar nonsense: "Jews are smelly, shake like jelly, covered in vines from arse to belly!" – just one sample from a very wide range. But we treated the name-calling as something entirely natural, like raindrops or hailstones. It didn't stop us playing together, even when we were a little older and beginning to take in the cracks that put our dispassionate trustfulness and sense of security at risk.

The yard was visited by itinerant knife-grinders, woodcutters and labourers covered in coal dust. I can see tinkers cutting out bits of metal with which to reinforce the damaged edges of enamel pots. I can hear the knife-grinders calling out "... scissooors... kniiives..." and my mother scrabbling around in the drawers of our kitchen dresser and her sewing machine. Of a Tuesday, which was market-day, we had organ-grinders with fortune-telling parrots that would pick fortunes out of a box. Itinerant traders – *bosniaks* – their spines curved backwards and with a basket perched on their bellies, would offer us cords and ribbons, elastic, buttons, cotton thread, penknives and cheap watches. Neckties hung round their baskets like Christmas tree decorations. From the women who came in from outlying villages, all dressed in their native costumes of billowing skirts and camisoles, mother would stock up on fresh, saffron-yellow butter wrapped in burdock leaves, as well as forest mushrooms, wild strawberries and bilberries. Occasionally, a certain crazy young man would come ambling into the yard. He was quite harmless, but would fly off the handle whenever the kids yelled Silly Billy at him before running to hide.

I couldn't make up my mind if the old man with the white hair and beard, wearing a worn, but clean dinner jacket, was a musician or a beggar. He would play a sad, interminable song about blue forget-me-nots on his fiddle. Genuine beggars would come straight out with their reason for being there; that old boy was probably letting his fiddle speak for him. There were several species of beggars. They included both men and women, and Gypsy women in gaily coloured skirts with gold, jingly earrings beneath their headscarves, which they tied in the manner of pirates. They would be surrounded by their dark-eyed, dark-haired, curly-headed children. In their throaty, deep, insistent voices they would beg: "Some change, give me your small change! Do! The Good Lord will reward you, dear lady! Give me some, do!"

Jewish beggars – *schnorrers* – wore a hat and they had beards and side whiskers. They would sit on the synagogue steps, waiting for worshipers to arrive for evening or morning prayers. They only ever ate dry bread with onions. One day I made so bold as to approach one old schnorrer and ask him why he was begging. I remember his reply because later I was jubilant at finding it, slightly differently worded, in the Tharaud brothers' *Rose of Sharon*.

"I beg in honour of eternal and almighty God. His brow is covered in dew and He keeps it cool in the fresh air of early morning. And what do you think: What day is the Almighty's favourite...? Saturday, when people don't work and even animals are allowed a rest. And everybody knows that our King David, before he became ruler over Israel and Judaea and was still leading an itinerant life, was observed begging in the homes of Philistines. If you don't believe me, go to the Book of Samuel and find verses five and six."[11]

The beggar was speaking in Yiddish, but I understood him, because besides speaking Slovak I had also learned German, but since I knew nothing whatsoever about the Book of Samuel, I asked my father if what the beggar had told me was true.

"That was a fine yarn he spun you, but I'm sure he believes it himself. He'll have a starving wife and a heap of hungry little kids waiting wistfully for him back home. It would have been better if he'd learned a trade, but he probably couldn't afford it, and old habits and religious prejudice are stronger than common sense," my father said, leaving me with the impression that he was talking more to himself than to me. As to the Book of Samuel, I learned nothing.

3

My parents were born in the Habsburg Empire – Mum in the southern parts, Dad in the eastern. They met during the last year of the Great War at Piešťany, where Mum lived and where Dad, an army volunteer, was recovering after being injured. Mum, an eighteen-year-old beauty, had black eyes and dark, dense wavy hair. Dad's eyes were green and dreamy, and his hair was fair.

When, like most children, we asked our parents: "What was it like when you were little?" their responses were filtered sufficiently to be left pedagogically and socially acceptable. From conversations among our elders and things we overheard by chance, we deduced that our parents had got married despite resistance from, and without the blessing of, Mum's domineering mother, who had been determined that her daughter should marry the banker who was one of her persistent suitors.

Mum had had a very strict upbringing, having to abide by endless prohibitions and observe the Commandments, most notably the fourth of the Ten: Honour thy father and thy mother... Her love for her father was overwhelmed by fear of her mother's tyrannical bad temper and by her own insecurity. Grandfather, Mum's favourite, said nothing in order to preserve peace in the home. I only ever saw him once, when I must have been about two. I can remember sitting on his lap with him lovingly stroking my hair. He died when I was twelve.

In 1918, after the war was over, my parents settled in the newly independent Czechoslovak Republic. One of its founders and its first President, Tomáš Garrigue Masaryk, was a Humanist scholar of world renown, a fighter for minority rights and a democrat convinced that the most important condition underpinning the democratic order was a sound education system under which children would be raised to become independent citizens with a sound critical faculty. I, however, only learned any of this after I started at the Jewish school in Liptovský Svätý Mikuláš. Because of its progressive teaching methods and the early introduction to foreign languages, the school was attended by not just children of Jewish families, but also pupils from better educated Christian families and even some of the offspring of Gypsy musicians.

Lessons at my school always began with a short prayer:

Almighty God, our Lord,
once more we are starting to learn.
Grant that this will benefit
not only us but others, too.
Amen.

My father's most deeply ingrained interest was music. He had a wonderful voice and could play a range of different musical instruments. He would have loved to become an opera singer. However, he married very young and had to feed his five children, born in rapid succession. His unfulfilled dream became transformed into a nostalgic unrest veiled by a sense for the practical, the application of common sense in a crisis, an unceasing interest in political developments, and prescience. To this day I can hear the exotic names of faraway radio stations, I can feel the warm, crackly smell of the overheating Bakelite of our wireless, which he listened to avidly. His running commentary left us children with a sense, and certain hints, of something unknown but decisive for us too. Father composed, was a precentor, and trained and conducted the male-voice choir, which included boys, that used to sing in the synagogue on feast days.

Mum was a bookworm. She would spend every stolen free moment with a book. She was radiant with glee the day she found in the loft a dusty wicker suitcase, crammed full of books. She was interested in art, wrote poems, and on the daily walks we took after dinner she would tell us stories that never had an ending. She had studied at a teacher training college. Besides Slovak, she was fluent in German and Hungarian and had reasonable French. She used to teach us songs, jingles and poems.

Hanging on the kitchen walls we had some decorative little cloth mats from Vienna, where she had worked for a time as a private tutor. One was embroidered with the text:

Nur einmal im Jahre blüht der Mai.
Nur einmal im Leben die Liebe.

I proved that these words of wisdom were not true by my rapid turnover of the boys I loved. They began when I was about ten years old. The object of my first crush was a young chimneysweep with smiling blue eyes twinkling out from his blackened face. Next in line was a boy who was illegitimate. He wore a sailor suit and reminded me of Little Lord Fauntleroy. His extraordinarily long, fair hair flowed over his sailor-suit collar and his twelve-year-old self was enveloped in an alluring nimbus of whispered petit-bourgeois gossip. He was followed by a certain young man whose unattractiveness was relieved by his skilful rendering of Tosseli's Serenade on the violin, and after him came a whole string of other inexplicably attractive objects of my infatuation.

On a different Viennese mat there was, within a wreath of notably thorny roses and green leaves, the following appeal, embroidered in red silk thread:

> *Grüss Gott, tret'ein.*
> *Bring Glück herein!*

Glück, good fortune, was something our young parents really did need. Right after their wedding, my father had to earn some money by taking occasional jobs. In the early morning he delivered milk and in the evening he studied. Although Mum was teaching, there was never enough money. I myself didn't experience this stretch of my parents' life, because once my father completed his studies and landed a permanent job, the family's economic situation gradually changed. Mum began buying us toys at the market on Tuesdays. I can still remember my first wonderful surprise: a bag full of balls. I have a clear vision of her, wearing a black velvet dress with a narrow waist and a bell-shaped skirt, taking them out of the bag one by one: yellow, green, red and blue ones, flying through space and bouncing around in the yard.

We began having our clothes made by a seamstress according to designs made by Mum. We would get new coats and shoes for spring and winter. Every year, a family photo was taken at the studio of Mr Jungwirth, one of the few people in our town who were in a mixed marriage, an offense that most of our fellow-citizens took a dim view of. If Lutherans and Catholics married, crossing the line, that was a sin, but even more sinful was it for a Christian to marry a Jew. The fate of the Jungwirth family illustrated the changes that were being played out on the European stage. Jungwirth, the photographer, was a Sudeten German, his wife one of the daughters of a poor Jewish family. They gave their children, both girls, German names. When the Sudeten Germans organized in the Nazi Henlein party began shouting "*Heim ins Reich*", Jungwirth, a member of the Nazi party, grew acutely homesick. He vanished, leaving his wife and his children with Wagnerian names without explanation and without money.

My seven-years-younger brother Ernest was, for us, a fair-haired, angelic, grey-eyed chimera. Like my sister Lila, he often gave the impression of a visitor from some distant planet. He was Mummy's boy and he reciprocated that favour. When we three girls began to feel rather awkward at being "still tied to our mother's apron strings" and began refusing to go out with her for an evening stroll, our brother went instead. To this day I don't know where I acquired the guilty presentiment that he was to die young.

Ever since childhood, Dalma, quick-witted, fleet of foot and pretty, had wanted to be an actress. She had an extremely good memory and even at the age of three Mum would send her to the shops. She would drag home a string bag full of groceries along the pavement behind her. She never forgot anything and as a reward for being so clever and for the aura that she spread about the shop with her kiddie charm, she came home with a paper cone full of sugar letters. At school the lads would fight to win her favour.

Dalma and I lived in the land of Quite the Reverse, ruled over by Queen Fantasy. In it were all the places, odours, features and people that we got from fairy tales or the love affairs retailed in the adult magazines we perused in secret. Its leading lights were the ladies in fashion magazines. Everything was different, more beautiful and better, but also worse, than in the real world with which, despite our everlasting games of "quite the reverse", we never actually lost contact. Lila refused to join in. She claimed her name was Ďuro and insisted that boys didn't play with girls.

As the eldest child, I was forced to re-enter the real world the most often. The magic words that opened the door back into it were the reprimands over the sins of my younger siblings. Dalma was already delighting in testing the limits that I had to fight for and pay the price of.

Lila achieved her ends by a special method. She paid for them with fevers. She could develop a high temperature practically on demand. One summer vacation, Mum decided that we would benefit from taking sewing lessons at one of the classier sartorial salons in Mikuláš. She resolutely brooked no opposition. At the "salon" we spent the entire time sewing shoulder pads. Dalma and I stuck it out for a month. Lila very soon started to turn yellow and swell up. While we two continued inhaling dust in the workshop, watching with revulsion the broad, brash and bulging backside of our seamstress "madam" and her snobbish courting of posh ladies, Lila, better developed physically than I, would go off for walks to such beauty spots as Sekerka or Nicovô with Viktor, one of the more "sensible" boys in our social circle. Whenever we tried to wind her up and asked if Viktor ever kissed her, she would reply scornfully that she and Viktor spent the time discussing philosophical and social issues. She made her own decisions as to what was useful to her. In defiance of Mum's wishes, she began making some money for herself by cleaning for the family of one of her friends, the mathematical genius Gideon. Gideon was in the habit of going through visitors' bags and coat pockets hanging in their front hall – his father was chief engineer at some factory – and if he found any letters in them, he would read them and then recount them to his friends in a cleverly parodic re-rendering. This twofold contravention of social decency was taken, in Gideon's case, as one privilege of being a genius.

During the next summer holiday, Lila took loving charge of eight goats and thirty angora rabbits. The animals reciprocated her care, which one of the goats showed by butting her non-stop until she fell into a pile of freshly cut grass, where it could enjoy repeatedly jumping over her. Whenever Lila went into the village for some shopping, all eight goats accompanied her and waited for her outside the shop. No one was allowed anywhere near Lila; the goats, her bodyguards, made sure of that. She would cut grass with a scythe, feed the rabbits, clean out the animal houses and cages, milk the goats and churn butter. In the village they called her the goat queen.

When Miss Schöntag, the best music teacher in town, convinced Father that I was musically gifted and would go far, provided I spent at least an hour a day practising my scales, my parents bought me a piano. In it they saw a guarantee of my future career, though I myself felt more a burden of responsibility, occasioned by that huge, chestnut-brown instrument.

Miss Schöntag, white-haired, cultivated, fastidious and strict, demanded discipline, precision and hard work. With her sarcastic comments and reprimands, which struck as crisp and staccato as a metronome, she could darken even the brightest summer's day. And since I preferred by far just to improvise, play by ear, not nurturing my natural gift the way one ought and so squandering her precious time, she passed me on, as she did with all her other less worthy pupils, to her less gifted, but pedagogically reputable younger sister, a widow with a baby son and tiny pension. The court where the sisters lived in a two-storey house with a courtyard gallery, had two large gateways. One gave on to Hlavná

[Main St.], the other led out to the parallel, unpaved backstreet where the gardens began.

I just loved those galleries. They were jolly and welcoming. But because I wasn't spending an hour a day practising my scales, which fostered in me an image of faded, dusty artificial flowers, and because the piano lessons cost quite a lot, I sensed that with every step up to the Schöntag gallery I was losing something of my parents' goodwill and hopes. Why that was so, when it needn't have been, I do not know. Too often I arrived late. I would waste precious minutes outside the dressmakers' workshop, which resembled a large greenhouse. To me it was like an aviary. Filled with greenery and birdsong. Among the branches of trees and bushes and around the large table, flew yellow and orange canaries. Two indentured lads sat on the large table. Sewing and cutting threads with some large scissors. The ruler of this aviary was the taskmaster, Mr Tuli, a sprightly little man who resembled his birds.

My musical career evaporated irretrievably the day my purse slipped unobserved from my pocket, and with it the money for my music lessons. Nobody believed that my distress was genuine and that I hadn't thrown the money away deliberately. I'd become a disappointment as a good daughter and decent human being. What had happened was a logical consequence of the actions of one who treated money earned "by the sweat of someone's brow" as casually as I treated my own talents.

4

For a long time we went about all dressed in the same sailor suits and coats with gold buttons, and when we tried to protest against such uniformity, the desire of us three older girls to assert our individuality was scuppered by the demand that we should exercise some self-restraint. Father had meanwhile succumbed to his longing to become finally independent and terminate his dependence on the leaders of the Jewish community of which he was cantor. A friend from Vienna (whose daughter with the umbrella had taught us how to play "black cook") talked him into setting up a place to make and sell smoked meat products, adding that he would find him an assistant and give him a hand with the business. Father had to borrow the money to buy the machinery involved and for the wages of a properly trained smoked meat butcher. Father's friend's advice, the assistant's ineptitude and Father's own lack of experience dissolved into an explosive cocktail that knocked the bottom out of the household economy. We couldn't fathom where Father had parted company with his common sense, and I think he himself was the most mystified and embarrassed. Embarrassed on account of his fata morgana and the fact that for years we had to pay off the debts by instalments. However, Mum remained staunchly by his side and protected him against any loss of confidence and the respect of his family. And no matter what a big girl I now thought of myself as, I couldn't help thinking of the malevolent influence of the black cook. It was just then that Hitler came to power in Germany.

Mum, on the one hand a naturally exuberant person who liked a good laugh and had a fine sense of humour, required, on the other hand, that her numerous commandments be meticulously observed: Treat all the children alike! Equal rights and obligations! No accepting "charitable" gifts from better-off fellow-citizens! Adhere to the rules of reputable behaviour lest even a hint of petit-bourgeois gossip or envy be directed our way! Keep educating yourselves! Be back home in the evening at the time set by Mum! Speak the truth under all circumstances! No swearing and do nothing to offend the Lord God! Avoid bad company and any examples it sets!

Mum's egalitarianism and the shortage of money were to blame for my not getting the ice skates I so longed for. She would have had to buy four pairs instead of just one. And so the walled ice rink between the town and the river became a romanticized dreamworld. Laughter, shouting, happy voices, snatches of Slovak, Czech and German operettas and hit songs came jetting over the wall into the wintery, snow-covered landscape beyond. To this day I can catch a gust of the glorious gloom that sprang from the sentimental German evergreen: *Reich mir zum Abschied noch einmal die Hände*, goodbye, goodbye and once more goodbye... Love, parting, tears, a long voyage across the ocean to America... Truly twenty-four-carat slush.

America used to be called the land of freedom and limitless possibilities. There anyone could do whatever they wanted, find employment, and, if they were lucky, even grow rich. "Amerikans", returning ex-pats, would build themselves fine houses and some even factories. This stoked our immature notions of happy endings in everyday life. We gorged on cheap paperbacks, Tom Shark, Karl May, Mark Twain, Fenimore Cooper and Harriet Beecher-Stowe. We collected and swapped photos of film stars. We mangled their names just as we mangled the words of hit songs from English films and jazz songs. We would go to the pictures for one crown and sit right in front of the screen, in the front row, and with our heads thrown back and our chins pointing forward we would be carried away to the Wild West and the adventures of cowboys or the love affairs, sad or happy, between beautiful, but poor girls, and the sons of millionaires, we would follow the bloody shoot-outs among gangsters against a backdrop of skyscrapers and admire the stalwart heroes of crime thrillers. Only once did I sit in the middle of a cinema for the full three crowns. I was given the money by Father's sister, Auntie Mala from Prague.

Auntie Mala attaches to one of the less pleasant consequences of Mum's being so high-principled. The American branch of the family, of whom we'd heard nothing for a very long time, who knew only about me and nothing about my four siblings, sent me a beautiful long, red silk dress with a wide frilled skirt. Mum took some scissors, cut it to pieces and made two pillows out of it. I was distraught and shed a lot of tears over what I saw as an unwarranted massacre. I could hear, coming from next door, Auntie Mala chiding Mum for her excessively strict observation of her principles and that it would be better if she taught us girls never to envy one another. After she'd had her say, Auntie Mala came to join me and asked if I'd like to learn to dance the Charleston. She had a warm alto laugh, vented as she showed me what to do with my legs. She performed with light-footed elegance in front of the bedroom mirror. In the end we were both dancing and laughing like crazy.

We were never short of food. We ate a lot of vegetables. These we bought from allotment-holding Bulgarians. We had our own geese. Chickens and eggs were cheap, sold by village women. We children would go foraging for wild fungi. And we used to pick sloes after the first frost. Mum made wine from them. There was a mineral spring that we visited, its waters health-giving and free of charge. Also healthy was the linden blossom from the tree in the yard; we would pick it and dry it and make an infusion from it.

We had a home help and, as things were back then, she was appallingly badly paid. But without her help Mum would never have got all the darning, patching, washing and ironing done.

Every morning, Mum would wash us in cold water, then furiously towel us dry and warm. We had a hot bath only once a week. We always went for a walk before bedtime even if it was bitterly cold and the snow built up into great walls either side of the front door. The evenings were white, all glitter with ice crystals, moonlight and stars. The frozen snow crunched beneath our snowshoed feet. Our hands were kept warm by freshly roasted potatoes in little pouches inside our gloves.

As early as November the town would be scented with pine needles. Sleigh bells jingled and the sound of church bells echoed all over the town. We strolled past brightly lit shopfronts that twinkled with little devils and angels wrapped in black-and-white tin-foil, and gaily coloured chocolate animals. We were drugged with the smells of salami, ham, smoked herrings and pickled fish issuing from delicatessens. We would pause outside them and in one we would see its rotund little proprietor, clad in white, and his chubby little wife, who was said to have to shave every morning, as they cut chunks of brawn or wrapped frankfurters and other goodies in greaseproof paper. From one of the street vendors Mum would buy ten chestnuts. Two for each of us. Such recollections of my childhood winters bring back the sight of my breath puffing in the hard frost of Liptov and the scent of the surrounding forests.

Father's inner restlessness drove him from place to place, from one flat to the next. We never asked why, in the space of fourteen years, we had moved eight times. We took it as a matter of course. I was only saddened once, when we left the flat by the school courtyard, where we stayed longest. It was like a when bird leaves its warm nest to fend for itself in the wide, wide world. And the world – that was the town, its people, their interrelations and quirks. Houses, gateways, courtyards, shops large and small, mysteries. The large, flat, white stones where the Garbiarka stream was wide, clean and transparent and where the womenfolk would come to rinse their washing beneath the trees; a sidestream of the Váh, smelling of fish and sheltered by willows. The Gypsy settlement across the river next to the end of the bridge leading from Vrbica to Iľanovo and Ploštín. Every bit of nature, every sign of life where there was something to discover, get to know, unmask.

When we came in from school, hungry, Mum would give us a

crown and say: "Pop round to Gerstl's and get some damson cheese." The gooey, dark-blue stuff was scooped from a barrel with a wooden spoon, tossed onto some grease-proof paper, wrapped up and twisted into some old newspaper. Damson cheese, spread thickly onto a nice thick slice of bread, was sweet and very filling.

Like all small grocery stores, Gerstl's in Nižný Hušták had a doorbell and smelled of yeast, cinnamon, gherkins and sundry southern spices. The sacks of flour, beans, lentils, peas and a glorious range of imported groceries on the shelves lived in a perpetual twilight. Having come out of the shop and through the gateway into the large courtyard, I was almost knocked out by the sunlight and so befuddled by the pervasive smell coming from the stables that I had to take care not to fall foul of horse hooves or wagon wheels. The wagons were for transporting flour and belonged to the baker, who owned the stables and four horses. The courtyard had a thick layer of scattered, yellow, rustling straw. From the balcony of the baker's white house hung baskets of dark-red begonias. The far gateway led out of the courtyard onto the road, which led past some council houses and half-built villas down to the meadows that lined the Váh.

5

When Mum discovered Victor Margueritte's *Tomboy* under my duvet (I used to read books at night using a torch), she started worrying seriously about my morals. She couldn't imagine that a probing and perceptive mind of any age has, even in a small town, plenty of opportunities to encounter and identify the pretence and hypocrisy that lurks beneath a mask of virtue.

Besides an interest in collecting cheap, but good pictures at auction, Mum had one other hobby: collecting freakish individuals who'd been excluded from normal society because they were either poor or oddly behaved, or at least were that way inclined. Trying to shield them suited not only her social sentiment, but also her craving to get to know people and hear their unusual and bizarre life stories. One told her how he'd been born on a large farm. With the money his siblings supplied to buy him out he had travelled the country and bought books on art and music. His goal in life was to become a painter and poet. His visiting card was black with the lettering in gold, which said simply: "Arnošt Láska [literally, Arnošt Love] Autodidact". He clothed his slender, bow-legged frame in billowing capes, lined with red, green or purple brocade, with a huge bowknot to match. Using his finger, he would do oil paintings of flowers, huge bunches of grapes and chubby girls sporting red bonnets. He used to read his first poem to us: "Thou art my flower, thou hast me in thy power, o, rose of my life, become thee my wife."

We gathered that he'd been born out in the fields at harvest time and that because of the rush they'd put him inside a large pot on a kitchen shelf and only took him out in time to be breastfed. He was convinced that the shape of the pot affected his stature as well as his short bow legs; he comforted himself with the knowledge that Toulouse-Lautrec's were even shorter. Mum had no inkling that his greatest passion was pornography and that he brought back from his travels a rich haul of pornographic books and magazines, photographs of different positions for having sex, and illustrated biographies of famous courtesans. While Mum was out, he would show them to me and my sisters and the maid. He would accompany his presentation with his creaky laugh and kept licking his drooling lips with his pink tongue. One day he treated us to a detailed account of how he'd raped a fourteen-year-old girl in a field. He was a frequent guest at the home of my friend Ľuda, in the room that her parents rented out to itinerant prostitutes. As protection against sexually transmitted diseases he would drink a liquid called Pitralon straight from the bottle.

We said nothing of any of this to Mum and only told her

everything the day we caught the painter and poet Láska trying to remove my ten-year-old sister Gréta's knickers. She threw the criminally depraved pervert out of the house and told him never to show his face there again. We never saw him again anywhere in the town.

Father left our upbringing to Mum. I can see him now, walking along the street with his stick. The sun is shining on his pale-ginger hair. He stops, leans on his stick and turns his dreamy green eyes to what's going on in the square facing the Town Hall, taking note of the people at the vegetable stalls or just staring idly. He's on his way to see his brother Samuel, who has just opened a lingerie shop. Any business is handled by my old Aunt Edita, while my uncle sits on a chair outside the shop, drawing pictures of the workmen resurfacing the street with asphalt.

Father adored his younger, very pretty, fair-haired sister Mala. He could have a good laugh with her as with no one else. They were like little children, spoke Ukrainian together and sang Russian and Ukrainian songs. Father's Russo-Jewish spleen, *khandra*, and his melancholia seemed like a remote echo, in some minor key, of the fate of his forebears, who had been persecuted and beaten and of whom the rest of us knew hardly anything. This echo came to me in one particular song that he used to sing:

A čo, ak môj cieľ je len lákavý prelud
A že moja loď možno nenájde dok
Kým slnko len na nebi nado mnou svieti
A hreje a sprevádza každý môj krok

A čo keď si budujem len vzdušné zámky
Že život je zriedka bez smutku a bied
Len vo sne je nádej na pokoj a šťastie
A nebo tak modré, že takého niet

And what if my goal's but a will o' the wisp
And my ship may be one that never will dock
As long as the sun shines high o'er my head
Warming and tracing each step as I walk

And what if my hopes are all castles in Spain
For life is beset with trials as we know
Hope and good fortune come only in dreams
Where the sky is so blue and the sun all aglow

Auntie Mala had married a Czech doctor. After Hitler seized Bohemia and Moravia they escaped from Prague to the Soviet Union. There they both died, somewhere in Siberia.

While Mum kept a close watch on our chastity, she had no objection to boys coming to see us. We would discuss politics and literature and recite poems together by heart. The arguments, both earnest and jocular, that we had in the course of our debates met with our parents' approval. "See, girls are just as clever as boys!" Father used to say.

Women have to learn to stand on their own two feet to become independent of their husbands and the latter's social standing. To reach that end they need to acquire an education. Knowledge reduces fear of the authorities and increases self-reliance. And you, as children of Jewish parents, are going to need that. Ignore the names you get called. Don't identify with them. People with prejudices, even those of whom you'd never suspect it, are often emotionally impoverished, many quite ignorant, having perhaps been indoctrinated since childhood, and possibly insecure, discontented and weak. They think they can win power and a sense of superiority by persecuting fellow-citizens who can't defend themselves – all this was instilled in us by our parents.

Like most children, I didn't like our parents' sermonizing, but these words of theirs have stayed with me all my life.

6

The lives of Father's forebears was vanishing in the mists of time. Years after the war, my uncle told me that they had come to Transcarpathian Ukraine (Sub-Carpathian Ruthenia) from Odessa, and the story told within the family was that they were descended from Khazars, a nomadic people that had spread from southern Russia as far as the northern Caucasus. These people were a mix of Slavs, Finns, Turks and Tatars. During the reign of Attila the Hun their territory stretched from the Don to the Volga and in the seventh century from the Urals to the Dniester. Under the pressure of periodic invasions from Christian tribes on one side and Muslim tribes on the other, most of the settled Khazars and all the Khazar princes decided to adopt Judaism. Their supreme secular and spiritual authority was the *khagan*. Knowledge of the Khazars and their regime comes from the tenth-century correspondence between Khagan Joseph and a Spanish Jewish cleric. The Khazars exhibited great tolerance for their Muslim and Christian fellow-citizens. Their empire collapsed in the eleventh century and its people dispersed in every direction.

I just wish I had a map of the routes taken by my ancestors over the centuries. The only thing I know for definite is that my paternal grandfather wound up at Jasinia, where he had a small farm. He grew maize and would send us the flour from which Father would make polenta. A few sheep and a cow provided milk and home-made cheese for the seven children. The family led a modest existence and couldn't afford the education that the children aspired to. Only the oldest one, their musically extremely gifted son, learned to play the violin. The rest had to rely on their own devices; they left home quite young and scattered all over the world.

During the Great War, Father's eldest brother, a soldier and promising violinist, developed gangrene and died. His second brother became a rabbi in San Diego and was said to speak nine languages. The youngest settled in Prague, married a piano teacher and completed a course at a commercial college. Later they emigrated to Leeds, in the UK, where, during World War II, his activity was so meritorious that he was invited to Buckingham Palace.

The one I knew best was Uncle Samuel. At the age of eighteen he went to Prague, took lodgings with an elderly widow for whom he did countless jobs, thereby enjoying his board and lodging free of charge. He used to sell fox paws to furriers and spent the money he made on training to become an orthopaedist. He painted in his free time. Hana, the eldest of Father's sisters, was a widow; she lived with her parents and provided for herself and her daughter by doing embroidery to order. The youngest, Mala, had dreamed of becoming a dancer, but ended up as a secretary. "Itinerant musicians and story-tellers were always welcome at our house in Jasinia. They would share our table and sleep on straw out in the shed," Uncle Samuel used to recall.

Grandfather came to see us only once. He took a horse-drawn cab from the station and brought us presents of a sack of maize flour and a round cheese the size of a wagon wheel. He told us stories and gave us advice for life: "Remember, children, the two worst sins that you must never commit: Never wake someone who's asleep, because, sleeping, they're in God's embrace, and never make fun of someone in the presence of others."

I promised to remember these sins, but the very next week I went and committed the first one. Granddad had fallen ill, he had a high temperature, his door was closed, from behind it we could hear him coughing and we were under strict orders to be quiet and not disturb him. Suddenly it was as if the whole house was sick and grumpy and sullen and I felt banished from it. And since I wished to see for myself what had brought this change about, I looked in on Granddad as I was on my way to bed. He was lying in bed, all wrapped up in his duvet, with only his spiky goatee poking out. The squeak of the hinges had woken him. He raised his head and saw me standing on the threshold in Mum's long, white nightie. In his feverish state I must have seemed larger than life and my arms inside the long sleeves probably looked like wings, I myself looking like the Angel of Death. "Go away! You're too early!" he shouted, sprang from under the bedclothes and crawled under the bed.

I never committed the second sin. Nor did I ever tell anyone about that other experience. Not even Granddad after he got better. This memory is all I have left of him.

My paternal grandmother also only ever came to stay once, when I was about five. Her name was Sima. It was after her that I got my second, unofficial name. In my recollections she's dressed like a Russian babushka. She's wearing a kerchief crosswise over her front, tied at the back, and a long, wide skirt. She's holding my hand. We cross the rear half of the square diagonally, past the well and then through what was called Makabea, between some new villas, out into the fields. We have to wait at the level crossing barriers. A train thunders past, puffing rarefied rings of smoke up into the heavens. The barriers rise, we cross the track and follow the grassy footpath along the railway embankment, then scramble up the hill called Sekerka. There, on the meadow that slopes down towards the railway, near the point where the hillside is divided by a wall of blackthorn and hawthorn, Grandma picks various medicinal and culinary herbs. I'm helping her and my hands take on the smell of different kinds of thyme. Ahead to the right, we can see on the horizon the outline of the dense, dark-green coniferous forest of Nicovô, where Maytime rag days were held, and where we would scrape gum resin from the trees, boil it in milk and sugar and munch it like chewing gum. Grandma makes little bunches of the herbs and hangs them out to dry against the white wall of the house. She ties red ribbons to our wrists to keep us safe from the evil eye. The song that went with that must have been written in a minor key.

I only ever knew two of Mum's sisters. Slim little Ilonka, a teacher, was dearly in love with one of her colleagues, but her mother insisted that she marry the owner of the local drugstore. He was only a couple of centimetres taller. He was a good man and a good father to their two little boys, and when Ilonka's tall, well-built true love died quite young, of cancer, Grandma proclaimed victoriously: "You have to admit I know what I'm doing!"

The name of the youngest sister seemed well-chosen prognostically. She was Bella and a gorgeous redhead. Of the brothers in that generation I only knew one, the black sheep of the family, the skirt-chasing Lev. He was interested in mystics, spiritualism, the Cabala, astrology, tarot, various kinds of divination and all the mysteries of the world. We had no idea where he got his money from, but if he happened to come to see us, he always brought costly presents for everyone. During his three-week visit, Grandma didn't mention him once.

When she was with us, Father's visits to his brother Samuel lasted longer. Grandma expected her grandchildren to kiss her ostentatiously extended hand. She only withdrew it after we'd all done our duty. In our land of Quite the Reverse, Dalma and I made no bones of what we thought of her. She was the one living prototype for the characters in our game. We assigned to her role of the wicked witch who, in the person of a beautiful and haughty countess with a great crown of hair and long earrings, would direct everything, hatch plots, set snares and render all beautiful things ugly. Lila maintained her stony silence and our brother was sorry for Mum. Little Gréta with her curly auburn hair and laughing turquoise eyes would imitate Grandma when out of Mum's sight. Even at the age of five she was good at playing various types of people, spotting their most typical features and acting them out to us in a way that had us roaring with laughter.

We needed no better theatre and were quite sure that, one fine day, she would become a famous actress.

7

When I was eight, the little town of Liptovský Svätý Mikuláš was a worthy 644 years old. By the time I was in my third year at school I had already learned just how great many figures in every field of culture and art this old town had given its country and the wider world. Its origins, however, lay in a much more distant past about which I knew just as little as about the past of my ancestors. The hills and mountains that encircle the Liptov Basin were silent in their lofty, untouchable majesty. Buildings, churches, mansions, halls, documents, pictures, excavations and castle ruins high up on the crags all bore testament to everything that had, generation after generation, gone on, got lost, changed or survived in some new form. But the town was alive here and now, every minute of our childhood present, and the villages scattered round about filled the air with the smells of ploughland, hay, stables and gardens. Ducks and geese dabbled about in streams overhung by shady willow trees. Fences, bell-towers, wells and the benches outside houses gave us a warm feeling inside. Main roads, tracks across meadows and between fields, footpaths shielded by lines of trees and bridges over streams were for us pathways to the intimately close unknown. And in our games the River Váh, that wanderer through the whole Liptov valley, quite dangerous for Slovakia's Odyssean raftsmen, was our Mississippi. Goats and geese grazed beneath the willows along its banks. Among the bushes on the islets washed by a current that smelled of fish, we were Tom Sawyers and Huckleberry Finns, and we would send paper boats southwards to join the Danube to cries of "Mark Twain". We would smear ourselves with mud and make Red Indians of ourselves. The number 1713, answering to the year in which Juraj Jánošík, the Slovak Robin Hood was executed, was the password to the secret hiding place of us outlaws, who took from the rich and gave to the poor. For a brief moment we could be the twelve falcons above the balefire on Kráľova hoľa,[12] even though there were only five of us. Towards evening, when church bells began to ring and cows began to make their way home from their pastures, we too, abandoned our eternal hunting grounds, where water turned into grains of sand and sand into water.

As a warning against alcoholism, a scourge that was one of the unresolved problems of the young republic, our school corridor had two large, framed posters. One carried an image of Martin Sober, the other one of Martin Drunkard.

The blue-eyed, laughing wife and children of Martin Sober had a marzipan complexion, red cheeks and a fine head of hair; Martin himself was a sturdy, broad-shouldered man, brimful of health and with an amiable expression on his face.

Martin Drunkard was all skin and bone. Shining out from his grey, gaunt face was his red nose, and his eyes of an indefinable colour were sinking into their deep sockets. Behind him stood his pale, scrawny, wrinkled wife and around him some greenish creatures with blank faces and droopy ears. That poster filled me with revulsion and fear and I used to walk past it with my eyes closed. However, the pictured reality that I avoided was something I saw for real in the family of my friend and classmate Ľuda. She lived in Nižný Hušták in one of the little two-roomed cottages. In one of their rooms there was a cobbler's bench, the kitchen, and beds and mattresses for the whole family. They rented out the other room, the bedroom, to prostitutes. In the main room lived and breathed six human beings, two adults and four children. It reeked of leather, wax, shoe polish, tar, sweat, grime, fumes from cooking and gin. Only Ľuda, the eldest child, was bright-eyed, chubby-cheeked and of a sound constitution. All the others had tuberculosis and looked like the pitiful little skeletons on the Martin Drunkard poster. Only in the tiny garden behind the house, among the begonias and dame's violets, marigolds and sunflowers could you get a breath of fresh air with a tinge of dill.

I had mixed feelings about visiting Ľuda at home. Curiosity mixed with anxiety, as I passed through the short unlit hallway, which reeked of powder and cheap perfume because it was also used by visitors to the bedroom where they were attended to on a double bed beneath a portrait of Ľuda's grandparents. A divan in there was used by a creature that differed from anything we had ever encountered previously. At first sight, it was a man, but he had breasts and his long black hair flowed down across his shoulders. He wore blouses with lace collars and poking out from under his men's trousers you could see high-heeled ladies shoes. He told us how he'd come from Prague, where professors at the university used to demonstrate him to their students. He explained that people like him were hermaphrodites, so called after the son of the Greek gods Hermes and Aphrodite. We were dying to know, but too timid to ask, if he also received visitors on the divan and whether and how he served them. I found Hermes and Aphrodite in the encyclopaedia of one of my friends.

Ľuda was forever laughing. She was good at school and a friend you could rely on. Her attitude to life – nothing human is alien to me – applied successfully to me too. She quit high school after the fourth year, but our friendship endured.

Another friend, Cecília, lived on the road leading to the station, in one of the handful of terraced houses with huge glass verandas and a spacious courtyard fairly divided up among the tenants. She and I would help each other with our homework. She me with maths, I her with German. My relationship with her was not as spontaneously natural as with Ľuda. I always had to be on my guard, she could be quite provocative, and I had to have closely argued responses to hand. But because I knew that, no matter how well supported by evidence, my defence would not help me break through her wall of unshakable conviction, I usually let Cecília speak. She was deeply concerned to see me saved from hellfire: my sole salvation was to have myself baptised as a Roman Catholic and so wash away the blood of the Crucified One.

Cecília's father was a tailor and their entire flat was soaked in the steam emanating from flatirons working on wet fabrics. Their walls were all covered in pictures of saints. Cecília collected them the way the rest of us collected actors and actresses. She had more in her pockets and as bookmarks in her textbooks, where they lay bleeding from their countless wounds, most notably St Sebastian. Her brother was a parish priest, and the whole family were supporters of Hlinka's Slovak People's Party.

Whenever we were in their front garden and Cecília was poking around in the soil and sowing grass seeds, I had this sense of her sowing her saints as well and that a wooden cross was going to spring up above each of them. A dove in mourning would sit on each cross, tinkling the little bell held in its beak to give notice of its own funeral.

Cecília, taller than I by a head, had a pale oval face with regular features, pallid eyes and a chestnut fringe. She would talk calmly, quietly, gravely and with urgency about the enemies of the Slovak people: Hungarians, Czechs and Jews.

"What have got against Czechs and Jews?" I asked her. "I could understand your rage at the Hungarians. If it weren't for the world war, they might well have Magyarized the whole of Slovakia. I've just been reading that after our liberation from their rule in 1918 only three hundred of the original two thousand Slovak schools were left. Only seven and a half per cent of teachers were Slovaks and only one per cent of civil servants. Which is why Czech teachers and bureaucrats came in to assist."

"Fine, but now it's time they went. Look at our grammar

school: scratch a teacher, find a Czech. And all of the type they've no use for back home. Stupid, unqualified. Anything's good enough for us, their ungrateful Slovak brothers. All top jobs have been taken by Czechs. They treat us like a colony. Everything's being run from Prague. Like we're a charity to be handled with condescension. For them, we're a nation of tinkers. And Masaryk, who declared us and himself to be Czechoslovaks, hasn't granted us the autonomy he promised. And the Jews? Sorry, but they're the ones who killed Jesus, they ride on the coattails of whoever's in charge and they're poisoning us with alcohol."

"But don't forget that Jesus was a Jew, and you could describe plenty of our Czech teachers as educated and inspiring pedagogues. And we do have some Slovak teachers as well now. Do you want me to spell them all out to you?"

"No, don't bother, because you need to stop and think as well," Cecília replied without explaining why I needed to. "There are about four or five of them, two of which are free-thinkers and freemasons. We need people like that about as much as we need the Jewish shopkeepers and publicans who rip our people off and besot them with firewater."

When Cecília had finished giving vent to her convictions without once raising her voice, we went back to our schoolwork.

In Nižný Hušták, not far from Ľuda's parents' house, there was a small lock-up, which we called the nick. The man in charge of it was a tall policeman, broad in the beam, he would often sit around smoking his pipe on the bench outside. I used to play with his daughter, Hanka, in their garden, which was full of roses, vegetable patches, peas and strawberries. They also had an orchard between the grammar school and the common. It was dark and smelled of cats, but it did have the advantage of a gate leading out onto the common, where travelling circuses would pitch their tents, swings, roundabouts, shooting galleries and stalls selling coloured balls, lollipops and pink candyfloss. I used to like sitting with the policeman and getting him to tell me about his prisoners. There was one in particular that interested me because I'd just finished reading Emily Brontë's *Wuthering Heights* and the object of my interest reminded me of Heathcliff.

"What? Him? He's an incorrigible smuggler," said the policeman. "Half Gypsy, half goodness knows what. That's all that black hair above his blue eyes. And those white teeth! Women and girls go crazy over him and keep him in hiding whenever he's wanted by the police. He won't be here long, we're having him transferred to a bigger prison. Yet he went to school and is forever writing things. He's already filled three exercise books and says there's a book to come out of it all. I dunno, but I reckon there will be."

One day I stopped by the barred window of the nick. It was a warm day, the sun was shining and the window was open. Heathcliff was standing behind it, his arms threaded through the bars, watching the people across the street.

"Why do you smuggle stuff?" I asked him.

"Because of the moon and the stars and because I know places beneath them where no one has ever been but me," replied Heathcliff, half Gypsy, half goodness knows what.

8

Mikuláš was a garrison town. There was a cavalry barracks at the north end, just beyond Vyšný Hušták, which seemed split clean off by some huge, wide kitchen knife, with just a few scattered houses like crumbs blown by the wind onto the road to Okoličné. On the southern side of the town, separated from Palúdzka by the Váh, a second large barracks stood by the road to Ondrašová. The troops would come marching out in long lines past the statue of M. R.

Štefánik,[13] singing an old marching song, the ground beneath their heavy boots groaning in time. As evening fell, the curfew signal rang out over the whole town. Some of the officers and NCOs lived outside the barracks and one of them, a warrant officer, was the father of my friend Dagmara. They had a flat in Nižný Hušták, which was to me what unknown continents must have been to the first explorers. Nižný Hušták had originally been a village and an echo of that had been preserved in the cottages with little gardens surrounded by low wooden fences. The cottages came to be surrounded by larger houses, factories, shops, the workshops of furriers, locksmiths, electricians and shoemakers, bakeries and large burgher dwellings. Nižný Hušták was home to numerous oddballs, crazies, exotic beings, be they Catholics, Lutherans or Jews, and these beings, to my mind, looked or acted differently from the townsfolk living round the County Hall and up in Vyšný Hušták. It was there that I first saw a human corpse and first heard of suicide. This was committed by Zita, a daughter of the second Hušták shoemaker, who hardly ever said a word and had never been drunk in his life. Zita, tormented by the prospect of growing into an old maid, had jumped off their roof into the gap between the houses and cracked her skull. "How come she didn't get jammed between the walls...?" their shocked neighbours wondered.

Dagmara lived in a house next to the poultry market and opposite the nick. In the corner of a quadrangle taken up by lines of tall, bench-like tables there was space for a circular booth with a roof like a Prussian helmet. Inside it sat the corpulent Júlia, who sold tobacco and cigarettes and spent her entire day knitting tight woollen dresses to order. I liked to pop in for a chat and I could only get inside, almost the entire space being filled with her great bulk, because I was as thin as a lath. She enjoyed having a natter and was forever sucking toffees. She would drop the wrappers on the floor and only gather them up in the evening before she shut up shop for the day. She knew who was going out, or no longer going out, with whom, who went out on trysts behind their husband's or wife's back, and who was the real father of this or that child. "My dresses are drainpipe-thin, they're perfect for slim ladies with a trim figure. But then they mustn't start putting on weight. Then everything becomes visible, even if they add a corset. But who cares, they place an order, I just do the knitting."

Inside Dagmara's parents' house there wasn't a single speck of dust. Their carpets were unrumpled and perfectly positioned on the highly polished parquet floor. All their stoves had been scrubbed and buffed till they shone like window glass, and anything at all that was amenable to cleaning just glittered and glowed. We would invariably sit in the kitchen, which, despite being impeccably clean, had a slight, indefinably unpleasant odour. The warrant officer's lady wife used to wear very high-heeled shoes and a blue fox boa around her neck whenever she went for a saunter along the esplanade with her fluffy little white dog. In her handbag she always kept the keys to the closet and to the cupboard through whose sparkling glass doors you could read the titles of much coveted sentimental novels by everyone from Hüttlová to Čárská[14] along with every volume published in the *Red Library* and *Blue Library* series of such literary trash.

I used to assume that Dagmara had an eye problem, because her eyes were always red and not once did it cross my mind that it could have come from crying. She never let on that her father used to beat her, merely saying she got punished if she had a mark lower than A for anything. The warrant officer's lady wife's chief concern was her little dog. She would comb it, doll it up with top-knots and gaily coloured clips, and she felt hard done by and ill-served by fortune. To me, a mere third-grade pupil at the Hodža *Realschule*, she would gripe about her husband's inferior status, which meant his stars were silver, not gold, forever heaving sighs at not having made a better marriage, but then she'd been young and foolish. Dagmara stood loyally by her lukewarm parents and her only wish was for her father to be transferred to a town with a ballet school. She was intelligent, sensitive and pretty. She moved with an easy grace. A born dancer in a household that never saw any dancing.

One day, the windows of Dagmara's parents' flat were all wide open, letting the street fill with wails of lamentation. I entered the dining room through the open door and there on the polished table top stood, between four candlesticks, an open coffin, in which lay the rigid corpse of the warrant officer, in his uniform with its silver stars. On a chair in one corner sat Dagmara with her head bowed and covering her face with her hands, while her mother was going round and round the table, wailing like a crybaby and screaming: "Oh God, what a beautiful white body he had... No one ever had such a beautiful white body as his..."

The warrant officer had fallen off his horse and broken his neck and they gave him a funeral with full military honours. Dagmara and her mother left Mikuláš. Dagmara never once wrote to me, so I never heard whether the town they'd moved to did or didn't have a ballet school.

Whenever there was a poultry market, women from the outlying villages would stand by long narrow tables surrounded by swarms of customers arguing over the prices of butter, eggs or the live chickens, ducks and geese that had their legs tied with bits of coloured rag. The lady who owned the tavern on the corner of Priečna Street and Nižný Hušták, one of the market's best customers, hauled off home a basket full of her fidgety squawking purchases. She herself was like a big black pudding. Summer or winter, she was always in short sleeves, she smoked cigars, and her voice was deep and throaty like a man's. She served and gave the orders in her tavern, ruling firmly over it and those who lived there. I used to go there to get jugs of beer for my dad. The publican looked desperate to take up as little space as possible –

"that shameless sinner", as his wife called him: he'd got their maid Petra pregnant and she'd given birth to the crippled Petruška, whose head looked like an unripe pear on a thin stalk, but with features that rather revealed who her father was. The woman didn't throw Petra out, but let her stay on with them as part of the household. Her son Oskar, who was a little older than I, was very like his mother, and that's all that can be said of him. Her daughter Isabella was a perfect match for her name: a thick mass of black hair, wild, sullen and attractive. She ran off with a cavalry captain when he was transferred to Prague. "Just as you might expect," people said. It was an interesting event, worthy of an opera *à la* Carmen, and talk of the "scandal" took a long time to fade. Mum wouldn't let me play with Oskar and I pined after the innkeeper's large garden, filled as it was with flowers and fruit trees.

A few houses to the south of the tavern was the home of the poorest of the poor Jewish inhabitants of the town. He was a porter at the station, a reclusive, taciturn little man with a drooping head and weary legs. His name was Salzberger and to me it symbolized the heaps of tears that no one had shed for him. He was widowed, with two children. I never saw him speak to anyone. He would come home wizened and worn and his daughter, Piroška, who acted as his maid and sometimes did other people's weekly wash, would be waiting for him by the door. She went about in second-hand clothes, laddered stockings and seriously down-at-heel shoes with holes in them. I never heard her say a word. The son, Pujo, was a neglected creature, thought to be a halfwit. One day he just cleared off to join the Gypsies in their settlement beside the river. There he was accepted and initiated into all their rituals. He went about with them, rode their caravans with them and had a good laugh with them. He became a white Gypsy and a human being.

The half-hidden stream, the Garbiarka, ran across a small stretch of open land on the edge of Nižný Hušták, just where the road bent round to the left and a footbridge across the stream led to the Klingerka, the southern part of the riverside meadowland where now stood the new detached houses of workers, tradesmen and lower- and middle-ranking office workers. Next to the footbridge, still on the Hušták side, stood the wooden house built very early in the nineteenth century by the legendary, stalwart, handsome and musically gifted first fiddle of a Gypsy band called Jožko Piťo. The story was that he had won the wood needed to build his house at card games played with the local yeomanry. He used to collect folk songs and would play them in versions of his own creation on his beloved fiddle. The house was also home to a member of the Gypsy band that for almost seventy years used to play for the citizenry at their socials, theatre shows or simply as and when, for the benefit of the guests in hotels and restaurants. Sometimes the front door of the house would open suddenly and there would be its occupant standing like a little figure about to give a weather forecast. His round face used to gleam with the smile he bestowed on every passerby. After the door closed, the sound of his fiddle would ring out from behind it, its tune accompanying the walkers all the way to the end of the street.

9

In 1936 we were living, for the second time, in the same house in Vyšný Hušták. First time it was on the first floor with the balcony and windows onto the central courtyard, the second time in a larger flat with windows onto the street. The daughter of the piano teacher who rented one of the floors at the back, begged me day after day not to do my piano improvisations with the window open because they could be heard in the street and the staff at the revenue office on the far side might think – God forbid! – that it was her playing.

Next to the rear courtyard wall there was a tall, ancient mulberry tree. Its branches reached up to the roof, and when the fruits, having progressed from green to white, then from white to red, finally ripened to dark-blue, we used to pick them from where we sat in the open kitchen window, as we watched the typographers behind the windows of the print shop that faced onto the courtyard. One of them, Rázus from Vrbica, had eyes that reminded me of lines from a song by Voskovec and Werich: "Holy Mary with her Baby Jesus, his blue eyes so very winning, whenever the thought of him crosses my mind, it fair sets my old head spinning, oh, yeah..." The printers would smile back at us in a kindly, friendly manner, and one of them used to take us into his garden in Vrbica so we could eat our fill of strawberries, and so that we could pick more to take home with us he even bought us a little wicker basket each.

Close to the main post office on the Vrbica road was a glazier's. There were seven children of whom the older ones used to come to our courtyard and we would go into their shop, which had a lovely smell of wood shavings and, hanging on the wall, various pictures including a framed portrait of the Virgin Mary, whom all seven children resembled. Their faces were like fine china with pale pink cheeks, and they looked like rather expensive dolls that had to be handled with great care. Iron steps led down to the workshop in the yard and when we jumped down them, they made sounds like a tambourine. I had this image that if one of the glazier's children accidentally went tumbling down them, he or she would be smashed into a thousand fragments.

The back gate out of the yard led out onto the road along the Garbiarka stream. That was where I first saw what a strike was like. It broke out at the Pálka factory opposite, where the workers had barricaded themselves in and their womenfolk were bringing them baskets of food, clean underwear and slippers. From the first floor, the men hauled the baskets up on ropes through the windows and then gave the women brief instructions as to what they should do and bring next.

The houses along the Garbiarka looked out on a small meadow, where they would beat their carpets and where we would meet up with the kids from the mixed Czech-Slovak family of a tailor. They used to eat fresh slices of bread coated in butter and jam and the youngest of them had quite a time of it as he tried to cram one such open sandwich into his gaping mouth, markedly outlined in jam. The tailor was painstaking in the matter of his self-improvement and all his walls were covered in shelves full of books. They were quite musty with the dust of all kinds of fabrics, as I discovered when I borrowed from him the collected works of the Czech writers Jaroslav Hašek and Karel Matěj Čapek-Chod.

There were roads, tracks and pathways leading from Vyšný Hušták to Vrbica, a village now merged with the town, which had always impressed me with its sense of cosiness, logs crackling in kitchens and warmth – things I have always cherished. I loved the mill, the bell-tower, the bridge, the cottages with long gardens that ran down to the meadow lining the Váh, the Garbiarka stream and its dabbling ducks and geese, everything that lived and grew there with roots reaching deep into the past and the earthy, animal aroma of the present, teeming with voices and purposive motions, impregnated and overarched with the tranquillity of traditions being upheld. Many years later, and despite the many cruel losses I'd had to cope with in life, I might suddenly be seized with momentary fond recollections of my early life lived in the atmosphere of enlightened tolerance that had ruled Liptov ever since Emperor Joseph II issued his Patent of Toleration in 1781. Tolerance manifested itself in the joint actions put together by different associations, of which Mikuláš had at least thirty. Choirs, drama groups, gymnastics and sports clubs, Scout troops, political, social, volunteer and other useful groupings involved in various branches of the social and economic life of the community, all of them centred on one or other of the three main confessions. Every year the town's schools got involved in the joint programme of dramatic and gymnastic performances called Akadémia. At one such Akadémia, members of the Jewish Arts Association, dressed in Slovak folk costumes, put on a Slovak song and dance show that was a portrayal of life in a Slovak village. I knew all the songs they sang, and more. I still sing them all even today. They are ingrained in my memory along with countless Slovak folk tales, many of which I have had published in book form in Danish. My own involvement in that show went no further than selling open sandwiches to members of the audience during the interval, dressed in the costume of Orava. Coming from one corner of the Tatra cinema, which was packed, I caught some loud whispering going on between two people I didn't know.

"Don't you find it a bit indecent for Jewish boys and girls to get dressed up in Slovak folk costumes?"

"Indeed so, you're right there. It's just more of their aggressive presumptuousness."

Their words stung me to the core, but I wiped them straight from my mind so as not to be infected by such animosity. But I couldn't erase the hidden shadow of darkness that they carried.

In the autumn of 1936, the evening after Yom Kippur ended (when all, even non-believing, assimilated members of the community, attend services at the synagogue, to cleanse themselves of all their sins by praying and fasting) a kosher butcher, returning home with his family after a full day of fasting at the synagogue, found their housemaid in their kitchen, lying in a pool of blood. The police, whom the butcher had contacted immediately, established that someone had slashed the girl's throat with one of the butcher's large razor-sharp knives. The next day, the town and the surrounding villages were awash, at least among their most superstitious and least aware inhabitants, with alarming rumours about ritual murder. The Jews have killed yet another innocent Christian virgin to drink her blood just like they kill Christian babies and mix their blood in the bread they eat at Easter. Long after the investigation was completed and the girl was found not to have been a virgin and her killer was found to have been her own jealous boyfriend, the rumours took an age to die down.

"It's just a reawakening of a dormant myth," said one of my friends, a couple of generations older than me, who'd once done a degree in theatre studies and now spent his free time on amateur dramatics. By way of example, one local young Jewish group had recently enjoyed great success with a performance of Karel Čapek's *White Plague*. A year before that, he'd chosen me to play Pony Hütchen in Erich Kästner's *Emil and the Detectives*.

Several days after the first night, when I popped into Hoffmann's pharmacy to get some aspirins, the pharmacist came round from behind his counter to shake my hand and say, "Welcome, Miss, and congratulations on a brilliant performance. You'll make a great actress one day!"

I found the praise a bit embarrassing, but also a pleasure to hear: it was the first time I'd been addressed as Miss. I left the pharmacy with my head held high and a feeling that I was entering maturity. And that feeling only grew after I was accepted into the "debating society", where older and more experienced young people initiated Lila and me into the complex world of isms. After the murder at the kosher butcher's, we discussed the source of the ritual murder libel and, in that context, the whole so-called Jewish question. An attempt at an explanation was made by Maťo and Karol. Maťo was a student at the University of Bratislava, Karol at Prague University.

Maťo

Scattered throughout the world, with no homeland of their own, the Jews were subjected – beyond the reach of any law – to every kind of persecution and condemned to living in ghettoes. What sustained them and gave them hope was their belief in matters spiritual. Additionally, their instinct for self-preservation from frequent forced exile taught them to engage in employments that they could take with them from place to place and carry in their minds. This included, for example, having a head for business, philosophy, languages and generally keeping their memories sharp.

Karol

And because there was no one to side with them, ecclesiastical and political propaganda used them as sacrificial lambs, held responsible for all the catastrophes caused by an inept or corrupt establishment; natural disasters, epidemics and any other misfortunes that were afflicting the people in whatever country Jews happened to be living in. They were accused of bringing with them the plague, a poor harvest or general poverty. They had murdered God, for which they bore eternal guilt. They are untrustworthy tempters, an alien element with no homeland, given to scrupulously defiling a nation's pure soul by their pursuit of mammon, their impure carnal appetites and their lust for ultimate power.

Maťo

All this is to be found in *The Protocols of the Elders of Zion*, which were fabricated by the tsarist Russian *okhranka* or secret police on the basis of widespread superstitions and latent antisemitism. Jews are alleged to have had a secret plan to create a Judaeo-Machiavellian world rule with the aid of the most abominable, bloody crimes imaginable. Just how deeply and often unconsciously rooted these myths are in the minds of even decent folk can be illustrated by one banal joke: If you say to anyone that something's "all the fault of the Jews and cyclists", most, and that includes Jews, will respond with: "Why cyclists?" If only people were prepared to acknowledge that Jews are like everyone else: good and bad, educated and uneducated, honest and dishonest, rich and poor, gifted and stupid, and recognize just how much they have contributed to the cultural development of any country where they've been allowed to settle and become involved in its daily round. I think and hope that the majority of people in this town and in this country actually know this.

Karol

Let's return briefly to the matter of ritual murder, or blood libel. Once, around the turn of the century, a Jew called Hilsner from the village of Polná, was accused of ritual murder. T. G. Masaryk travelled to Polná to see the scene of the "crime" for himself. A professor of sociology and philosophy, Masaryk set about studying the criminal law and wrote about his findings and his conviction that the charge had been constructed out of falsehoods, prejudices and superstition, to the Vienna *Neue Freie Presse*. The entire German and clerical press labelled him a traitor suborned by the Jews. There were noisy student demonstrations at which he was maligned as a lackey of the Jews. For a time he was even banned from lecturing by the Ministry of Education.

"For me, that campaign was an horrendous personal experience. What made me feel most ashamed was the villainy of it," Masaryk said.

A year later, the rising impact of Nazism in Germany had begun to trouble the whole of Europe. Émigrés in Czechoslovakia gave accounts of the crimes and concentration camps of the Third Reich and people sought to assure one another that they were exaggerating, and that nothing of the kind could ever happen here, in our democracy. In our club, where we mostly discussed art and Czech, Slovak and other literature, and read poetry and listened to classical music and jazz, we began discussing various social structures.

Some of our members were Marxists, some had dallied with anarchism and nihilism and would read the works of Marx and Engels, Lenin, Kropotkin and Bakunin. They tried to explain to the rest of us the difference between philosophical and vulgar materialism. For the Communists, the Soviet Union represented the ideal, because it had eliminated poverty and social injustice and because its ideology and the future were structured on a scientific basis. Revolution and class hatred were major means to achieving a noble objective. Those members who favoured humanism were, in their eyes, sentimental, petit-bourgeois softies.

We youngsters, fourteen- and fifteen-year-olds, were a cocktail of the natural reaction of youth to the "dictatorship" of the parental generation, and of resentment at all narrow-mindedness, social inequalities and the exploitation of the ignorance caused by poverty. We sought to demonstrate that we weren't petty bourgeois conformists and had no desire to be "softies" by not cleaning our shoes and wearing only blouses and skirts. I launched my irreligion with the prayer: "Dear God, please be not angry with me for no longer believing in Thee." But the threat of Nazism, together with our reading of *The Brown Book*[15] and Hitler's *Mein Kampf*, added purpose and direction to our immature revolutionary-romantic ideas.

The most interesting participant in our debates was Alex. It was in his flat that we met. He was the most widely read and had a mastery of quite a number of languages. In addition to art, history, the social sciences and philosophy he was also interested in the psychoanalysis that had inspired the Surrealist poets. He lent me Freud's *Totem und Tabu* and from his bookcase I helped myself to Kant's *Die Kritik der reinen Vernunft*. The former I only grasped in part, while the sheer effort required to understand the latter gave me quite a headache. However, psychoanalysis added spice to our sexual curiosity. It enabled us to employ Freud's sexual symbolism "scientifically", construe our dreams, watch out for slips of the tongue and make fun of those who made them. We learned by heart a certain poem by Kästner in which going up and down stairs and riding in a train were Freudian symbols of physical love. Alex, a gifted, witty young man who formulated his questions and answers with precision and acuity, had a tendency to withdraw suddenly inside himself, fall silent and become quite remote, as if he'd only been with us by mere chance. There was in him something mysterious, secret and captivating and I felt greatly honoured when he asked if I'd go for a walk with him. One walk led to many more and each one ended in an old, abandoned, military cemetery. The skewed headstones were weathered and green with moss. They stood or lay among grass that was full of weeds, among straggly bushes and old trees, among whose ancient branches tweeted, twittered and sang a host of birds. The site was dominated by the sad, beautiful, melancholic echo of all the unfulfilled promises that the young war dead had left in the world of the living. We used to sit beneath a weeping willow on a fallen gravestone surrounded by tall grass and Alex would tell me all about Bakunin's revolutionary catechism and his collaborator Sergei Nechaev.

"All too often we are unaware of the most intimate driving forces behind our choices, thoughts and actions," Alex would tutor me. "We need to be careful not to yield – for reasons concealed from us – to the dogmatic, blind fanaticism of Nechaev or other theorists like him. Nechaev preached that everything that exists had to be ruthlessly destroyed so that something totally new could arise from the ruins of the old social order. The state must be annihilated and there must be total chaos. Revolution has just one single objective: to see everything, including our own selves, crushed and pulverized by our own hands. No more love, family, friends, children, gratitude and trust. The cold passion of revolution scorns the sympathy and weakness of what is called humanism and rejects adherence to the laws, agreements and promises of morality."

I used to listen very closely to what Alex had to say. His words became engraved on my memory, but I was too young and immature to be able to put them in their proper historical and ideological context. Then suddenly, after one of his pauses, he surprised me with a sudden outburst – I'm a sick man, the doctors have said I've got cyclical paranoia – I couldn't fathom why such a clever man needed to make himself interesting and it upset me that he was doing himself down in my company like that. But Alex had been speaking the truth. In Switzerland, where, following his adventurous escape there hiding beneath a railway wagon, they issued him with a residence permit, he committed suicide just before the war ended.

10

One of our temporary flats was opposite the Haas leather works. The works was owned by an old gentleman with a long, pure-white, beautifully manicured beard, who was swathed, for reasons unknown to me, in an aura of well-earned respect. He had withdrawn into his private world, leaving the works to his three sons. The youngest of them ran it, living right next to it, just inside one of the huge, red, arched gateways that led to the tannery. We called him Brčko [Little Quill – a common nickname for people with abundant fine curls] because he looked like a curly-headed bear on rubber legs and his vertical and horizontal dimensions were only half those of his brothers. He was an amiable man who liked chatting, but he was hard to understand because his words ran away with him and he spluttered as he tried to keep a grip on them.

I used to go into the tannery yard, which was covered in scattered oak bark, and I would stand, filled with curiosity, but also slightly stunned, in front of the huge tanks of tannin and leather dyes. The sudden thought of what might happen to me if I fell into one gave me quite a jolt. On my way out I always helped myself to a lump of potato sugar from the barrels under the gateway; it was used, I've no idea why, in the treatment of raw hide.

The workmen used to wear long, wide aprons and hobnailed boots as protection. For me, the sound of their regular, resonant footsteps was the clearest signal that the workday wasn't over yet. I used to talk to them in a kind of conspiratorial tone, which sprang from my romantic notion that I was contributing to the cross-class understanding that was going to bring the fulfilment of my dream of international brotherhood and equality.

"So, my lass," Brčko began one day as we bumped into each other in the gateway. "You interested in politics?"

"And aren't you, Nuncle?"

"Sure, I am interested in politics, but politics is more interested in me. I steer clear of all that because when things go bad, they always point a finger at people like me and say: This is all your fault. Which is why I think Jews should stay clear of politics."

I was fifteen and treated Brčko's attitude as opportunistically evasive.

The rear factory yard was surrounded by a high wooden fence, painted red. I used to like resting my back against its sun-warmed planks. My feet would be lost among the weeds as I gazed at the Garbiarka, stained brown with waste from the tannery, though at other times it could be so clear that it flashed in the rays of the sun and you could see every stone or pebble at the bottom along with gaily coloured bits of broken pottery and old pots, mostly white and full of holes. The railway line ran parallel to the stream and twice a day an old, asthmatic train came puffing by, hopper wagons hauled by a huge engine. From there it was only a short walk to the Klingerka, the new settlement built to the south on the meadow beside the river, where most of the houses had been built and gardens created by their owners. After their day's work they would tend their vegetable patches and feed their rabbits, or pig if they had one. Those who had a goat would go and collect it from beneath the willows lining the Váh.

I attended the M. M. Hodža Grammar School,[16] where I didn't study much but, thanks to my good teachers, learned a lot nonetheless. I only got top marks for foreign languages and Slovak. My parents, disappointed by my lack of success on the piano and how I let my musical talents fester, were even more upset when the lovely man who taught Slovak asked Mum if there wasn't perhaps some problem in the family, given that such an intelligent pupil was getting so few good marks. They were embarrassed and all the more cross for having no reason to heap praise on me. I felt sorry for them, and for myself. I knew they only hounded me out of their care and concern for their children's futures. I was conscience-stricken and felt permanently stuck in a vicious circle. My own explanation for it all was that, as the eldest child, I was the guinea pig of very young parents who lacked experience, that their unreasonable expectations and demands applied only to me and that this was why I was such a rebel, perhaps unconsciously. But it is also true that I loved books and everything else had to give way to this passion of mine. I never stopped reading, day or night, and during the summer holidays I might read as many as three books a day. In the morning, I would be sleep-deprived, worn out and often unprepared. My unfocussed behaviour, which left me unready for lessons, was only aggravated by my being, thanks in part to the novels I read, forever in love, sometimes with three boys at once. I was mesmerized by a fanatical addiction that saw me apprehend things and people with great intensity. I felt twinned with Nature, the clouds and infinity.

My first serious love was Milan, a boy in my class. We both tried hard to fix a date, but invariably had to abandon the idea at the last moment. Thanks to one composition assignment for which only Milan possessed the necessary background material, we did finally arrange to meet beside the Váh. I arrived slightly early, to give me time to find an ideal spot under the trees and settle down on the grass, posing like a film star in a love scene. As I waited, my heart was beating aloud, my breath tinged with orange from the sweets I'd been eating, I was sitting erect with my head tilted rather fetchingly and my feet stretched forward. Finally I spotted him approaching with the book under his arm and his head as bare as a yellow Greek pumpkin. The sun shone through his ears and illuminated his scalp, now shorn of the thick, curly, light-brown hair that had contributed to his allure. His lovely head seemed to have shrunk to some scalp hunter's trophy. My love collapsed like a deflated sponge cake. Milan handed me the book and looked at me with honeyed eyes.

"I can see what you're thinking, but the thing about hair is that it usually grows back," he said, then he turned on his heel and left.

I wrote my essay and returned Milan's book, now surplus to requirement. My love came back a few months later, along with his hair.

I ruined my second chance myself, under much more dramatic circumstances: at a party arranged by us pupils, unbeknown to the school authorities, in a neighbouring town.

It was wintertime. The whole lowland and all the hills and mountains were white. The roads were covered in snowdrifts. And the snow kept coming, thick and fast. The dance hall at the inn was warm, filled with laughter, joy and expectation and the smell of pine needles and wafts from the kitchen, where some geese were roasting. All my classmates came. Only Milan was missing. Turn and turn about, all the final-year students from the forestry college took me onto the dance floor. The wide skirt of my new, sky-blue lace dress was like a tulip in full bloom. It twisted and swung as it picked up the rhythms of waltz, foxtrot or tango. But disenchantment was lurking behind every upsurge of delight in the dance and the foresters' interest in me.

Suddenly, the door flung open and there stood Milan, slightly drunk, his coat unbuttoned and covered in snow. Flakes of snow were melting on his eyelashes. When he spotted me, he threw his arms towards me and yelled: "Hey! Orchestra! Play Violetta!" Violetta translates the Hungarian name Ibolya. He stepped up to me and whispered: "If only you knew..." Suddenly my knees turned to butter and my heart started pounding so loud that everyone must have heard it, my throat seemed to have a knot in it, I was overcome by something akin to a fainting fit and was afraid I might be about to fall to the ground in full sight and melt there like heated jelly. I pushed him away at the very second when the thing I craved most had been about to come true.

The tipsy Milan lost his balance and fell flat on the floor, then everything fizzled out. The music, laughter, joy and passion. Everything was lost forever and as cold as the ashes of a dead bonfire. For Milan it must have been an unexpected, embarrassing and undignified blow at the very moment when he had finally picked up the courage and was all set to act in the presence of his classmates and their guests.

After a moment, Milan got up off the dance floor, suddenly sober, stiffly turned his back on me, took a few steps and finally sat down between two girls who sought kindly and, where I was concerned, maliciously, to console him, and he began to write a letter. He addressed the envelope, in strikingly large letters, to a woman known to be an opponent of sexual restraint. Someone suggested I sing something. I knew that my alto could, if I let it, ooze sensuality, and I decided give my song my all – love, explanation and conciliation:

Nebanovala by,
keby nemusela,
keby ťa šuhajko,
rada nevidela.

A ja nebanujem,
že tvoja nebudem,
ale ja banujem,
ako ťa zabudnem.

She wouldn't repine
if she didn't have to,
if she, young swain,
did not so love you.

And I'm not repining
that I'm not to get you,
I'm merely repining
'bout how to forget you

However, my song had no effect on Milan. He spent the rest of the evening just as cold and remote. I mourned his loss and never did forget him. My unfulfilled, romantic student love would smoulder and flare up as a backdrop to all my future relationships. It only died out for good many years later, after I received a letter from Milan in which he rued our immature ineptitude and timidity.

You can find a plug to fill any gap and my plug was a medical student who attracted me by his truly handsome exterior, the long catalogue of virgins he'd laid and the blazing eyes of married women. He was six years older than I and left his grammar school girlfriend for me. He wrote a letter to each of us from Prague. Together we went to the school porter, who would place any letters on the ledge of his cubby-hole on the ground floor. In my letter it said that I was his chosen one; what it had said in the other was plain from the dirty looks directed at me by my rival.

The medic came home for the autumn break and was the first to kiss me the way adult males kiss. That took place behind the three crates that were piled up inside our gateway. My mother caught us at it and yelled severely and for all to hear: "Iboja, what are you doing! Pull yourself together and get inside!"

Mum's humiliating proceeding put paid to my relationship with the medic. But that wasn't the only contributing factor: I'd imagined he would smell like fresh oranges, but before our date he'd eaten his fill of garlic toast. When I admonished him, he replied huffily: "You don't expect me to eat violets just for some woman's sake, do you?"

The third object of my interest was a twenty-eight-year-old ethnologist. We'd met on our bikes, I on my way from Mikuláš to Okoličné, he from Okoličné to Mikuláš. I had a puncture and he offered to repair it for me. I took a shine to him because he looked like the French actor Charles Boyer.

Our trysts were in secret. When I asked him, he let me have a puff of his cigarette as we lay in the grass on the bank of the Váh. The smoke, along with my joy at the ethnologist's very presence, made my head spin and thus I learned to smoke. We went on long hikes in the hills and dales, during which he taught me not to be ashamed of the least aesthetic of human needs.

Mum thought I was taking those hiking trips with a whole gaggle of young folk. She certainly wouldn't have let me go with a single adult male. Goodness knows what might happen! But we only ever kissed and between one assignation and the next we would write each other poems, in Slovak, German or French. In every respect these meetings were educational. The ethnologist was only in town for a longish visit and after he left I did miss him, for about a week.

II

I was in the habit of lying out in the grass on the hills beyond the railway embankment. All round the horizon the Tatra Mountains reared high and in their embrace I used to read, or watch the clouds flying by, or the people outlined behind the windows of passing trains, or, behind the trains, like a farewell, the slowly dispersing rings of smoke. Everything carried with it the perfumed aura of an eternity that, in a form unknown to me, went on and on beneath the endless firmament, beyond seven mountains and seven rivers.[17]

The Váh was not one of those seven rivers. It did not live solely in my imagination. In the meadows that line its banks the town lived out its free time to the full. Young folk bathed to great bursts of laughter, much shouting, questions and answers flying this way and that above the current, boys and girls got to know each other better, ducks, geese and goats grazed the grass and there lay I, studying, but, above all, devouring one book after another. Kitsch and fine literature alike disappeared down the funnel of my bottomless curiosity. And when I found in some book words whose meaning I couldn't grasp, they were a promise that one day I would be also able to open with impunity the door to the thirteenth room.

On the far side lay the Gypsy settlement. Hovels knocked together from boards, planks, odd bits of wood carried down by the river, and sheets of iron. Among them the Gypsy children would run about, scraggy horses would graze, there'd be open fires and over it all a hotchpotch of colours and noises. It was across the river, actually quite close, but remote and imbued with a frightening attractive force, which would steer well clear of having crossed the bridge to Il'anovo to go and pick primroses on the stony, grass-decked hillside beyond the Gypsy settlement.

The sun was also shining down warm on my deaf-and-blind absorption in Sinclair Lewis's *Babbitt* and one of the goats began to munch, unobserved and with gusto, my Latin dictionary. It was saved for me by a passing young stranger, who introduced himself as a doctor who'd just begun working at the hospital in Palúdzka.

"That book you're reading, it must be interesting, certainly more interesting than your Latin dictionary," he said as he sat down on the grass beside me.

I closed my book, revealing both its title and the author's name.

"Do you read a lot of foreign literature?"

"Anything I can lay my hands on."

"And do you read any Slovak literature?"

"Of course, Slovak and Czech, prose and verse. Presently I'm most taken by the verse of Nezval and Surrealism, because it's so surprisingly full of unexpected images, ideas, flights of fancy, so unfettered, original and universal, unconventional and unbound by tradition..."

"Either you've read that somewhere or you're one of those who find Slovak poetry too traditional, too attached to the native sod, maybe a bit too patriotic and provincial..."

"You said that, not me, but why such acrimony..."

"I'll give it to you straight, because I love my people and its creativity, and I know what it has had to go through, and because now's the time for us to make a show of our patriotism and assert our sovereignty, with our own political rights, and to shake off the label of a nation without a history."

"Forgive me, but to the best of my knowledge the Slovaks joined the new Czechoslovak Republic voluntarily."

"Yes, because they wanted to be rid of the stifling embrace of the Hungarians while also being a counterweight to the three million Germans in the Republic. That was conditional on the autonomy promised them, but not delivered. From the outset, Andrej Hlinka tried to force the government in Prague to fulfil that promise. The world accepted Czechoslovakia as one state and one nation. But there's no such thing as a Czechoslovak nation. And the Czechoslovak people is nonsense!"

"Does that mean you're opposed to coexistence with the Czechs in a common state?"

"No! I'm not opposed to the Czechs. I recognize the high level of Czech culture and scholarship and I respect the effort put by the Czechs into the preservation and cultivation of Slovak culture before the birth of the Republic. But the time has come when it is essential for our coexistence to be played out on the basis of an agreement between two separate nations. In a nutshell, for us to cease to be a kind of colony managed from Prague."

The young doctor's dream came true thanks to Hitler and the unwillingness and unpreparedness of Britain and France to go to war "on behalf of a small, unknown sausage-shaped country", and to their naive, cosy notion that compromises with Hitler in the interest of preserving "eternal peace" were possible. There were even those who warned against the plague looming over Europe, but then, why break one's back and try to leap when it's easier to grovel?

Hitler was determined to wipe Czechoslovakia off the map and used Germans and pro-German lobbyists in the West as a spearhead. By resorting to his SA- and SS-like strike forces, Konrad Henlein, the leader of the Sudeten National Socialist Party, provoked bloody clashes in the border region and complained that the government in Prague was failing to observe minority rights and that German and other minorities were entitled to return home.

On 29 September 1938, seventh months after the Anschluß that united Austria with Germany, Hitler, Mussolini, Chamberlain and Daladier signed the so-called Munich Agreement. Czechoslovakia had to cede Sudetenland to the Third Reich.

Surfacing from that time, which is played out before my eyes on an old, damaged, brown strip of film, I have a clear image of my father. He's sitting on a kitchen chair, unravelling his green foot-rags. He's glad to be back home, but feels ashamed that we had mobilized but then lost everything without having put up a fight, saying something said later, with minor changes, by the French politician Léon Blum: "We've gained some relief, but our pants are full."

However, Hitler had more cards up his sleeve. One of these was the Slovak separatist movement headed by the Catholic priest Jozef Tiso. On March 14, 1939, Slovakia's independence was declared in Vienna. At the same time, President Beneš's successor, the aged Emil Hácha, received orders to visit Hitler in Berlin. At a meeting held at night, under the threat that Prague might be bombed, he was forced to sign a document according to which the two heads of state agreed jointly to maintain order on their respective territories. The following day, Hitler entered Prague. The Czech Lands were proclaimed to be the Protectorate of Bohemia and Moravia (Böhmen und Mähren), under the protection of the German Reich. In addition, Hitler seized the highly developed Czech arms industry.

At our club, Alex, who was the first of us to have read *Mein Kampf* and now listened to the news on a range of radio stations, would give us quotes from the western press as an ironic commentary on their own blindness:

Eternal Anglo-German cooperation.

Peace preserved, the Parisians rejoiced.

Are we really to believe that Hitler's ultimate goal is genuinely as blood-curdling as is sometimes alleged?

But Hitler has said more than once that he has no intention of attacking France or England.

Peace in our time!!!

Peace in our time lasted eleven months.

12

In April 1939, one group of grammar school pupils started wearing uniforms of the Hlinka Guard.[18] They were proud of their polished boots and puffed up to bursting point with their sense of superiority and power. I was very surprised and dismayed when even Milan came into the classroom in uniform. I hadn't expected that of him. It took away the universal humanity that, for reasons unknown, I had ascribed to him, and brought him close to fascism. Mária, a new girl in town following her brother-in-law's starting work at the Tatra Bank, mounted the platform and declaimed, "I'm proud of you boys. You're doing the right thing!" I went over to Milan and whispered, "You too, Brutus, my lad...?" I don't know if it was my words or his intrinsic otherness that killed off his leaning towards that trend in politics. He only appeared once in uniform, on the day when one of the girls in our class, from a well-known Lutheran family, used the break after the first lesson to write on the board, in large letters "President Masaryk – we shall remain true to your legacy."

Things were still at that early stage when ominous changes start to loom, when the old was still mingled with the new and various things could be said without adverse consequences. It was also the last year in which Jewish pupils were allowed to graduate from high school. I was still over six months away from my eighteenth birthday. During the eight years of my studies I had been so little involved in anything, perhaps also from a sense of vulnerability, that no one in my class had really come to know me. I was allowed, however, to take the school-leaving exams. Then suddenly a minor miracle seemed to strike.

Faced with the board of examiners sitting at their table, I suddenly felt as if a curse had been lifted, as if I had become unchained. I performed with confidence, answering all the questions effortlessly, possibly also because I was certain that no one was going to twist them in front of witnesses. I did ask the young Latin teacher the meaning of one or two words, then I translated the required text with ease and fluency.

I was among the best of the best and the examiners puzzled over the marks in my pupil's record book. "How is this possible?" one of them asked our form mistress, a teacher of Slovak, with whom I'd had problems because of her fossilized lack of imagination or any sense of psychology and the impression I'd formed that she'd just learned the things she was teaching by heart. The history teacher, a Czech who quite liked the new path being taken in Slovakia and whom I didn't like because he had a nasty, sarcastic streak, came over to me and said, "Congratulations, you were excellent!"

Was I delighted at this "triumph"? Certainly, but only briefly. My success only afforded a moment's intoxication that evaporated the moment I came down the school steps and re-entered daily life as lived in the Slovak State.

The consequences of the Munich Agreement left most of the betrayed and democratically minded citizens of Bohemia, plus a handful of those in Slovakia, with the impression that the sole friend and sole political guarantor of their survival was the Soviet Union. There was barely a single Czech poet who didn't give vent in their verse to their anger, bitterness and new outlook on the future of Europe, her betrayers and her saviours. At our club we eagerly discussed the political situation and what to do about it. Some of us decided, where possible, to join in the secret resistance against fascism. For the soul of someone with my background and for those who didn't accept the government's programme uncritically, these were inhospitable times, battered and tattered by blows of every kind. I seemed to be seeing the times from a distance, in rapidly changing images as caught through the windows of a moving train, at whose destination I could only guess, while knowing it boded no good for me. And it seemed as if the person feeling, seeing and hearing everything was merely my double.

Nothing was as it had been. Everything had been tossed about. Only shards were left. What had been necessary and normal was now unnecessary and abnormal. Trust, tolerance, peace of mind, joy, friendship, certainty, laughter, sadness and tears had become targets of violence. All doors had been flung open to ignominy, degradation, thievery and the violation of the intimacy of private life. The previous legal norm no longer applied, ethical standards had lost their value, truth had become untruth and lies had become truth. Only my hope and my self-assurance remained unimpaired. And there was also the consolation that sprang from the actions of good people, and those who could not be bought in the dangerous circumstances that now prevailed. But these were all mere feelings, a reflection and – under the magnifying glass of my impressions – a concentrated radiance emanating from all the injunctions, dictates and imperatives issued by the new regime. A regime that had adopted and enhanced the laws of the Third Reich.

13

Concerning injunctions, dictates and imperatives

In 1940, the so-called Central Office for Economics elaborated a plan for the removal of Jews from the economic life of the Slovak State and the transfer of their property to Aryan ownership. Legalized theft, labelled "Aryanization", was based on the racialist theory of the right of the Übermensch to "de-Jewify" society, i.e. cleanse it of its noxious, inferior elements. Citizens split into Aryanizers and non-Aryanizers.

Thieving also went on in other ways: Hlinka's guards in black uniforms and jackboots would carry out random house searches. They were looking for objects of value, hidden treasures, clothes and jewellery. They would leave hung about with carpets and curtains, their arms full of pictures, mats, vases, china, cutlery, typewriters, radios and even items essential to daily life.

During one search, which also involved some former acquaintances or people I barely knew, but who would say hello if we met in the high street, presumably thinking me worthy of their attention, but now going by the slogan "Just take what they've bagged!", I was standing, arms folded, leaning against the table. I stared with revulsion at the open wardrobes and the crumpled underwear hanging there, the drawers that had been taken out and thrown about, and at the empty shelves and the books tossed all over the floor or kicked into a corner. I felt totally alienated and suddenly nothing mattered.

"You're just common-or-garden lowlife. You should be ashamed to be thieving like this in public!" I said, totally indifferent to what consequences it might lead to.

They glanced at me, laughed and marched off. I was perhaps the only one there feeling such shame at their barbaric goings-on.

Jews were banned from swimming pools, skating rinks and sports grounds. They weren't allowed in the cinema. They weren't allowed to visit Aryan households and Aryans were forbidden to receive Jewish visitors.

People who failed to observe this ban on contact with Jews were nicknamed "white Jews".

Jews were not allowed out in the evening. Jewish children could only attend Jewish schools. Higher education was off limits.

You needed a special license to travel and could then occupy only the last carriages of trains. On buses, Jews had to stand on the rear platform. If there wasn't enough room for Aryans, Jews had to alight and make room.

Jews were not allowed to keep dogs, and they had to wear a yellow star sewn onto their clothes over where their heart lay concealed. Jewish tenants had to move out of their flats if some non-Jew showed an interest.

After the Hitlerite Nazi model, Jews were superfluous, eradicable victims of fascistic megalomania, exposed to every kind of degradation and treated as non-persons. And I, one of those imperilled by such inhumanity, but with my soul untouched by the injustice and the abusive name-calling, moved through the present as through a mist, and my sharpened senses seemed to be taking in what was going on all by themselves.

To this day I can see the huge black inscriptions on walls, kiosks and empty shop windows: "Jews to Palestine!", "Jewish shambles!", "Jews out!" To this day I can hear the screams of old men having their beards yanked and the pounding of jackboots. And I can still hear creeping into my memory, as if by the back door, the words "Let's toss all the Jews of Kežmarok into the stream" (in Slovak it rhymes). I don't recall any similar chant relating to Mikuláš, but if it had crossed their minds that it rhymes with "goulash" I can well imagine what they might have done with it. All the louder do I recapture the refrain of the Hlinka Guards' marching song: "Let's draw their blood by cut and thrust, by no means shall we be the first..." and I have a clear vision of the creepy, bare, junk-shop-like image of the room inside County Hall where we handed in our jumpers and coats as "winter aid", and my ears still fill with an echo of one sentence uttered by the interior minister from the balcony of that same County Hall: "We'll soon wipe the grin of the Jews' faces..." which seemed to be foretelling the transports to Poland, to Auschwitz etc., which began in March 1942.

While it was still possible, and even for a short period after it was banned, we would steal out at night with coloured chalk in our pockets. On walls and fences we would write or post up calls to fight fascism and we slipped illegal leaflets through people's doors and into their yards. We would hold secret meetings by the Váh and, concealed beneath the willow branches, we would quietly sing:

Možno, že to všetko nie je pravda,
že je to iba zlý sen.
Čakám na svoje zobudenie.
Čakám na nový deň.

Maybe none of this is real,
maybe it's just an evil dream.
I'm waiting for the day I wake,
and for this to in the past have been.

14

"You need to bribe the notary," said my father.

"But how, Dad? I've never ever done anything like that!"

"If these were normal times, I'd never ask anything of the kind of you, but if you want to avoid deportation, you have to have a try. Lila got a travel permit solely on the basis of a telegram that spoke of her terminally sick "fiancé". We can't afford two terminally sick fiancés in East Slovakia. So get going."

"And what if the notary throws me out?"

"He won't."

"How do you know?"

"I know and there's an end of it. Here's your ID book, I've put a 1000-crown note in it with just half a centimetre showing. I'd give more, but haven't got any. Now go!"

Father had a plan, each stage of which had to be carried out down to the last detail. In East Slovakia Lila had met up with a people smuggler, whom Father had found via some folk he knew, and she's agreed with him on the date and time for crossing the frontier into Hungary. The date on Lila's travel document had had to be forged so that we could travel together.

I set off, regretting that my childhood angels weren't carrying me down the steps. I hauled myself across the square like an overloaded little donkey. I glanced at the books in Klimeš's bookshop. They all merged before my eyes into a gaudy blur. Making several detours, I was getting ever closer to taking an unpleasant, but necessary step. I opened the huge yellow door of the law court, my heart pounding. Slowly I walked along the stone-paved corridor. On the left there was a door bearing the inscription *Notarius publicus*. I wavered as I stood in front of it, but the awareness of my responsibility for a happy outcome to Father's rescue plan forced me to open it.

Sitting at the typewriter on the office desk was a blonde female clerk. I knew her and that made me feel a bit better, while also giving me a fright. She looked up at me.

"Hi, Iboja... How may I help you?" she asked in a neutral tone of voice.

"I'd like to speak to the notary."

"Wait a moment, I'll see if he's available..." she said, then she got up from her desk and crossed to the notary's office door, which she opened.

"It's all right, you can go in," she announced.

"How may I help you?" asked the notary, a man with sleek black hair, parted at the side. Beneath his pointy beard I could see a red bow tie peeping out from his snow-white collar.

"I need a travel permit, please," I said, passing my citizen's ID book to him. He glanced at it, reached for it, stood up and went off with it into a back room. He was back in no time, handed me my ID, now freed of its 1000 crowns, opened the door and called: "Milka, be so good as to issue a travel permit for the young lady. I've signed it, so you do the rest."

"For how many days?" Milka asked me. "I need to know the name of the town you're travelling to and the date of your return."

"I'm going to visit my family in Trebišov for three days," I replied, hoping that it wouldn't dawn on Milka that Trebišov was close to the Hungarian border.

Milka saw nothing suspicious and with the travel document in my pocket I hurried back across the courtyard, into the street and home, amazed at how easy it was to bribe a public official.

"People are like the times they live in," said my father, to whom I remain grateful to this day for the determination and self-control that overlay all the pain, doubts and fears for our future and also for his unshakeable belief in our ability to find our way through a jungle rife with labyrinthine hurdles.

Father set out his plan: the only country where we had any hope of surviving as fugitives was semi-fascist Hungary. In the other surrounding countries fascism was in full sway. We were to take only the barest essentials with us. Underwear, nightwear, two blouses, two jumpers and the most basic sanitary requirements. Our parents had had blue gabardine costumes made for us and grey woollen coats with a fishbone pattern. The coats had an A-shape cut, buttoned-on hoods and wide belts, which tightened the bottom half into a bell shape. In our new outfits and grey walking shoes we did look elegant. Elegance was part of the plan.

"You have to act with self-assurance, as if you were used to being waited on, especially when you go to a hotel. Nobody will ask you awkward questions and they'll be polite to you. Clothes make the man, as you know. When you reach Trebišov, find a hotel, leave your things there and go to the smuggler. You've got his address. The crossing and the money are all sorted out. The smuggler will help you exchange Slovak crowns for Hungarian pengő. It's a bit of a problem you not speaking Hungarian, so you'll have to stick to German. You're from Austria, orphans in search of relatives who live in Hungary. It's a pretty poor excuse, but I haven't come up with anything better. When it comes to shopping or food, if possible look out for shops or taverns with German-Jewish names.

"In Budapest, which is your goal, we've got some distant relations, two brothers whose young mother died, after which they were brought up by my father's first wife. I wasn't born then, but I remember them being mentioned later with the names Dudi and Feri, and that their surname was Ferenczi. The boys were taken to Budapest by their father after he got a job there as a porcelain painter. We rarely heard anything about them and latterly nothing at all. You must try to find them.

"If you do make it to Budapest and do find the Ferenczis, send a telegram at once with the text 'Uncle is well again'. If you end up settling somewhere else, your telegram should say 'Auntie Klára has had her operation'. Sign both telegrams 'Pali'".

"Rudo, the neighbours' son, has an aunt in Budapest and he's given me her address. You can turn to her as well when she gets back from a trip to Debrecen. You're to slip in her letter box the address where Rudo will find you after he's smuggled out two suitcases of summer and winter clothes for you, as he's promised. As you know, Rudo's a rather adventurous young buck. He's already smuggled out into Hungary, he didn't tell me how, whole wagonloads of farm machinery, and he'll be helping you not just as a friend, but also as a bit of a lad."

As I was wondering where my parents had found the money for this extremely costly enterprise, I remembered we'd been sent some dollars from America, unfortunately too late and not enough for all of us to make the trip across the sea. Father had given my uncle, who was about to emigrate illegally, his share, and Rudo may have helped him sell some of the dollars.

15

A new flag is flying from the County Hall balcony: a double-barred cross on three stylized waves[19] – the symbol of the clero-fascist Slovak state. Not long ago we were a democracy and now we're a dictatorship. Many people have adapted to the new order. Some with relish and Schadenfreude, others implicitly – they have children and need to provide for their subsistence, but there are others who remain as they have always been and evince their disposition with a smile, a hello, by not looking the other way and by secretly helping those in need.

As one walks through the town, the world looks quite ordinary, as if its face has not been scarred with black and dirty-red exanthema and yellow stars. The same old well is still there in front of the County Hall. The butcher still stands outside his shop, legs apart, hands beneath his bloodstained apron, looking up at the sky and holding his face out to the rays of the spring sun. The dairy is still exuding the sharp, cool smell of sour milk and bryndza. Tunes from operettas come streaming out of the open, net-curtained, first-floor windows above the pharmacy. The tender leaves of the young acacias flicker in the gentle breeze. Before long, the lindens will be filling the air with their scent.

Children are walking or hopping along the pavements as I turn the corner from the square towards Vyšný Hušták in the company of Kubo (not his real name, just a shortening of his surname), who is about to complete his military service at a Slovakian Army works unit in Liptovský Svätý Peter.

I'm fond of Kubo and admire his profound knowledge of human nature, acquired from his having studied art and literature while simultaneously studying medicine. Surrealism is tailor-made for his perception of our paradoxical times, when what's called "normal" is more absurd than the worst nightmare. He battles with its cruelty and dehumanization with black humour, self-mockery and the strong language with which he fights back against the awareness of his own possible demise. What surprises me most is the unshakeable self-respect and hope that his attitude radiates. He has blue eyes set in a handsome face, thick, light brown hair and a deep voice filled with a penetrating and all-embracing sensuality.

"Given that so many priests are so fanatically in favour of

fascism, and that our president is a prelate with good relations with the Vatican, then even the Good Lord must be shielding them. And those friends in the third Reich are so clever: they got rid of unemployment and overcame at a stroke all the problems that democracy had failed to solve, so it's no surprise they kow-tow to them..." he says.

We've reached the northern edge of the town close to the protestant orphanage and cemetery. There's a small square patch of grass with two dark-red benches beneath some ancient chestnut trees. We've just got time to sit down for a quick chat. Two Gypsy women have emerged from the narrow alleyway between the fire walls. I know they must have first crossed the bridge, then passed by the old tower dating back to the time of the Turkish invasions, the bell tower and the cottages and gardens in Vrbica.

"I should go so I'm not late back to the camp," says Kubo, glancing at his watch. "My train's due any moment."

We hurry off and make it to the train in the nick of time.

Kubo waves to me from the window and shouts: "Till we meet again!" and I shout back after the moving train: "I'm looking forward to it!"

But I looked forward in vain. Shortly after we met, his entire camp went down with some infection. I wasn't to see him again until the day before I left for Trebišov.

It's been raining all day. Gutters are overflowing, raindrops are streaming down windows, running down tree trunks, flicking off branches, spattering against walls. The street is awash with rainwater. There's a wind blowing and the air is unpleasantly cold and damp. Kubo is leaning against next door's fence trying in vain to light a cigarette. His dark-blue uniform is all crumpled. His sleeves are too short, leaving his bare wrists poking right out. Standing beside him, I get a whiff of mothballs and chlorine. I'm angry with myself because the sight of his appearance and condition has taken the edge off our meeting. "God, you're an idiot!" I tell myself, but I can't help it. The rain, wind and all the rest has turned the world into a junk shop and left me genderless.

"Do you think I don't know how I look and how you're seeing me?" Kubo says. "They disinfected me with my clothes on and like them I've shrunk and I stink. I've come from the hospital in Ružomberok, where they treated me for pneumonia. My train leaves in forty-five minutes. So will you see me off? I can't stay here. I mean to disappear."

We're half-way to the station and just as I'm turning to Kubo to tell him that I shall also be elsewhere before long, I spot the Hlinka guards. Three of them. They've come up silently from behind, surrounded Kubo and now they're kicking him with their gleaming jackboots. Kubo tries in vain to protect himself, but is grossly outnumbered.

"Go home, bitch!" one of them roars at me. But I don't go and become witness to Kubo's utter degradation. Three pairs of black arms lift him up high like a figurine and drop him flat on his face. They tramp up and down his back and keep hitting him with their coshes.

"Stop! Stop that! Leave him alone, you bastards!" I shout. But the guards ignore me, adjust their uniforms, tighten their belts and depart, chortling and mouthing off: "Serves him right, the stinking Jew! We should have slung 'em out long ago!"

For a while Kubo remains prostrate. Then he arduously sits up. I can tell his body is hurting all over. His face is a network of cuts and scratches, but finally he manages to sit up, take out his handkerchief and wipe the blood and mud from his face. His handkerchief isn't big enough, so I offer him mine. He takes it, but without looking at me. He checks that his teeth are all right, but with such detachment that I feel excluded from his proximity.

"There'll be nothing left of us," he says, and he knows that I know what he means.

16

Father, Mum, Dalma, Bábo and Grétka are standing beneath the old mulberry tree in the yard of the last house opposite the Jewish cemetery, which we all called home. It was March 1942, after the first transport from Mikuláš to Poland. I just had time to catch sight of those being transported, young folk, not much older than me. Many of them were newlyweds who'd thought that marriage would save them from being carted away. Rumours were rife and any drowning man clutches at straws. They sang as they walked along in lines, comforting themselves that they weren't alone, that their lot was being shared with others, that there was solidarity among them. Lila and I totally rejected any such solidarity, because it was being manifested against a background of utter humiliation. Which was also why, as we parted from our parents and siblings beneath the trees, we called back "Good bye and see you soon!" one last time from the gateway as we waved a fond farewell. We hadn't wanted to part at the station, where everyone would have seen us, and we felt safe in the belief that we would be back.

To play safe, we bought return tickets. The train was late. There were other passengers sitting or standing about in the waiting room and on the platform. So as to avoid their gazes, we'd bought some illustrated magazines, in which we eagerly buried ourselves. When the train finally pulled in twenty minutes late, our own stress and disquiet were also set in motion. With beating hearts we boarded one of the end carriages and found a compartment in which there were only two other passengers.

Towns and villages swept past, one station after the next. By the time the train stopped at Poprad it started to rain. Flowers were beginning to peep out from under the leaves that had fallen on the embankments the previous autumn. Through the open window we could scent the earth as it woke to springtime. Just before we reached Košice we heard noises coming from the next compartment, shouting, crying and a voice that was trying to restore calm.

"Papers and travel passes," came the order from the door of our compartment that had been slid open. Two Hlinka guards were running checks.

"Okay," said the one who'd just checked my permit.

"This date must have been falsified. We need to take a closer look!" said the one checking Lila's papers. We were saved by a scream coming from the next compartment. The two guards dashed off to see and never came back. But when the train stopped at Košice, the passengers carried from it a woman who was covered in blood, and the Hlinka guards led off the man who had stabbed her.

"And they were supposedly on their honeymoon..." said one lady as she returned, distraught, from the platform to her seat on the train. When we finally reached Trebišov, it was nearly evening. It had stopped raining and the moon was up. Neither Lila nor I have any sense of direction and so we let ourselves be seduced by the red neon lights of the Hotel Excelsior directly opposite the station and made straight for it across the railway lines. We trod the gravel and stepped on the sleepers. Our footsteps echoed into the darkness that was shot through by the light of the moon.

"What's that, over there to the right...?" Lila whispered, pointing to a line of freight train trucks with small, barred windows. Eyes watched us through the bars as if trying to ask us something. The people in the train trucks, if they were people, were silent. They struck us as emissaries of Silence.

We crossed the railway lines and just as we were about to follow a short row of young weeping willows to reach the footpath opposite, a few lines from a long-forgotten poem came back to me:

*Ten clivý večer
rozprávali stromy,
že najsmutnejšie z nich,
keď hovoria,
sú vŕby.*

*That wistful evening
the trees were saying
that the saddest of them,
when they speak,
are willows.*

A photo of me at 18 years old.

On the outskirts of Liptovský Svätý Mikuláš. The only photograph I found in a pile of trash when I returned home in June 1945.

A street in Mikuláš in the early 1930s.

Barnes were used for storing leaflets.

BOOK 2

FLIGHT

I

We reached the pavement down a narrow passage and crossed over to the hotel. The pale-green plaster was crumbling away from its shabby walls and the letter C in its grand, red, neon name was hanging head down. We'd let ourselves be drawn to this cheap place attached to the station, but we had no desire to go looking for something better in a town we didn't know. The wide door with rounded windows in its upper half showed signs of being frequently kicked, and the part round the handle was smirched. On the black-and-white imitation marble tiles in the lobby, a Gypsy woman was wiping away some muddy shoe stains with a wet rag. At the desk sat a thin fellow wearing a shapeless, outsize brown sweater. His eyes of an uncertain shade peered at us from above the pale, thin whiskers beneath his long red nose. He had a chequered woollen scarf wound several times round his neck and a blue beret on his head. He coughed and hawked and blew his nose into a crumpled dark-blue handkerchief, which he then stuck back in his trouser pocket. Standing on the counter next to him was a small cage. Inside it, a green parrot was turning somersaults round a horizontal perch. I enquired if we might have a room with a bath, to which the thin chap replied: "I do have a room free, but not with a bath; the shower and toilets are along the corridor. Will you take it?"

We exchanged glances and nodded. Playing the *grande dame* here would be ludicrous.

"It's on the first floor, number eleven," said the cold-ridden receptionist as he took a key on a pear-shaped tag from the wooden screen behind him, then he raised the flap of his counter and asked if he should take our suitcases.

"We're only staying one night," I said stiffly.

The fact of the receptionist's bow legs could not be concealed even by his broad, wrinkled trouser legs. The walls of the staircase shone with an oil-based, grey-green paint. The smell of cabbage coming from the kitchens also struck me as grey-green. "Come back! Come back!" squawked the parrot up the poorly lit stairwell, and I had a brief, but acute craving to be back home. This was driven away by the man's words as he unlocked room 11: "There's hot water in the kitchen and the restaurant serves hot meals until 10 p.m."

The room was pleasantly surprising. Everything in it was white. Wardrobe, mirror frame, beds and luggage shelf. Only the hangers inside the wardrobe were of various colours and sizes. The woollen blanket on the bed was orange and the pure white duvets beneath it lifted our spirits a degree or two. We brought jugfuls of water up from the kitchen, washed our hands and faces, combed our hair, left our bags on the bench, locked the door, returned the key and went out into the street. "Come back! Come back!" the parrot squawked after us.

In the hotel restaurant a Gypsy band was playing. A heavy drizzle was descending on Trebišov's one long, almost deserted street. The air was saturated with the scent of trees and of the damp soil of spring. From behind the brightly lit windows of taverns came the sounds of voices, laughter and the clinking of glasses. Most of the shops had their blinds drawn down. In the rows of houses, broken here and there by side passages or tiny gardens, indoor lights were glinting through the fabric of their curtains.

Number 157 at the far end of the town was a whitewashed building with green window shutters. Its front was almost completely hidden behind the branches of an old pear tree. There was a thin sliver of light beneath the front door. A lamp behind the window lit up the parti-coloured squares of glass. The door had neither bell nor knocker. We hammered on it.

"Come on in! Door's open," came a man's voice.

We pressed the handle down, opened the heavy, squeaking door and went straight into a large room, where a man in his underwear was sitting on a readymade bed. He had some brown check slippers on his feet. His soft, fleshy belly caused his singlet to billow. We exchanged hellos, remained standing and waited for him to offer us something to sit on. He didn't, but launched instead into an obviously prepared address: "I've been expecting you, but I have to tell you first of all that nothing's going to come of our arrangement. These last few days the border guards have caught twelve people. I'm sorry, but under these circumstances I can't take you across, and I don't even want to. It's too great a risk for me. Maybe I'm a coward, but you just try and find someone with more guts than me! And don't try talking me round. I wouldn't do it for three times the amount we've agreed on. I realise what a pickle I've got you into and I feel a bit embarrassed. So, you better go now!"

We backed out through the heavy oak door into the wet street with its meagre lights. Disappointment seemed to drip from us along with the rainwater from the overflowing eaves. The way back seemed a lot longer than the way there. We didn't speak. As we approached the hotel, Lila broke our shared silence, charged as it was with our private thoughts. "We'll think of something tomorrow, I'm sure," she said.

The cold-ridden receptionist was asleep at his counter. We woke him up and asked for our key. With no cover over his cage, the parrot was wide awake and screaming: "Come back! Come back!"

"Shut up, stupid, can't you see they're back already!" the disgruntled ex-sleeper snapped at it. He struggled to his feet, handed us our key and covered the cage with a red headscarf.

We slowly climbed the stairs amid the boiled cabbage fumes that, as the day had progressed, had condensed into a quite unpleasant odour. We agreed that we'd rise early and start looking for a solution to the near-impasse in which we found ourselves. We got undressed, did our teeth and went to bed.

We were woken by a noise: someone was hammering at the door. I glanced at my watch: two o'clock.

"Who's there?"

"Inspection," came the hoarse reply from the receptionist.

"What inspection? How dare you wake us up like this!" Lila shouted.

"You didn't register properly."

"Couldn't it have waited till morning?"

"No. The police carry out checks even during the night."

"Have you brought the registration form with you?" Lila asked and, the receptionist having confirmed that he had, she got out of bed and opened the door.

He came in, closed the door behind him and leaned against it. "I know why you're here. You want to escape to Hungary. I could report you, and whether I do or don't, that depends on you."

"Out! Clear off this instant, or *we'll* report *you* if the police really do show up. Close the door behind you and don't even think of waking us up again!" Lila managed to say with such force, conviction and outrage that the receptionist slithered back out, closing the door behind him. We listened as his footsteps receded, waited for about thirty minutes and then stole out into the corridor to check what chances there were of concealment or escape.

The back door was open. Steps led through the empty kitchen out into the yard, where there were some outbuildings that might afford sanctuary in the event of some dire peril. But the rest of the night passed uneventfully and we managed to sleep until six-thirty.

The place in reception previously taken by the skinny fellow with the awful cold was now occupied by a stout, red-faced woman. We paid our bill and left the Excelsior. The sky was overcast and Trebišov was just as drowsy as we were. The only signs of life in the street were a horse and cart, a milkman with his cart laden with cans, a handful of workmen on their way to work and, across the way, a tavern that was open. We crossed the street and went inside.

There was a handful of early-morning habitués at the tables and rather more began drifting into the canteen area. There were some older men, perhaps widowers or old bachelors, and people on their way to their offices. They shared the morning papers out between them. There were cardboard beer mats on the red-and-white chequered tablecloths. We played with them while we waited. A waiter in a red-and-white striped waistcoat brought us some breakfast. Slowly we ate our rolls with butter and apricot jam, drank our white coffees and looked alternately at a newspaper and the now rather livelier street outside the windows.

Time had stopped still and we were at a loss as to how to set it back in motion.

"Iboja, quick, pay!" Lila suddenly whispered urgently, then she rose, crossed to the door, charged across the street to the pavement opposite and began talking to a young man who looked vaguely familiar.

I paid, crossed to join Lila and realized that I knew the young man from Mikuláš, where his father had a job at the county court. His name was Martin, but we called him Rusty because of his curly, copper-coloured hair. As we chatted, Martin explained his presence in Trebišov: his father was working there as a judge. "And what are you two doing in Trebišov?" he asked in tones that suggested he suspected what the answer to his question might be, a suspicion bolstered by the words: "I think it would be best if you came home with me."

On the way there, he assured us that his father would definitely help us, that he knew plenty of people-smugglers from his courtroom and he knew which ones could be trusted.

"But for a reputable judge that would be an illegal procedure, a crime that could get him locked up," I remarked, but my words carried not a hint of disapprobation. Far from it! I was glad that this deus ex machina had appeared on the scene to set our stalled time back in motion.

"Abnormal times demand abnormal actions on the part of reputable people. I know my father's attitude. I know how he views what's going on here. He's a decent man, a practising Christian, Lutheran, and loving thy neighbour is something he takes seriously. Trust me. He'll find you someone to get you across the border, and I even know who. His father's Slovak and his mother Hungarian. For years he's been crossing the border in secret and taking supplies to his poor relations. He's more an adventurer than a smuggler. But I'll tell you now, he won't get you into Hungary for nothing; he needs money!"

It all turned out exactly as Martin had foretold. His chubby little mother immediately offered us a warm bath and some lunch, and his father, informed in advance by Martin, had found us a helper. The day would have passed in perfect harmony had it not been for one minor unpleasantness: my elegant new, grey shoes had left me with a painful blister on my right heel. Martin's mum offered me some shoes of hers, but she had size 35 and I was a 37. She cleaned my wound, stuck a plaster on it and tied it round with gauze. After dinner, our unknown helper tapped out the agreed signal on the kitchen window. We put on our coats, packed our bags, thanked our kindly hosts for their unexpected assistance, which was given at great personal risk, said our farewells, and set off into the dark of night with our smuggler.

2

By the light of the lamp in the kitchen I had a brief, clear sight of the man described by Martin as more adventurer than smuggler. Tall, broad-shouldered, with a weather-beaten but pleasant, sharp-cut face, he was to me the embodiment of a smuggler as I had mentally painted one after the romanticized figure of "Heathcliff" from the Mikuláš nick. He welcomed us with the words: "Never you fear. I know the border like the back of my hand!"

We left by the back gate. It had stopped raining. The way was lit for us by the moon. Via a small spinney of spruce we came out into the fields, where the wind was blowing unimpeded. Wet lumps of clay kept sticking to our shoes. We scraped them off with bits of wood and flat stones. The blister on my heel was still playing up, but I gritted my teeth to ignore the pain. In the dark among the trees of the dense forest that had now emerged before us after we'd crossed the fields, stood a well-concealed cabin. The smuggler passed through the trees and unlocked the cabin door.

Its loud creak disturbed the silence beneath the star-filled night sky. In the dark, the smuggler moved around as silently as an animal and he came back out with lumps of bread and smoked ham. He put them in his rucksack and said, "The bread's gone hard, but it's still edible!"

We carried on, forcing our way through brambles and bushes. Twigs kept lashing at our faces. Something in the trees let out a screech. We'd woken a sleeping bird. We proceeded through patches of mist. Rainwater dripped incessantly from the trees.

"Your coats are ideal, dark-grey and barely visible in the dark, and your hoods hide your faces well," the smuggler commented. Suddenly he fell silent, stopped in his tracks and raised an arm to signal that we weren't to move. "Hide behind the trees," he whispered.

In the moonlight, the figures of two border guards and their angled rifle barrels were silhouetted against the sky. One of them was trying to light a cigarette. The flame flared up and died. We stood there, silent and patiently waiting. After the man had finished his cigarette, he and the other disappeared into the forest.

"Now!" said the smuggler. "Two steps and hit the ground. There's a main road ahead. We need to crawl across it!"

We lay on our stomachs and, slithering like lizards, we crossed the road and crawled into the woods on the far side. Having got back on our feet, we shook off all the dust and dirt. We walked on through a pine forest and I felt as if some alien being was writing in white chalk on a blackboard somewhere inside my head: I'm following my nose through an emanation of ploughland in a hot-green darkness, along soggy paths, between dark tree stumps into a night filled with mute shadows on grass, snow-whitened in the moonlight.

The pain of my blister rose in proportion to the time we spent wandering beneath the night sky, as far away as possible from human habitation. Somewhere a dog barked. Dawn was breaking and we could detect the outlines of cottages, stables and barns. The scent of spring suddenly seemed to intensify. We came to a halt by a ditch filled with rainwater. The smuggler jumped across it, then turned to face us with an outstretched arm. "Jump!" he said.

We jumped across the ditch and found ourselves in a quagmire full of squelching mud. It spurted up as high as our coat hems.

"Welcome to Hungary!" said our helper, a broad smile baring his gleaming white teeth.

We clung to field boundaries. The sun was just rising as we entered the yard of a large farmstead.

"There's a cowshed over there," the smuggler said, pointing. "Go inside and have a rest. I'll come for you as and when necessary."

On our way to the stable we heard him banging on a window and calling out: "Borodabácsi [Uncle Boroda]... Borodabácsi... Rise and shine! Borodabácsi!"

We lay down in some straw. The cows stood patiently in their stalls, chewing the cud and swishing flies away with their tails. Worn out and sleepy, woozy with the animal warmth, the smell and the fumes coming from dung and manure, we heard, just before we fell asleep, the sound of a window being opened and a deep, gravelly male voice saying: "Hang on, I'll be with you as soon as I get my pants on."

After about an hour the smuggler came to get us. He led us off into the kitchen, where there was a grumpy woman in slippers with a tasselled woollen square tossed over her long, yellow, flannel nightdress. She was stoking the range with logs. Borodabácsi, the middle-aged, red-faced farmer, brimming with health, was seated at the table as he offered the smuggler a tot of plum brandy.

"Borodabácsi will take you to the nearest town inside Hungary,

Sátoraljaújhely, where the annual fair happens to be taking place. He'll change your crowns for pengő for you and you can give him something for his trouble. Anything else you'll have to take care of yourselves," the smuggler informed us.

We paid him 2000 Slovak crowns and, having thanked us, he wished us all the very best, said good-bye and left. I felt immediately that the atmosphere in the unfamiliar kitchen had gone cold, despite the gaily crackling logs.

The lady in the nightdress still hadn't said a word. She silently set on the table before us two plates of scrambled eggs, two thick slices of buttered black bread and a pot of white coffee.

"They have to be out of here as soon as possible, you know what the town crier said and what was reported on the radio. They might come for us and lock us up!" As she pleaded with her husband she was tugging at the tassels on her scarf as if she meant to yank them right off. "There was also that piece in the paper."

The farmer thumped the table with his fist. "Do shut up! Find them a couple of heavy woollen scarves instead. They need to be wrapped up tight when I drive off with them," he ordered his wife.

By the time the farmer had hitched up his horses and as his wife was hunting for some heavy woollen scarves, we had finished our generous breakfast. At the realization that we'd soon be out of there, the farmer's wife mellowed, wished us success with our endeavours and consigned us firmly to the care of the merciful Lord God.

With our stomachs full we felt idle, sleepier and even more fatigued. We felt frozen in the biting cold of the morning air. We drew our coat belts tight, tossed our bags into the hay wagon, clambered aboard it, wrapped ourselves tight in the heavy woollen scarves and sat down on the wagon floor. The wagon set off, rattling its way along gravel tracks through several villages until it reached the highway. The regular clip-clop of the horses' hooves only made us even dozier. We snoozed almost the entire journey.

On the main road, other wagons were jolting along before and behind us. Some men and women were on foot, with huge baskets on their backs and smaller ones slung over their arms.

"Won't be long now and we'll be in Nové Mesto pod Šiatrom," the farmer announced. "And there, in the hurly-burly of the marketplace, no one will even notice you."

3

One of the impositions laid upon the emergent Slovak State was the cession of a piece of its territory to Hungary, hence Nové Mesto pod Šiatrom had become Sátoraljaújlely. The people here spoke Slovak. This was certainly encouraging, but the thought that we couldn't rely on any one of them brought us back to reality. So we had to stick to our father's advice and speak only German.

The hay wagon trundled across the marketplace, awash with carts, people, cattle, stalls, tables, voices and shouting and pulled up in a side street. There, the farmer exchanged our Slovak crowns for pengő and received his reward. Our money had shrunk to a ludicrously tiny sum.

We handed back the woollens, climbed down from the wagon and suddenly we were alone in a Hungarian town with no knowledge of the language beyond *nem* and *igen* and a few mangled lines from Hungarian songs.

The pubs and coffee houses on the marketplace were open or in the process of opening. Gypsy families were sitting on the church steps with children of all ages and their noisy chatter mingled with the general hubbub, the turmoil, the cries of the sellers, the cackling and clucking, and the haggling and wrangling over the prices of the wares on offer. We stood in the midst of this gaudy hurly-burly, looking for any German-Jewish names on the pubs.

"There!" Lila whispered as she nudged me. Her eyes were

directed to the name plate above a patisserie bearing the words "Ernyei József". And because one of the Jewish solicitors in Mikuláš was called Ernyei we headed straight for the shop in question.

The bell on the door tinkled as we entered. I went up to the counter and, in German, asked the lady in the white coat whether we might have a cup of tea and a roll or a slice of cake. The eyes of the neat, grey-haired lady took in our worn, sleep-deprived faces and dishevelled hair, then she looked down and saw our muddy shoes and my heel, bandaged with a filthy hankie. "You needn't say anything. Follow me," she said and led us into the room behind. "Stay here. Have a wash and comb your hair, and clean your shoes and coats. There's some soap and a towel by the basin. And some toilet paper on the table. Wet it and use it as a sponge. I'll fetch some tea and sandwiches."

The shop doorbell announced the arrival of some customers and the obliging lady went back into the shop. Having served the customers, she brought us some tea, bread and cheese and a German-Hungarian phrase book. "You need to learn the simplest phrases in Hungarian. But first rest awhile and I'll have a word with some trustworthy clients about how we can help. One of them has to take you home with them. I can't, because my grandchildren are living with me, and the lady who looks after them. She might let something slip, and that would not be good either for you or for me."

We washed from top to toe in cold water and felt the fresher for it. We lay down on a wide bench and fell asleep. Having slept for two hours, we got up, sat at the table and opened the phrase book.

"*Jó napót kivánok*," Lila read. "Good day."

"*Jó estét* [good evening]."

"*Kezét csókolom* [I kiss your hands]."

"Boy, hold my horse...!"

"May I offer you my arm, dear Madame?"

We looked at the book's title page and found that it had been published in 1895 by the Austro-Hungarian Imperial Military Publishing House.

"Here's something a bit more useful," said Lila. "*Olyan álmos es fárad vagyok!* [I'm so tired and worn out!]"

When the patisserie lady came back she brought with her 150 pengő that she'd coaxed out of some trustworthy customers.

"Have you had a look at the dictionary?" she asked, and when we repeated the phrases we'd learned she tried to correct our pronunciation, of which Hungarians would at once have said that it was "*tótos*".[1]

For lunch we each received a plateful of goulash and another 150 pengő. We were feeling more and more drowsy and, having waited in vain, our hopes of finding hospitable, but also fearless, people burst like a punctured balloon. We had become fugitives excluded from normal life and dependent on the help of strangers.

The day was coming to an end and the patisserie to closing time. A grey fatigue was beginning to consume us. We were abandoning all hope of further assistance when suddenly the shop doorbell rang, the door into the back room opened shortly after, and an old lady in a billowing skirt came in. "Gather up your things, my children, and follow me," she bade us. "First you need a good sleep!" she said as we entered the hallway of her house. She took us to a bedroom. She made up her own double bed for us, remarking that she was a widow and now slept in it alone. She offered us two of her own nightdresses, wished us a good night's sleep and left the bedroom with our clothes slung over her shoulder. On the way through the town we'd told her the story of our escape and about our plans. She had listened attentively and with compassion.

When she came to wake us it was already late evening. Our blouses, underwear and stockings had been washed, our jackets cleaned and they were all, together with our skirts and overcoats, slung across two chairs. We got dressed and the old lady took us into her vast kitchen. A fire was blazing away in the stove. The table, with a white table cloth and candles burning in tall candlesticks, was laid for us and some guests, two girls and four young men.

"We've bought you tickets to Budapest, and these young people will take you to the station." She pointed to one of the girls and said, "Juliška's my granddaughter and her friend is Veronka. The boys can make their own introductions."

We had meat soup and boiled chicken with rice and knotted white rolls, and the young people summoned by the old lady to assist taught us some Hungarian words and the proper way to pronounce them.

"*Leves* [soup]," said Veronka, pointing to the contents of my plate. "And bread is called *kenyér*."

"Sh... sh... sh... *utazni* ... [to travel]."

The old lady suddenly hid her face in her hands and burst into tears. "Dear God, why is there so much evil in the world?"

"*Sírni* [to cry]," said Juliška as she began wiping the tears from her grandmother's face.

We were walking across the poorly lit town. The boys a few steps ahead of us. The police and gendarmerie had been carrying out roundups of late. At the station, the voice coming from the loudspeakers was saying words that meant nothing to me. Juliška whispered that the train to Budapest that had just pulled in was full of recruits and that in half an hour, at midnight, there'd be another one. We decided to travel with the recruits.

All the compartments, and the corridors, were full of tired recruits sleeping on their small, black wooden suitcases. Lila and I fell asleep and only woke up when the train braked and squealed to a halt at Debrecen, where all the recruits alighted. Us apart, there were only two passengers left in our compartment. One was a middle-aged man with a huge grizzled beard, wearing a green overcoat and tall laced boots. You could see how he was relishing his fat cigar, puffing out the smoke and watching it disperse. The other passenger was a lady dressed entirely in black. A black veil dangled from her hat, covering her face. She alighted at the next station and no one else joined us. Lila and I didn't dare speak. With our eyes closed, we sat there in the train as it thundered off into the darkness. As the guard clipped our tickets, he asked something that I didn't understand, and I replied with the only sentence I'd learned to say in Hungarian "*Olyan fárad és álmos vagyok* [I'm so worn out and sleepy]". The guard asked no more questions and I noticed the pricked ears and attentive eyes of the man with the cigar. The door having closed behind the guard, he said something in Hungarian. I told him I didn't understand and only spoke German, that I was from Vienna and that we were tourists. I thought it unwise to pretend I was an orphan and risk saying the wrong thing.

"*Schon gut. In Ordnung* [Very well. All right.] So you're tourists from Vienna," our sole surviving fellow passenger replied in German. "That doesn't bother me. Be who you will, but you can tell me the truth. I won't let on."

Let's hope he's not a cop or secret policeman, flashed through my mind, but he chatted on, explaining that he was a commercial traveller on his way to Budapest and that he'd already helped several migrants, and that he would help us, too, if we wanted.

"Why don't you believe me and why do you want to help us?" I asked.

"For a start, you're not speaking Viennese German. Secondly, I know people. And thirdly, I'm a Jew. Don't be afraid. I've got two daughters and they're in my passport. When we get to Budapest and there's a check, I'll present you as my daughters. But you're going to have to get hold of some papers and proof that you deregistered in some other town so you can get ration coupons," he advised us.

Up until then no such practical problems had so much as crossed my mind, and now I had, swarming inside my head like bees, vague intimations of the unexpected and unimaginable exigencies and hindrances that lay ahead.

4

We were overcome by fatigue and fell asleep, only waking when the train clattered to a halt at Keleti Station in Budapest. Raindrops were trickling down the misted window. It was raining outside. We donned our coats, got our luggage down from the rack and followed the good-natured commercial traveller into the vast, black-and-white-tiled station concourse. From out of the crowds of travellers amid the pillars of the concourse two gendarmes emerged, sporting hats with rooster feathers, and they made straight for us.

What now, flashed through my mind. *Is our journey to end before it's even begun?*

"Good morning, Horváthbácsi! [Uncle Horváth] Are these your daughters...?" one of the gendarmes greeted our companion.

"Good morning. At last I've managed to persuade them to come with me and let me show them Budapest," Horváthbácsi replied, and his calm and the civil tone of the gendarme dispelled my momentary fit of panic.

The gendarmes smiled at us and disappeared amid the throng of passengers arriving and departing. At a kiosk, Mr Horváth bought us a street plan of Budapest, and after we'd come down the broad, white steps onto the pavement and into the drizzling rain, he called us a cab and said good-bye. He probably thought his good deed done, because he turned his back on us and walked off without once turning to look back. He left me with a sudden sense of emptiness, like the dismay of a child at having its only toy stolen.

We were standing on a street in an alien city of which my sole impressions had come from things people had said and from the pictures in *Színházi életu*, a theatre and film magazine that a neighbour used to pass to Mum after she'd finished with it. The people around us were speaking in an incomprehensible tongue. We couldn't even understand the shop signs and posters, and the map of Budapest would only have been of any use if we had even the slightest sense of direction.

The cab driver replied to our questions in broken German and his expression spoke of his uncomprehending bewilderment when we asked him to find either Ferenczi György or Ferenczi Ferencz. His dubious expression only intensified when he saw the knotted hankie low down on my not exactly clean, laddered stocking.

"I'll find them if you give me an address," he said. Having explained that we had no address and having repeated Father's story about orphans looking for their relatives, he shook his head sceptically. "Ferenczi is a very common name. Do you want me to take you round them all? Have you any idea what that would cost? Look, there's a phone book in that booth over there. Have a look and select one Ferenczi and I'll take you there. Then we'll see," the cabbie explained.

We entered the booth, opened the phone book and found the Ferenczis. We scoured the pages of small print, one name after another, and decided it didn't matter which one we chose. I closed my eyes and put my finger on the page. Ferenczi György, porcelain and glass wholesaler, was what lay beneath my finger. The taxi driver took us there and it transpired that this Ferenczi György was Father's Dudi. In that moment, an inkling of the existence of guardian angels flew across my mind.

We paid the cab driver and entered the shop. Sweet-scented curly wood shavings were poking out of open wooden crates. In a glass cage in the corner of the room sat Dudi, at his typewriter. He had a square, brick-red face above his snow-white shirt. Our announcement must have caught him on the hop and he hadn't yet had time to recover from his clearly unpleasant surprise, because he indignantly protested his horror that parents could send such young children abroad, forcing them to live off the charity of strangers and exposing them to all manner of perils. Dudi's voice, fretful at first, gradually grew calmer as we spoke. He was slow to get over the shock and embarrassment at having lost his self-control, but eventually lapsed into silence. After a moment of silent concentration he invited us to go and sit in the back room and wait for the decision of the family council. They needed to agree as one on how to handle this unexpected problem.

While Dudi and the rest of the family, summoned along by phone – his wife and her mother, his brother Feri and his wife – held their consultation, we waited in the large stockroom behind the shop. It was full of crates, open and partly open, tissue paper, unpacked items of porcelain and glass, and the scent of freshly sawn deal. There were two young people at work there. Ági, a young woman who herself looked like a china doll, was checking over the wares, and when we came in she was blowing through the little rubber tubes of some perfume flacons. She could just about manage in German and translated our responses for the errand-boy, Pali. It became clear as we talked that our views on many matters were alike and they both promised to introduce us to some young Hungarians who were opposed to the rising influence of fascism in Hungary.

"The quicker you learn Hungarian, the more easily you'll fit in," said Ági and she began teaching us there and then. She named every item in the room in Hungarian. She remarked that we must surely be hungry and gave each of us a salami roll and a glass of milk. By the time the family council had completed its business and called us in, we four young people had become of one mind beneath the unspoken slogan "Outcasts of the world, unite!".

The family council had decided to split responsibility for us between the brothers. Lila was to live with Feri at the other end of the city, while I would be here, in the street where the shop was. When I asked if we might not stay together, Feri's wife Zsuzsa said, "No! Your presence places us in danger and splitting you up will make it easier to cope with any problems that might arise. It's on the radio every day: people found harbouring illegal aliens face time in prison. And do call us Uncle and Auntie!"

5

We left the shop. Lila and Auntie Zsuzsa turned right, Auntie Maró, her mother and I turned left. Maró, a slim, grey-eyed woman with a regular oval face and thick chestnut hair swept back into a knot, and her white-haired, cultivated, youthful-looking mother took me off to a grand, Baroque building. Through its wide door with crystal windows we entered a hallway inlaid with marble. On the steps we were joined by a third woman with a full bag of shopping.

"This is Erna, our cook," the white-haired member of the family pair introduced her to me. Then she added: "You can call me Auntie Sári."

I walked on in between the two women as if they were leading me into a courtroom. I accepted the situation with the patience of alienation. I was missing Lila. "Keep going! They're trying to help you. Just be thankful you're alive!" my inner voice chimed up. It did cheer me up a little, but couldn't drive away the sheer exhaustion of the last few days.

The family lived in an eight-roomed flat. The kitchen and the maid's quarters were at the end of a long corridor. Erna the cook had one of the five bedrooms. They put me in a large, high-ceilinged room next to Erna's. The room was cold, but it had a freshly waxed parquet floor, Persian carpets and white furniture with gold beading. The windows had two sets of curtains, one flimsy and one of heavy red velvet.

Both women did their best to be welcoming. Maró led me to a large, green-tiled bathroom with an enormous built-in bath. She ran me a bubbly bath and asked me to strip off because everything I had on was in urgent need of washing.

"I'll lend you anything you need, but first we have to tend to that foot. There's shampoo on the little shelf under the mirror and you've got some towels on the chair next to the bath," she said before leaving me to myself. Half an hour later she was back with an armful of lingerie, clothes and stockings; she inspected my foot, sprinkled it with some disinfectant powder and bandaged it up. She waited while I got dressed and put my cleaned shoes on. The dress was a little long and wide at the shoulders, but with the belt drawn tight it looked acceptable. After Maró had blown and combed my hair, a warm wave of affection surged within me. It dipped slightly when Maró asked if I hadn't forgotten to clean my teeth.

"Come with me," she urged. "I'll take you to meet the family."

Sitting in a rocking chair in the living room was an old, bald man with wrinkled features and a limp, fleshy mouth. His lower lip drooped half-way down his chin and the corners of his mouth were bulging with saliva. Auntie Sári spoke up in German from her leather armchair: "This is our Granddad, the family wiseacre. There's no question to which he wouldn't have the answer."

"Who's the girl?" asked the wiseacre, watching me through narrow, slanting eyes of uncertain colour.

"A distant relation of Gyuri's," said Maró. "She'll be living with us until she learns to speak Hungarian, then she'll have to stand on her own two feet."

"What? Learn Hungarian? That could take a year or more! How old are you?" he asked tetchily.

"Nearly nineteen."

"And they let you leave home just like that? To roam around in foreign parts? Call your parents responsible?"

"Her sister's also here, she's a year younger. We've put her up with Feri. It's not been easy for them," his wife, Auntie Sári, butted in.

"And we're supposed to look after them? Why us? God knows when this'll end, and then we'll get the blame anyway. What's for lunch? I fancy a steak." In response to his wife's reminder that it was hard to get good quality beef on a ration card, he said grumpily, "All right, all right, but there must be quite a bit left of that half side of veal in the freezer...!"

"Stop worrying, Dad, you'll get your veal chop," Auntie Sári sought to calm him before calling out: "Where are you, my little angels? Where are you, children?" The door to the adjacent room flew open and in ran two small boys.

"Bandikam! Puczikam! Come to Granny! And speak German the way your young lady tutor taught you."

"Who's that girl wearing Mummy's dress?" asked the younger of the two, glancing at me with his large blue eyes. "Our new miss?"

"There now, what a good idea, clever little Puczi! You do take after Granddad. The girl is called Ibo and she's a distant relation of your father's."

"If she's distant she's foreign, and I don't want us to be looked after by foreign girls!" Bandi yelled, pinching my thigh and thumping me in the belly.

"Stop that, Bandi! And show our visitor some respect!" Maró chided her elder son.

I noticed that throughout this scene the wiseacre had been rocking away and shaking with silent, mischievous laughter. Under the pretext of showing me round the rest of the flat, Maró led me out of the living room and apologized for her father's behaviour.

"The older he gets, the grumpier and more disaffected he is, but it's all down to senility. He's not been our wiseacre for a long time."

Out of the response to Bandi's question was hatched my employment: I became the new "miss" and my task was to look after the boys. They weren't the worst – quite sweet, spoilt, wayward. I had my work cut out with them, but they did teach me to speak Hungarian: they made fun of my pronunciation, corrected me and made me keep repeating words until they sounded right to their ears. Erna, who, in the absence of a maid, also acted as cleaner, taught me some Hungarian songs, sayings and recipes. I couldn't have had better teachers and my Hungarian improved detectably by the day. The Fates had fortunately endowed me with a faculty for languages.

I still wasn't allowed out and when Uncle caught me one time, during one of my rare visits to the shop with the children, chatting to Ági and Pali – actually I was asking them to send my parents a telegram and gave them a scrap of paper bearing the text and their address – he made the point that I shouldn't go hobnobbing with an errand-boy. I knew it was risky for me to leave the house, but Erna covered for me when I popped into the tobacconist's on the street corner for my stock of seven Egyptian cigarettes, one for each day of the week. I used to smoke in bed in the large cold bedroom and liked to watch the smoke curl slowly up to the ceiling high above. I had an uneasy conscience, but Lila was far away, having been sent to Lake Balaton as someone's companion, so the fat, white, aromatic cigarette was my only close friend.

6

I used to chat to the members of the family, I ate at their table, sharing their rations of meat, eggs, butter and rice, I used their bathroom and toiletries, but my sense of dependence stood between us like an invisible wall. I helped Erna in the kitchen, peeling the vegetables and drying the dishes. During one of our conversations she said, "You mustn't feel remorseful. Don't feel conscience-stricken about eating them out of house and home. They've got more than enough of everything, and money will buy you anything out in the villages and on the black market."

At the tobacconist's I met a young Yugoslav, the owner's nephew. We discussed what was going on in Yugoslavia. He said he was a *četnik*, not siding with Tito. And because all I knew about the Balkans was that the Ustashe was a criminal organization, that its leader, Ante Pavelić, was a rabid fascist and a friend of the Third Reich, and that Tito was a partisan hero fighting against the Nazis, it struck me that being a *četnik* meant having nothing to do with anything. I had no idea how wrong I was. The young Serb was nice to me, attentive, and despite his detachment I did like him. I only went to the tobacconist's once a week. It felt silly and embarrassing only buying one cigarette a day.

I hoped that Lila as the companion of a friend of Zsuzsa's was all right. That she was starving and being grotesquely abused I learnt only the next time we saw each other.

I had learnt Hungarian well enough to read the books in Ági and Pali's library. Steinbeck's *Tövis és borostyány* [*The Grapes of Wrath*] and *Jean Barois* by Roger Martin Du Gard were my first conquests as I battled with the new language. I absolutely gorged on the verse of the great Hungarian poets Petöfi and Ady, and even the words that I didn't fully grasp were music to my ears.

During one of my permitted jaunts out I went to visit Pali's mother. Since her husband's death she'd been earning her keep as a cleaner at big company offices. She always felt cold and would walk or sit around wrapped in a thick woollen blanket, and the last thing she was inclined to do was talk. Pali preferred us to meet at Ági's. Ági's flat was furnished with a pale shade of oak wood furniture. Her cotton cushion covers and curtains had a floral pattern. Any odd spaces she filled with house plants. And as you entered, you got a faint whiff of Molnár-Moser perfume. Ági had a perfect figure, a very pretty little face, long, thick fair hair, curling at the ends. I found the fact that she'd secretly married a medic, Tibor, the son of aristocratic parents, just as romantic as Pali's mum's being a cleaner. At Ági's, I made the acquaintance of Jani, Sanyi, Petyes, Józsi and a very fat young man called Oszi, all of them members of the illegal Communist Party.

Maró spoke highly of my Hungarian and regularly let me out of the house. During one such jaunt Pali and I were supposed to meet up with Oszi.

"Can you trust him?" I asked Pali.

"What makes you think we can't? Because he's fat?"

I had to admit I hadn't thought of it in those terms, but only because I couldn't imagine him in circumstances that called for a speedy escape to hide from the police.

"If he looked like Ági's Tibor, you wouldn't be having any doubts."

Pali was right about that, too. My uncertainty regarding Oszi's abilities were supported by the atmosphere in his family environment. Two pale, permanently agitated women – his divorced mother and her sister. Their entire life had been focussed on Oszi. They had spoiled him and were forever fussing about his health. They were very (if not too) grateful if ever someone wanted to make friends with him. I found all the sentimental pet names and accolades that they showered upon him, even when talking about him to us, quite distasteful. To me, it felt as if that tide of mawkish verbiage was an attempt to veil the bitterness and shame at the failed product of marital bliss that had been short-lived. Everything in their flat was immaculately clean. Not a speck of dust anywhere. Little mats, bits of lace, knick-knacks, paper flowers everywhere. The perfect environment for secret meetings.

"It would never occur to anyone that Oszi's a member of the resistance," Jani once told me.

Ági persuaded Maró to let me go with some friends to a concert. A mandolin band was playing at the great hall of the Workers' House of Culture. I sat in the middle of the third row among people who were eagerly expectant and in the mood. I glanced at the programme. It consisted of old and new Hungarian tunes, some of which I knew from Erna. I noted the presence of uniformed police inside the venue.

"They're at every cultural event put on for the workers. You may be sure there are some secret police here as well," Jani whispered to me.

Silence descended, the orchestra played a czardas, followed by an old Hungarian dance tune. It was greeted with a great ovation. I glanced back at the programme. The third item was *In Angol Park*. As the mandolins began to play I looked up sharply and opened my eyes wide.

"Relax!" Ági whispered and she pinched my hand. The title *Angol Park* disguised a familiar tune from the Russian film *Cirkus*. And the band's offering under the title *In the Desert* was actually a ballad about the revolutionary hero Vasily Chapayev, played to the beat of a czardas. The audience cheered and roared and clapped and stamped their feet. I noticed that even the policemen were clapping. The medley of genuine and fictitious Hungarian music included, under false titles, the Florian Geyer song and, under the guise of *The Boy Scout March*, the tune of *Solidarity Forever*. We sat there thunderstruck, we felt as if we'd overdone the champagne, but in the turmoil of this incredible event my head was spinning with thoughts of hubris and nemesis and the fear that it could all turn out disastrously. Surely the police knew they were being made a mockery of. It could end with all the exits being blocked. However, nothing of the kind happened and the audience left, chatting aloud and laughing. We eight young people went to wash down this daring, artful event with a glass of wine. I got home late, hoping to slip into my room unobserved.

That hope failed. After breakfast and a period of tense silence, Uncle Gyuri asked: "Where were you gadding about last night? How can you dare come home so late? Don't you realize the consequences that could have for the whole family? This can't go on. What were you up to?"

Without thinking twice I handed Maró the programme.

Gyuri snatched it from her hand and began to read it. "Such unheard-of irresponsibility, attending a railworkers' concert at the Workers' House of Culture! Are you out of your mind? In your situation and at a time like this to go mingling with Bolsheviks? Ági will pay for this! We have to decide what next."

The atmosphere around the table was below zero. I knew that my action could well end badly. I berated myself for being so foolish. How could I have been so foolish as to show them the programme and so expose Ági and Pali to Uncle's wrath and its consequences.

After a two-hour stroll with the children my time was my own and I walked across the city towards the Danube. Smoke from the steamers' funnels drifted across the water. The slim silhouettes of the bridges reared up high. The acacias along the embankment were emitting a heady, sweet scent. Up by the Citadella I lay down on a bench and looked up into the sky and at the towers, the trees and the birds. Margaret Island was a lush green colour. On the opposite bank of the river the Halászbástya [Fisherman's Bastion] was outlined in the haze like an unfinished drawing. A week previously I had posted my address to Rudo's aunt and was wondering if she was now back in Debrecen.

"Pity you weren't in," Erna said on my return. "You could have met a young man from your town. He left two suitcases here. They're in your room, and he left you a note on the table."

"I'm here for a few days. Living at my aunt's flat," Rudo had written, also leaving me his phone number.

Maró and I were sitting over a coffee in the kitchen. She reported that the family had decided to summon Lila back to Budapest. She'd be arriving in a week's time. My Hungarian would help us get by on our own.

"You're clever girls, both of you. I do hope you appreciate how hard for us it is to send you away, but it's for the sake of our children's safety and their future. But you'll have God on your side!"

I could tell it wasn't easy for Maró to be passing on the result of the family consultation like this.

"You shouldn't have gone to that concert!" she said reprovingly, looking at me through tearful eyes.

I phoned Rudo. We agreed to meet at Hősök tere [Heroes Square], from where we'd go to his aunt's place. His aunt, wearing a man's suit and with a man's hat on her head, collided with us in the doorway. She said hello in her deep alto voice and apologized for being just on her way into town, but said that her friend Erzsike would look after us.

"They live together, Auntie's a lesbian," Rudo remarked.

Erzsike, a monkeyish little creature with big brown eyes and a tiny chin that receded into her neck, made us welcome and brought in a plateful of sliced cake and some tea.

"Your parents received your telegram and are very pleased you got here safely. Everyone there is well and hoping to see you again soon. The suitcases contain summer and winter clothes. They have asked me to keep in touch with you and I've promised to do so for as long as it's possible."

In answer to his question as to whether all was well, I said, "Tell your mother and father that we're fine and they needn't worry about us."

Erzsike came and sat with us and told us that her friend with a grown-up son was going to be living with them in one of their two rooms, and that he had also left Slovakia. This announcement precluded any help: I couldn't ask her if she had room for me and Lila as well should the family throw us out on the street.

7

Lila returned from Balaton. We were standing in a Budapest street in the bright June sunlight, wearing floral summer skirts and the clogs that Zsuzsa had bought us as a farewell present. We each had 25 pengő in our pocket. We'd been given the money as we left, with the remark that all hospitality was now over. Pali promised to keep our suitcases safe. Ági's attempts to find us some accommodation had so far failed.

We didn't know Budapest. We didn't know whether the ID books that Ági had got for us were forged or just borrowed, so we couldn't use them to get ration cards. One way or another, our predicament had to be sorted out. We decided to look for somewhere to live. We criss-crossed the city. The houses lining the streets in this or that quarter betrayed the social standing of their occupants. In the quarter where we found ourselves late in the afternoon, factory sirens began announcing the end of the working day. On the entrance door of one large apartment building we spotted a white label bearing the legend "BED AVAILABLE on the third floor".

"We might just be able to afford a bed," said Lila. "Let's give it a try."

We climbed the long, dusty, unwashed stairs. Here and there the plaster was peeling off the patchy walls. We found the same label as on the ground floor. We rang the bell. The door was opened by a corpulent, shoddily dressed, middle-aged woman with a shock of greying black hair. Tied across her open dressing gown she had a filthy chequered apron. She was having a cigarette and blowing smoke rings with her lower lip. She measured us from top to toe and asked us what we wanted in a deep, almost masculine voice.

"I see. You want to rent a bed... Well, if you don't mind there being eight beds in the room, seven of them occupied, and that you'll have to share it, then come on in," she said. The rent was low, but we could stay there under one condition: we had to promise never to utter a word about what went on in the flat.

We took the eighth bed in a room where the other seven were occupied by two girls in training, four working women and a prostitute. From things the tenants said, and from our own observations, we inferred that our landlady was a black marketeer, taking in and selling on items acquired by theft, and that she had frequent male visitors with whom she played cards long into the night. In the vacuum in which we found ourselves the prohibited had become permissible and anything that contributed to salvation was acceptable. We warmed to our landlady, she was kind-hearted, not at all bothered by our status as unregistered fugitives and from time to time she gave us small sums in cash.

The girls rose early and came home exhausted in the evening, and although our chats with them were few and far between and quite brief, we relied on their loyalty.

We talked most with the gorgeous prostitute, Magda. She

spent her days at home. We were surprised to find she enjoyed what passes for quality literature. Otherwise she killed time washing or ironing. In the evenings she went to night clubs. Once a week she was visited by an elegant man who brought her flowers and books, gifts that she received with unconcealed disdain. She spent some weekends at his villa. It was quite exciting to observe how the relationship between these two complex characters evolved, their instinctive mutual disparagement, vindictiveness and battle for supremacy. They reminded me of Strindberg's plays.

Magda's visitor knew how she made her money and she reminded him constantly that he was to blame for her moral degeneracy. He followed her like a shadow and she sold herself on the street before his very eyes, which otherwise wasn't her normal practice. This was her punishment for how he'd abandoned her when she fell pregnant with his child. The baby had been born in the hospital where they let Magda work as a cleaner in return for board and lodging and assistance at births.

To be the mother of an illegitimate child was seen as shocking and Magda hadn't wanted to go back to the little town where everyone knew her. She'd looked for work and eventually found a poorly paid job as a dishwasher at one of the posher Budapest restaurants, where she later became a waitress. In order to be able to pay for the baby's keep at a distant relative's, she'd begun to bring certain older, comfortably off gentlemen home with her.

Lila and I wondered if Magda's confession was just another cheap, sentimental story of the kind prostitutes told their romantic clients in explanation of their chosen livelihood. But she was a good friend to us and when autumn came and we needed some stockings she bought some for us.

Magda's son's father was an engineer. While she was pregnant, he was offered a well-paid job in Argentina, which he took. Having returned five years later, he found Magda in the restaurant where he was about to have dinner. After much begging, she showed him a photo of his child and he suggested that they both come to live with him in his villa with a garden. Magda declined, but she did accept his offer of financial support for his son. She set aside part of the generous sum for her son's education.

Magda had continued with her, as she saw it, life of freedom. She'd continued to visit night clubs. At the Susogó bar, where she once even took Lila, she had fallen in love with the homosexual who became her pimp. He had exploited and bullied her to the point where the lovelorn Magda had slashed her wrists.

Among my memories of the time I spent as an illegal in Budapest, two names shine out like neon signs: Susogó (the whispering place) and Zserbo, the name of a super patisserie, where ladies in fur coats went for coffee and the best cakes in the city, and where the glass steps made sounds like a musical box as you mounted them. I don't recall the tune, but I do remember that Magda once took us there for slices of chestnut cake.

After Ági had found me a place to live at a milliner's, a friend of her mother's, our sister Dalma began to share Lila's bed. She had crossed the border into Hungary from Rožňava and reached Budapest after quite an adventurous journey. She had been found, hungry, on a park bench, by the Czech carer of a mentally defective child. She had taken her home and hidden her in her room. One of our acquaintances, an émigré from Slovakia, later spotted Dalma in the street and brought her to Lila.

Going about Budapest with Dalma had its dangers. She was the youngest of us and extremely pretty. She moved with a grace that was unintentionally inviting and she resembled the Hungarian film star Zita Szeleczky. She turned men's heads and people would often stop her in the street to ask for her autograph. The first sentence that she learned to pronounce to perfection was: "Nem vagyok Szeleczky Zita."

The bed at the milliner's stood in one corner of the large kitchen. The kitchen windows gave onto a narrow yard with a high wall. The room was constantly dim. The bed linen reeked of food. I only ever saw Alica, who rented another bed, in the evenings, when she came home to sleep. She never let on how she passed her days and she took great pains over both her appearance and her apparel. The little table beside her bed was littered with cosmetics, and her clothes were packed so tight in the narrow wardrobe, for which she paid extra, that she had to iron them every morning.

Rudo's aunt Mady found me a job in a dressmaker's workshop that made lingerie. Thanks to the initiative of my mother, I, on finishing high school and after the introduction of the laws that banned Jews from any further or higher education, had learned to sew. The pay was poor. I had no ration cards and the only thing we could buy without them was fruit. We were often hungry. When things were at their worst, we got help from our friends. It sometimes happened that I fainted from hunger and I was afraid lest it happened outdoors and attracted unwanted attention.

One day, the milliner's kitchen was filled with the aroma of freshly baked bread rolls. She would bake them first thing in the morning, while we, the lodgers, were still asleep, then leave them on the table. The smell of fresh rolls churned my stomach. After Alica had completed her lengthy matinal toilette and left, I couldn't resist the temptation, helped myself to a roll and ate it.

"Who stole my roll?" asked the milliner that evening when she came in from work.

"Surely you don't think I need any roll of yours, do you?" Alica, who'd come home early, replied scornfully.

"So it was you, you stole it, you thief! I'm not having you here if you steal! You have to move out! Tomorrow!" she bellowed at me.

I confessed to eating the roll. I knew the milliner's over-reaction was due to the fear that went with harbouring an illegal immigrant. The roll merely provided her with the excuse she needed to be rid of me, along with a decent excuse to give Ági's mother. That the one roll had turned into an entire baking tin I only heard later from Ági.

I packed my few goods and chattels, left the house weary and sleepy, and entered the park nearby. I wandered up and down all the paths until late in the afternoon. I registered neither colours nor smells, and I didn't hear the birds singing. I didn't want to bother my friends who, if it wasn't too much trouble to them, would readily have offered to put me up.

A lady in a green outfit walked past me. She was eating an ice cream and strolled off idly through the trees. After a short moment, she came back, glanced round and, finding no other bench, she sat down at the other end of mine. She finished her ice cream and wiped her mouth with her handkerchief. We sat there like that for a while. Two taciturn female strangers, each lost in her own thoughts.

"Forgive me for intruding," said the lady in the green outfit. "You look so pale, are you all right? Are you feeling hungry perhaps?"

I looked at her as if she'd just woken me up. She had a frank, amiable expression.

"Yes," I replied instinctively.

"Stay here and wait for me," the stranger said. She stood up, left and in ten minutes she was back with a pot of yogurt and two rolls with ham. "There. Now tell me what the trouble is. You can trust me."

I believed her, possibly for want of any other option. "I've nowhere to sleep," I told her.

"Are you a migrant?"

Unsettled and weakened by my momentary loss of optimism

and touched by the surprising kindness of a total stranger, I explained my predicament to her.

"I'd invite you to my place, but unfortunately I can't. But you know what? I'm going to try to find you something. Be here tomorrow morning at nine."

She was waiting for me as I entered the park at nine on the dot, and she handed me the address that was to become my future sanctuary. It was a pokey little hole beneath the stairs of a Baroque townhouse. But it had a door and a lock. It was dark inside even during the day, but at least there was a light bulb next the bed, the only item of furniture. There was no water either, but Ági, who was still working at the glass and porcelain wholesaler's, let me have a shower and wash my undies at her place. And Pali didn't just deliver his uncle's wares, but also messages between members of our group.

There were two of us assistants at the dressmaker's workshop. Eighteen-year-old Edita and I. Mostly we made men's shirts. Edita would sing as she worked and she taught me lots of Hungarian folksongs and hits of the day. Once, as she was telling me all about the life and songs of the popular Hungarian songstress Katalin Karády, it dawned on me in the context of one of her hits, that I was actually living in a country at war; that Hungary, along with Germany, Slovakia, Italy and Romania, was fighting against the Soviet Union, that I knew as much, but that in my transitory and alien existence it affected me only remotely, as if from afar. The hit song was a love letter to a soldier, out there somewhere beneath the stars and amid the snows of Russia, where death lay in wait for him. The melancholy and the elegiac sweetness of the tune stirred in me a vivid sense of gloom at the stupidity of mankind.

The workshop had been set up inside the large burgher apartment of our head craftswoman, the hunchbacked Mme Eva. She was the daughter and eternally gaping wound of a prosperous Budapest family, renowned for their good looks. Eva's family had swathed Eva in luxury, compassion and pity, but nothing they did could magic away, for her or their own good, that damned hunchback. Eva had torn free of the protective mesh of her family's care and taught herself to sew. She had set up the workshop and become independent. She hadn't shaken off attempts at creating an illusion of normality, but maybe she didn't really want to. Eva's beautiful sister had a perfect figure and crowds of admirers, one of whom she would lend to her. Edita was convinced they paid him for it.

Every Tuesday and Friday at two in the afternoon Eva would start getting ready for her date. She had a perfumed bubble bath, a cosmetician took care of her pretty face, a masseuse gave her an all-over massage, and a hair stylist combed her thick chestnut hair. At two minutes to four she would be standing, gloved and hatted and dressed in way that concealed her handicap as well as possible, all ready and waiting.

At four on the dot, a carriage would draw up outside the house. Eva went out to the street, the coachman held the door for her and helped her into the enclosed coach.

"That chap waiting for her in the coach, he reminds me of Jean-Pierre Aumont," said Edita.

"You've seen him?"

"I just happened to when he drew back the curtain. They drive around for a couple of hours, apparently discussing art and literature, which Mme Eva is interested in."

"Do you think there's at least a bit of romance in it all?"

"No, because I know that after she comes back from her rendezvous with Jean she just wanders from room to room in tears. She knows the whole thing is just a put-on."

While I was sewing lingerie, my sisters were canning eggs. They'd been found the job by the landlady. The preservative powder dissolved in water, but it also got into their lungs, made them cough and burned their eyes. The owner of the cannery only hired "black", unregistered, labour, paid very low wages, and my sisters used to go to bed hungry.

The house porter's wife, who kept order throughout the building, including my little cubby hole under the stairs, was a fat, cantankerous harridan with huge warts on her cheeks and chin. She treated me with disgust and loathing as if I were some beggar and made it obvious that I had no place there, in her house. She guessed that I was in Budapest illegally and was placing the other occupants, and her job, in jeopardy.

I spent my last weekend at liberty in the company of my five friends Jani, Petyes, Pali, Sanyi and Józsi. They took me on a trip my train to Dunakék, where the young workers' movement met.

Groups of young people would sit on the grass by the Danube, chatting, laughing, playing guitars and singing. All around was the gently undulating countryside. We strolled through the woods, among the hills and villages. We drank milk fresh from a cow. The jangle of church bells floated over houses and cottages and across fields fragrant with hay.

At one farm we bought some potatoes and, as evening drew nigh, we roasted them in the ashes of the fire above which we'd already grilled some bacon, skewered on twigs. With relish we munched on black bread drizzled with bacon fat.

After supper we lay down in the hay beneath a dark-blue starry sky. I didn't feel like sleeping at all, but the boys wrapped me in a blanket and sang me a lullaby.

Next morning, while I was still asleep, Petyes fetched some milk and fresh butter. We breakfasted on buttered bread and milk from Petyes' aluminium tumblers.

We washed in a stream and chatted about what was going on

inside Hungary and in the wider world and what, perhaps with our assistance, the future was going to be like. We got the train back to Budapest in the afternoon. We split up promising to meet again before too long.

Early in the morning the day after, two secret policemen came to get me; they took me with them to my two sisters and then arrested all three of us in the name of the law and led us away.

8

Through the wide door of a grand imperial and royal[2] office building and across a spacious entrance hall filled with citizens brought there willingly or unwillingly by blue-uniformed policemen, we were led into a room lined with packed bookshelves. Sitting at a desk was a fat, red-headed fellow with whiskers. His chubby, pink double chin dangled over his collar and part of his tie. In front of him, on some unravelled greaseproof paper were lumps of fresh ham and half a loaf of white bread. He was chewing away as he stared at us with his watery pale-blue eyes. He wiped his greasy lips with his big hand and barked at the policemen: "Scram! I'll deal with 'em!"

The policemen having left and closed the door behind them, he shot us a look of disdain, kept us standing by the door and went on shredding, munching and swallowing large chunks of food. When he was done, he screwed the paper into a ball and tossed it in the wastepaper basket. "Right, my little beauties, did you think we wouldn't find you? That we're idiots? That we didn't know where you were and who you are? Well, you're here now and what little we don't know we'll have you fill in for us, by fair means or foul!" he said in a false, fawning tone of voice that seemed surprisingly disproportionate to his great bulk.

"How do you want to force us to make a statement, not I hope by torture?" Lila asked.

He went all red in the face, which swelled up like a balloon, leapt to his feet and yelled back in a high-pitched voice: "Shut your mouth, you piece of vermin! Your Slovak Hungarian has given you away anyway. Show me your documents!"

We placed our ID books on his desk.

"Either you stole these or tampered with them. You're not Zádor Éva, and you've never been Megyessi Mária!"

He stood up, came round from behind the desk and stood facing us, legs apart. "I'd really like to just squash you like insects!" he hissed. He stood with one big, heavy shoe on my foot and would certainly have pressed down hard if a uniformed policeman hadn't appeared in the door to announce: "They're waiting for them. They're to be photographed and their prints taken."

After two days spent in a cell with a couple of prostitutes, who shared their cigarettes and life experiences with us, we were transferred to Rombach, an internment camp full of fugitives from all over central Europe and the Balkans.

The camp had three dormitories: for men, women and the camp administrators. The third one was where the border force operated from. The open space between the buildings was paved with stones and in the middle there was a well, where the internees could collect water to wash themselves and their clothes. They lived and slept on triple bunk beds that stood all crammed together, creating a closeness that inhibited any unmentionable goings-on. Here the prisoners either became unusually close friends or they feuded and squabbled over next to nothing. We became friends with women whose lives were totally different from anything we'd encountered previously. People with an uncertain future, relegated to a bed in an internment camp, lose their inhibitions when they come together, frequently going back to their past and revealing secrets that in other circumstances would have remained hidden. We listened to their stories with amazement and accepted their "eccentric" confessions without judging them. They broadened the scope of our tolerance.

The men and women would meet out in the yard. They grew closer and they became estranged, they accused one another of infidelity and then made up again. Everything amounted to a feverish replication of normality except that here there was also talk of escaping, of fear of what the future might hold and of the rumours that there were going to be transports to destinations unknown. The talk included narratives in which those being transported got shot at the Polish border or were relocated in ghettos. But for all these cares and despite the loss of their identity, most of the internees still harboured the hope of a return to normality and common decency.

Supervision of the camp was in the hands of the border force. How it was run was in the hands of the internees themselves. They were headed by a former butcher, Gubi. He had two deputies. One supplied false ID papers in return for sexual favours, the other didn't mess with anyone or anything, acted with propriety and gave the impression of being a thoroughly decent person.

One day I received an order to report to Gubi. He was lying on his bed in his vest and underpants. He had his hands folded under his round, podgy, shaven head. His arm and leg muscles were coated in grease. His eyes looked like cherries that had been thrust into strawberry cream and his little round mouth looked like a red forest slug.

He addressed me by the name under which I'd had myself registered at the camp. "Mira," he said, "come and sit here on the bed."

Because I made no move, he repeated his invitation: "Stop

standing there like a statue! Sit down on the bed. I need to tell you something."

"I can hear just as well standing up," I replied.

"Don't be afraid. I don't bite!"

Cautiously, I sat down on the bed.

"I don't know why I've got this feeling that I can trust you and confide to you all the things that are troubling me, like how much I miss my mother, how wretched I feel without her and alone. I feel like I'm icing up without her. There's no one on earth who can replace her warm embrace."

Tears filled his cherry-like eyes, and his lips and chin were quivering with emotion.

"But you've got a stove there in the corner. Why don't you light it if you're that cold?"

"How can you be so unfeeling? A stove's no substitute for my mum, it can't warm up my soul and my heart," he sobbed, and the tears streamed down his chubby cheeks into the gap between his chin and his vest. "I was hoping you'd stand in for her, warm me up, and that we might be able to help each other."

"Looks awfully like you're in the wrong job and out of your mind, I'm off."

"What? You dare to refuse my help? D'you think you're the only woman in the camp? Surely you realize the good you could do yourself by being obliging, don't you?"

Gubi's tears dried up as if by command. He got off the bed, gave me a shove, opened the door and chased me down the steps. "I'll show you who's boss here!"

He stood by the steps, arms akimbo on his broad hips, stuck his belly out and bellowed for all to hear: "The whore Mira will be cleaning the toilets for the next week!"

For eight days I scrubbed the toilets and their filthy wooden floors, inhaling the stench of faeces and musing on the camp rumours that Gubi was an informer in cahoots with the police, that he took bribes and would offer to help frightened women in return for sex.

Every once in a while the camp had visitors, each of which was the volunteer helper of a given group of prisoners. Me and my two sisters' visitor was an amiable little middle-aged man. We called him Endrebácsi. He was answerable for us and he would take us into the town with him and treat us to cocoa and cakes at the restaurant where he played cards.

One day they began, unexpectedly and with no obvious plan, to convey the internees to the Polish, but also to the Yugoslav border. The threat of deportation hung over us like the Sword of Damocles. No one knew the purpose of the transports. The first to disappear were German and Austrian émigrés and, with them, three young men, our closest friends, who were blessed with tolerant quick wits and sharp analytical minds. When we heard that they'd been shot, it was as if the bottom had fallen out of our world. The transports went on and on, the camp was emptying, and the day came when it was our turn.

9

We were sitting on wooden benches, guarded by two Hungarian policemen in dark-blue uniforms. Rumours throughout the train had it that we were on the way to Poland. Every word whispered, every new report, served only to deepen our uncertainty and extend the bounds of our fears. It was dark outside. The rhythmical clatter of the wheels drowned out our latent disquiet and sent us to sleep.

We were woken by the noise of doors being flung open and rapid footsteps out in the corridor. The train braked sharply and came to a halt.

"What is it? What's happening?" I gabbled.

"An order's come from Budapest to change direction. Now we're heading for Uzhhorod in Subcarpathian Ruthenia," one of the policemen told me. His large brown eyes mirrored his sympathy. The other policeman was seated motionless with his back against the wall, staring into a void.

The train had stopped, the early morning was grey and misty. We gathered up our things, took our suitcases down from the rack and left the train. I don't know if we walked or were driven, or how we reached the prison at Uzhhorod. I'd begun to accept these changes with a listless equanimity, but also with the secret hope that each one was the last.

The prison was in a state of chaos. Those in charge weren't ready for our arrival. Everything was being done at random or any old how. Men and women were sitting or standing in a long corridor. The bunks in the cells to the right were occupied by the prisoners who'd been here longest. Any free bits of space were taken up with mattresses. Police kept arriving with freshly arrested Hungarians, Poles and Ukrainians and taking prisoners off to court. They were all being charged with minor offenses such as prostitution, theft or vagrancy.

Through the large windows you could see out from the corridor into the yard, which was surrounded by a high wall and overlooked by the crowns of tall chestnut trees. Their yellow and rusty-red leaves were falling at the slightest breath of wind. It was autumn.

My clothes were in a mess. I'd been wearing the same stockings for three days. I felt disgusting and grubby. The mattress next to mine was occupied by a Polish aristocrat. Every evening he would kneel down on it and pray to the Virgin Mary. His nose was long and thin and the threadlike black eyebrows above his grey-green eyes looked as if they'd been put on with pen and ink. His eyes, like his mouth, wore a permanent expression of disdain. I couldn't fathom how he managed to look so dapper the whole time. In the morning, the white shirt in which he'd slept looked freshly ironed. When the light went out, he began to kiss my feet in their unwashed stockings and mumble something unintelligible in Polish. I tried silently and resolutely to snatch my unwashed feet from his grasp without waking my fellow-prisoners. In the morning, he acted as if I was a total stranger. He would smile at us with his arrogant smile and look at us as at something dirty and slimy that had crawled out of the sewers. The fight for my feet happened night after night and only stopped after I gave his nose such a kicking that it was covered in blood, his white shirt also getting spattered.

In the end cell a woman sat on her corner bunk bed dressed all in black. Her legs were spread so wide that you could see she wasn't wearing knickers. Where her stockings ended there were the pink patches of her bare thighs and everything between them was exposed to curious onlookers. Men would stand by the open door of her cell, gawping, laughing and exchanging lewd comments.

We three sisters became quite friendly with a horse thief, a simple, red-faced man in his forties, who enjoyed a good laugh and regaled us with tales from his life of crime. He warned us that we were likely to be marched across to the Hungarian-Slovakian frontier to be abandoned there or handed over to the Slovak border guards. Using a purple crayon that he first licked, he drew us a primitive map of Ostrov on a page torn from a notebook; that was an area that had once been Slovak and where he thought we were most likely to be taken. On his map he marked out roads and footpaths, added in the names of villages and said that he knew Ostrov like the back of his hand.

The police were constantly taking prisoners away and bringing them in, including two Polish brothers. Filek, the younger one, was sick. His brother Andrzej asked if he could have a mattress in his cell. Filek was shaking all over. He lay helpless on his mattress, in a sweat and clutching a small flatbread to his chest.

One evening, Andrzej and I were standing at the barred window looking out at the sky above the prison yard.

"So far we'd been lucky and thought our luck would last. Now it seems it hasn't. First we lost our way, wandering this way and that, and when we finally found the right road Filek fell ill, grew sluggish and started to despair of being saved. And now we're here. God knows what tomorrow has in store, if anything!" I tried to cheer him up a bit, then realized he wasn't listening.

"I need to take a look at Filek," he said and left me.

Early next morning they took him away. Filek couldn't move. They left him lying there on his mattress. He complained he had a terrible headache and was very thirsty. I brought him a cup of water from the tap in the corridor. I propped his raging head up and dribbled the water between his dehydrated lips.

"I'm going to die, I know I'm going to die," he whispered, his teeth chattering. "Take my bread... Take it, but don't eat it. It's got some gold inside!"

One of the guards summoned a doctor, who found that Filek had typhus and need to go to hospital. His flatbread with its baked-in gold lay on his chest as they carried him out.

The following day, Lila and I were marched to the border. For reasons unknown, they declined to recognize Dalma as our sister and she was forced to remain in the Uzhhorod prison.

10

The barrack square at Sobrance was encircled by low, ochreous garrison huts, stables and a two-storey administrative building with green doors and window frames. The first impression it left me with was an odd echo of the Habsburg monarchy that I'd never known. Both ends of the square had a line of ancient chestnut trees. The air was redolent of fallen leaves, horse manure and the smoke rising from three open fires. Huge iron cauldrons were suspended over the fires. Some border guards were sitting on tall three-legged stools, using long wooden spoons to stir the plum jam in the cauldrons, which were bubbling away, boiling over and spitting the dark gunge all over the place.

"It needs boiling without sugar for eight hours till it thickens," a young soldier told us, and he suggested we sit on our cases next to the fire. "The air's cold and it won't be dark till gone nine," he remarked.

The other border guards were smoking, chatting or doing and saying nothing. They took no notice of us. Only János, as the young soldier was called, was curious to know where we were from and what we did back home. He told us he came from a small farm and wanted to study architecture; he was saving up and, God willing, his dream might come true one day. After a few hours had passed, we had become such good friends that he gave us his address and asked us for ours.

"God knows where we'll be tomorrow and what our address will be," I told him, but from some irrational sense that we might somehow make time stop still and drop anchor back home I gave him our address in Mikuláš.

"Will you write back if I drop you a line," he asked, and when we nodded he smiled and said he looked forward to a letter, but that now he had to go, but he'd be back.

One of the guards handed each of us a three-legged stool and a wooden spoon. So we sat there, stirring the jam and keeping warm by the fire. It began to get dark, I kept mechanically stirring the cauldron and had a feeling of merging slowly with the grey light into an interminable half-sleep, from which I was woken by a sense that we were being stared at. Leaning against the door of the building opposite was a tall man who was staring at Lila. When he caught my eye he frowned, tightened his belt, straightened his shoulders and stuck his chest out.

János came back with a present of a loaf of bread, some cheese, salami, a cup of apricot jam, a thermos flask of tea, a small knife and some paper napkins. We thanked him for this unexpected act of generosity and divided the supplies into two canvas bags.

"Who's that chap over there?" Lila asked him.

"Lakatos. One of the vilest petty officers."

"I hope he won't be coming with us to the border, I'd much rather you came!"

At nine in the evening János was all set to lead us to the border. At the last minute he was joined by Lakatos. Both had rifles slung across one shoulder. We came out of the barracks onto the road. It led into a wood, beyond the wood onto some ploughland, its soft black earth all churned up, then into another wood. Beyond that there was an expanse of meadowland, partly boggy. Wherever the water seeped up it reflected the moonlight nicely. That also glinted on the bits of metal protecting the corners of our cases. When János made to take the cases from us, Lakatos bawled at him: "Idiot! You're not their servant!"

In a clearing surrounded by old willows Lakatos grabbed Lila by the shoulder, turned her to face him and hissed: "You're coming with me!"

"Leave her alone!" János protested.

"Shut up and mind your own business!" Lakatos yelled back at him.

But by this stage Lila was putting up her own defence. She scratched him, bit his hand and kicked him in the crotch. He hissed with pain and doubled up with a rasped: "You bitch! You tart! You swine you!" And having straightened back up, he bellowed: "Into the bog with 'em... Into the bog. Quick march, one two, one two. Into the bog...!"

"That's against the rules," János objected.

"What rules, you blithering idiot! We've been ordered to march them to the border and that's what we're doing. But these two bitches have tried to escape!"

He cast a menacing glance at János, unslung his rifle, aimed it at us and drove us ahead of him into the bog. We sank up to our ankles in the mud. One after another we dragged our feet out of it. We left our heavy suitcases lying in the mud. Back on dry land, we had mud squelching in our shoes and plopping off the bottom edges of our coats. We went forward with our feet soaked and caked in mud. Beyond the expanse of meadow was a wood and at its further end we could see, through the thinning undergrowth, the moonlit grey of a tarmac road. We lay down on it and remained there squashed flat against the surface. We pulled our grey hoods down over our foreheads. It crossed my mind that we were lucky to have them, and that our shoulder bags were dark blue. Some sentries were standing in a knot of fir trees at the edge of the wood having a cigarette. Floating across the sky, until a moment before full of stars and a bright moon, came some dark clouds. I glanced at my watch. Half past ten. The wood was completely dark. The sentries finished their cigarettes.

Two Slovak frontier guards passed along the other side of the road. They were so close that we could hear them talking. After they'd gone and disappeared among the trees, we crawled back into the woods on the Hungarian side. We were shrouded in the dark and cold of the heaving September air. In the wood, we scraped the mud off our shoes and did the best we could with our coat fringes. We were freezing cold. In my pocket I had that little map that the horse thief had drawn, but we had no idea where we were.

We strode off into the darkness. Walking fast so as to warm up a bit. We'd no idea if we were going right or left, north or south. A cloud had hidden the Pole Star, but even if it hadn't that wouldn't have been much help, given our hopeless sense of direction. We avoided woods so as not to get lost like hapless children in fairy tales. We stuck to fields and meadows until we came to a halt outside a three-winged grange, white and looking as if it had been sugar-glazed. It was as silent as an enchanted castle. We paused in case a dog started barking, but there was not a sound and nothing stirred. Silently, we entered the yard and let ourselves be guided by the odour of stables. We opened a stable door. It gave a slight creak and our faces were bathed in the warm aura of cow dung and milk, sugar beet and straw. Next to the far wall was a kind of shelter overhanging two pallets on which two boys were sleeping beneath stripy duvets. The moon lit up their rosy, sleep-flushed faces and almost pure-white hair. I touched the shoulder of the nearer of the two sleeping boys. He opened his eyes, but could probably see no more than my hazy outline.

"Sorry for waking you," I said in Hungarian.

"Has something happened?" he asked.

"No, no, nothing has happened, I just wanted to ask whether we're in Hungary..."

"No, you're in Slovakia..." the lad replied.

The other boy was still asleep.

"And where's the Hungarian border?"

"That way." The boy pointed. "Over there," he said, as if answering a question about the way to the nearest pub..."

"Is it far?"

"No, about five hundred metres. But be careful, there's gendarmes with dogs there."

We thanked the boy for the information and fortune for the miracle, and scuttled off. We didn't speak. Both our minds were on the almost surreal scene we'd just been through.

We needed to reach the border while it was still dark. Starting to rise out of the faint morning mist were the outlines of church spires and houses. Here and there a dog barked or a cock crowed, but we encountered no gendarmes. On a little wooden footbridge over a ditch just outside the village there were two soldiers with rifles. The failing darkness behind them was like a solid wall. One of the soldiers placed a finger to his lips and said: "Psst!" We walked past them and they didn't look round.

It was getting light. The peep of dawn was filled with birdsong. We could make out the hills, dark tree trunks and hints of foliage, and the dew on the grass. And we could hear the clanking of milk churns. Two lads wearing army forage caps came cycling past down an avenue of poplar trees. One shouted in Hungarian: "Step on it, Karcsi!"

We were in Hungary.

On the horizon the sun appeared behind a clump of tall, shaggy grass. We'd found an open patch in the middle of a dense alder carr and hidden there. We wiped our hands and faces with paper napkins soaked in the tea from our thermos flask. We ate some bread and cheese. Keeping the salami for lunch. We put our jumpers under our heads and rested. Cocks were crowing in the village nearby. We could hear hammer strokes coming from a smithy. Somewhere among the branches a chaffinch was going pink-pink-pink. I remembered that was a sign of good weather to come. Tr-tr-tr would mean rain. We had to stay in hiding until sunset. Nearby, someone was playing on a shepherd's pipe. Then the church bells began to ring. Our stockings and shoes were now dried out enough for us to get more or less rid of the remaining visible bits of mud. Being so weary, we fell asleep and only woke as darkness was falling. We got back to our feet, tightened our belts and left our hiding place.

II

The barns reminded me of huge mild-mannered animals. Bats were hurtling about in the dark after their prey. Somewhere a field mouse squeaked. We kept stubbing our toes on humps and anthills hidden in the grass and on clods and stones in the fields. I had a moment of dread about what would happen if one of us twisted an ankle or broke a leg, but quickly fought back any such idea. Now we needed to find our way through an unfamiliar landscape to a retreat somewhere between heaven and earth in a damp September night. We traipsed on steadfast and in silence as if we knew where we were headed. We paused when the silence of the night was broken by the trundling of some wheels. We decided to go after the sound. It led us into an avenue of poplars and disappeared in the dark.

We were brought to a halt by a footbridge over a stream. Taking shape ahead of us in the moonlight was a silvery grey track between two rows of the compact outlines of some cottages. We crossed the bridge. Silence reigned. No light in any of the windows. The only light was a narrow strip coming from under the stable door of the first house on the right.

"We need to try and get a bed for the night. Shall we both go, or just one of us?" Lila asked.

I went. I held my ear to the door and heard voices, a man's and a woman's. They were speaking Slovak. Aha, I thought, we must be in that Ostrov place the Uzhhorod horse thief was on about. I didn't knock; perhaps I was loath to cause the night to stir. I opened the door. It creaked and the two people inside looked at me in fright. They were an image of comfort and warmth. The man, who looked about forty, with a face sunburnt and windswept, was leaning against a cow with a lantern in one hand. The woman was sitting on a chair, peeling sweet corn into a large basket. The cob fell from her hands into her lap.

"God bless the work of your hands!" I said by way of greeting.

"May he just," the man replied.

"Goodness, girl, you frightened the life out of us! Where did you spring from at this time of night, and alone?" the woman asked me.

"I'm not alone. There are two of us. My sister's waiting outside. We wanted to ask if you'd be kind enough to let us spend the night in the loft or maybe here in the stable."

The man glanced at me with his concerned, kind blue eyes. "Call your sister in. No, leave it to me," he said, going straight out through the creaking door into the darkness outside.

"Forgive me, but you can't sleep here. I'm sorry, but we've got little children and they might go and let the cat out of the bag. About us having strangers visiting. People are nosy, and some are quite untrustworthy, they'd start asking questions and stopping by and soon the whole village would be alerted. Recently the gendarmerie's been doing house searches, looking for fugitives from Slovakia. Don't you worry though. We won't tell on you. I'll find you somewhere to sleep, but first let's all go inside." The woman shook her long skirt out and smoothed it down, the man doused the lantern and all four of us left the warm stable, passed through a short stretch of autumnal nocturnal cold and went inside the house proper of a smallish homestead. We entered its large kitchen. The farmer's wife turned up the wick of the guttering oil lamp and undid her blue scarf with its design of pink flowers. Her thick chestnut hair was twisted into a long plait. She was slim, with a narrow waist and she moved so gracefully in her long skirt. She lit the stove and set a large pot of water on the hot plate. Meanwhile, at the large oak table, her husband had been cutting some bread, spreading each slice with a thick layer of home-churned butter, and he also sat a chunk of cheese on a plate. I felt inordinately grateful to these kind-hearted, hospitable people, regretting that their sort didn't make up the majority of the world's populace. They knew we were fugitives, and they knew why. They had taken us in, no questions asked.

"We can tell from your coats that you're townsfolk," said the homesteader, and his wife suggested we clean our coats and shoes, wash our stockings and dry them next to the stove.

The man opened the door. "I'm going to get Peter Meissner. He sleeps in the annex, so I don't need to wake his father. They've got a big farm; it'll be a lot easier for you to hide there," he said.

We were sitting on chairs with wickerwork seats and soaking our feet in wooden tubs when the man came back with a young, curly-haired redhead.

"You can sleep on the hay in our loft, but my dad mustn't know. Today's 20 September, the day before Yom Kippur, a feast of penitence and fasting that my dad observes strictly. But I'll do what I can," the young man assured us. Then he began asking where we were from, what our names were and what we were intending to do next. Both he and our hosts listened closely to our replies.

"We need to get to Budapest, that's what matters most now," said Lila.

"You've got a horse and cart, Peter. How about you drive the girls to Uzhhorod and buy them train tickets to Budapest?" the homesteader's wife suggested.

"Great idea, but I won't be able to carry it out, unfortunately. Being so religious, my dad definitely won't allow it. All living things, including horses, have to rest," Peter explained.

"First thing in the morning the day after tomorrow shepherds will be taking their sheep to market, to Uzhhorod. You could go with them," said our host.

Logs were crackling inside the stove. The soft yellow light of the oil lamp made flickery shadows on the ceiling. On the table lay a bible with a silver clip. It had been in the family for over two hundred years, they told us, and they also warned us that the children wake very early.

"You just go and lie down in peace; I'll see to them," said Peter and we two, washed, brushed and well-fed, thanked our hosts for their magnanimity, donned our cleaned coats, picked up our bags and followed Peter out into the dark.

It was only then that we felt the full effect of our fatigue and the cold autumn air. Peter led us round the barns, past the church and cemetery and over the fields to his father's farmstead at the far end of the village. The cold rays of moonlight fell onto the stubble fields and the scattered knots of trees silhouetted on the horizon. We silently entered the main yard and Peter took us through to the barn. There we climbed a ladder up to the hay loft, took our coats off and buried ourselves in the hay. That warmed us up and gave us a sense of security. We slept soundly and the crowing of the cocks woke us only briefly. When I opened my eyes and looked at my watch it was ten o'clock. Peter brought us a half-damp towel, some bread, milk and half a roast chicken and the promise of more food at dusk.

"We were supposed to be having the chicken after the fast, but we've got plenty of food as it is, enough for three days. I've told my father about you, but without letting on that you're hiding here, but I did ask if I could have the coachman hitch up the horses and drive you to Uzhhorod. He wouldn't hear of it, since Mum's death he's grown ever more closed in on himself, like never before. It looks as if he's doing penance for something. Poor chap, I sometimes feel quite sorry for him. I've got a friend in Uzhhorod and I've managed to get him on the phone. He'll buy you tickets for the train to Budapest. So tomorrow morning it'll be me going with you!" Peter said, then he left so that his father wouldn't start looking for him.

12

We set off while it was still dark. Scattered clouds were racing across the sky. Between them constellations still twinkled. Long, hard grass stalks lashed at our legs. The night smelled of horses and the creaky little wooden footbridges over the streams seemed to echo to their whinnying. In the silence that followed, space just expanded and expanded.

In the yellow-green shade of first light we spotted the shepherds. We proceeded to follow in their footsteps. Briefly we lost sight of them, but when the sky turned pinkish we found them again. Their sheep were guarded by a dog while they sat on some boulders around a campfire. They reminded me of the fairy tale about The Twelve Months.[3] We exchanged greetings with them. They offered us space beside their fire and said they were waiting for a friend who'd got delayed. The shepherds were silent, smoking, and they didn't ask us any questions. We sat with them for a while, but then took our leave and carried on down the road that Peter had originally not taken. His friend in Uzhhorod was waiting for us on his doorstep. He had with him the train tickets to Budapest. After quite a long chat in the friend's flat, both lads accompanied us to the station. We promised we'd all meet up again in happier times.

The train arrived at Keleti Station at seven p.m. On the way, we'd learned that a blackout had been ordered in Budapest, and a curfew: after nine in the evening no one was allowed to be out in the street. That left us with two hours to find a bed for the night.

We went out into the streets of Budapest and stopped at Pali's. Only his mother was in. Wrapped in a blanket and miserable, she told us that Pali was staying with friends in the country, that Ági and most of our friends were in jail for illegal activities and that Oszi was in hospital following an attempted suicide. Nothing but dispiriting news over which we just didn't have the time to grieve.

"Suppose we try to find Endrebácsi at his usual restaurant," Lila suggested after we left the house.

We hurried through the streets of Budapest at the end of the day. Time was flying. Mady lived a long way away, and without Endrebácsi's help we should be forced, before the blackout, to find a passageway, outbuilding, an open pub or a space under some stairway. But how? We didn't even have any borrowed IDs or any forged papers. But luck was on our side. Endrebácsi was indeed at his usual restaurant, having a game of cards. Spotting us, he signed, by a movement of his eyebrows, for us not to speak. He said something to the people he was playing with, got up from his table and left the pub. We'd been waiting for him outside the door.

"Well hello, girls! I'm glad to see you!" he said, grabbing each of us by one arm and scurrying with us down a side street.

"You aren't going to like this, Endrebácsi, when we say why we were looking for you. We need help. We've got nowhere to stay the night and it's not long till the curfew," Lila explained.

"Okay, come on. We have to hurry," he responded and all three of us launched into a breathless search for a bed, mattress, some floor space, anything where we might lay our heads. We went in and out of passageways, up and down stairs. We scoured back yards, back streets and back alleys. Nothing.

"No papers? Sorry! We've got small children to think of!"

"No! Not even for one night. Sorry, it's just not on!"

"We don't know who they are and without papers, now, when all foreigners have to register – no!"

"That you of all people should be putting us on the spot like this! We'd never expect that of you!" Then doors slammed in their faces.

Men with their shirt sleeves rolled up, in their socks, their terrified wives behind them, children crying and voices: "Who is it? What's going on?"

And nosy neighbours behind half-open doors.

It started to rain. The pavements were covered in a layer of soggy fallen leaves. In the coffee houses and restaurants waiters were stacking upturned chairs on the tables. It was ten to nine when an acquaintance of Endre's, a widow, rented us a little room because her shortage of money was graver than her fear. Endrebácsi paid her a month in advance and gave us a small amount of cash in hand: "That's a start!" he said and hurried off home to his bed-sit in the next street.

During the day we had the whole flat to ourselves. The kitchen, one large room and one small one. We had a wash in the kitchen sink. The widow worked as a sales assistant in a bakery. She would bring home whatever leftovers there were of the day's bread and cakes. The flat was an annex tacked onto the rear wall of a large department store. It had a sun deck with wooden stairs leading down into the yard. There, between two tubs containing oleanders, stood a bench and a table. A washing line was stretched between the walls. That was where we hung our own washing when the sun came out.

As far as possible we stayed in the flat or the yard, but we needed to get hold of some false IDs. Out in the street there was the risk of bumping into agents from the border force who knew us from prison or the camp. So we decided to alter our appearance. Lila suggested that we bleach our hair, so without further delay we bought some hydrogen peroxide at a pharmacy nearby.

Lila's hair looked nice even after being bleached, but the fair locks that now framed her olive complexion made her look too conspicuous. The effect of my own colour change was horrendous. My hair was like a mass of straw and it looked no less cheap after I borrowed the widow's scissors and cut it short. When the widow saw me, she let out a yelp and said I looked disastrous and that we must find alternative accommodation as soon as possible.

We went to seek advice from Mady. She gave us something to eat and said that we could come any time we liked, but that we couldn't move in with her. The bed of her friend and the latter's son was now additionally occupied by the son's girlfriend. On the way back we bumped into Karol, a man who, like us, was in Hungary illegally. He had a room in the large flat of some widow, which she let him have in exchange for doing all the cleaning and taking her two greyhounds out for walks. He said that one of us could live with him, while for the other he'd be able to fix up a place to sleep in a greenhouse in Buda. I opted for the greenhouse. It was in the large garden of a mansion. There, under the care of the gardener, a group of four fugitives were already living in a summerhouse. The gardener knew who he was protecting, but the gentry to whom the property belonged were spending six months abroad, part of the time in Switzerland, at Davos, and the rest in Monte Carlo. Their sympathies were pro-German and they had influential contacts in high places.

Michal, one of the fugitives, made some money by baking cakes with a mock chestnut filling. He made that out of beans, margarine, sugar and flour. His raw materials came from a pastrycook friend who worked the black market. The gardener supplied us with eggs and fruit.

Three of the fugitives lived in the summerhouse, Michal and I in the greenhouse. The only cover I had was a thin blanket. I was freezing cold and Michal offered to warm me up. He was quite a handsome lad. I let him cuddle me, but he wanted more. I explained how disastrous it would be for me to lose my virginity and fall pregnant then of all times, after which he sobered up and calmed down. We then spent the rest of the night in bed together, keeping each other warm.

Our friends in the summerhouse knew a lithographer who

forged documents for a pair of émigrés, who then sold them on to interested parties. It turned out that I knew one of the sellers. I tried to emphasise our common predicament and sway his conscience, but in vain. In the end he suggested a compromise: he'd let me have some ID papers if I let him see me naked, but he even agreed to when I promised him just a sight of my breasts. He drove me to some woods on the moped that he'd bought with earnings from the sale of forged papers. In the tall grass beneath a spreading old oak tree I took off my blouse, sat down and let him survey the upper half of my body.

"How come you pretend to be a model of virtue when you don't wear a bra!" he said in a peevish, disgruntled tone as he drove me back from our outing. I couldn't be bothered to explain that I had no need of a bra and that I didn't have money to throw away on that or any other such luxuries. It crossed my mind that out there in the woods he could have raped me. My forged papers had cost me relatively little and I had to resign myself to feeling defiled.

13

A couple of times a week, Lila and I would meet up in Karol's room and on one such occasion Lila told me that Karol had paid for her forged papers. Despite all the warnings of our émigré friends, we used to go for short, and later longer, strolls into the city, even daring to go to Andrassy Street, the poshest and, for us, dangerous, main street of Budapest. On one such stroll a deep voice sounded from behind my back.

"Welcome back, Canary. Surely you can't have been thinking your new bleached hairdo would make you unrecognizable, can you?"

A large hand gripped my shoulder, turned me round and there I was, face to face with an agent from the border force. Lila was stopped from escaping by a second one, but she did manage to pop in her mouth, chew up and swallow the flimsy bit of paper on which we had the names of our friends. We spent the rest of the day in custody.

At the crack of dawn, we were taken off to be deloused. The city was deserted as we marched through the early-morning streets between two policemen. Some houses were beginning to wake. Bedding was being aired in windows. The clatter of the first trams of the day somehow heightened the feeling of cold. Dairies and bakeries were radiating the smell of sour milk and fresh bread.

Delousing took place in a great hulk of a building with a number of arched entrances and windows set like eyes in deep cavities in its walls. We weren't alone. Fellow creatures, as if picked out of refuse, collected from rubbish dumps, hauled out of holes, drains, passageways and basements, were standing with us in a large bare room, waiting. In tiny cabins we had to strip and hand over all our clothes, which were then marked and deloused. A burly female with broad, coarse, expressionless features raked mutely through our hair, combed it and repeatedly parted it with comb and fingers. They showered and disinfected us in a room with a stone floor. Everywhere reeked of chlorine and cheap detergents. It was a gross, pungent smell.

Once the procedure was over, now dressed in our deloused clothing, we were admitted one by one into a large lobby area. There I got a good look at our fellow delousees. The sight of them filled me with distress and sadness. They blinked in the light, pale, almost colourless, deprived now of everything that had given them warmth and protection. Lonely abandoned women, tramps, alcoholics, the demented. One man had a smile like the Mona Lisa, but for those dispensing the requirements of the law he evinced nothing but utter scorn. After we'd traipsed out into the morning city streets I saw him from behind. He had a limp and his back radiated defiance and provocation. Gorky and Dostoyevsky sprang to mind. We, too, had become dispossessed, excluded from "decent" society, like those who would shy away from us in the mist of the streets, disappearing round corners, down holes and in hiding places, beneath staircases and down in basements. The police took us back to Rombach, where Gubi greeted me with: "The whore Mira's back."

Gubi's desire to avenge his injured vanity was limited to three days and three nights. One of those nights is etched on my memory. During a raid by some Russian planes we had to remain in a cellar. We stood resting against a wall and I was glad that I had, next to me in the total darkness that was being pierced by the sound of explosions, Gubi's amiable sidekick. I was all the more surprised, then, by Gubi's sidekick's indecent attempts to touch various parts of my body. I tried to fight him off without speaking but with success, and in the brief pauses between explosions and the thunder of anti-aircraft batteries the silence of the darkened cellar was broken by his suppressed howls of pain.

The following day we were taken to a different camp, set up in what had been a Budapest school building. As we were leaving, Gubi's deputy passed close by me and said, sort of casually, "Tomorrow we could all be dead."

14

Szabolcs, the next camp, was also run by border force agents and interned prisoners. The camp warden and one of his deputies were decent folk, though another one was a primitive, power-seeking, malevolent individual, as were his wife and sister-in-law. They were always lurking, watching our every step, dishing out orders, criticizing, and making sure that we observed all the regulations and did nothing to jeopardize their time off, meat rations or permissions to go on dates in the evening.

Barányi, the older agent, was given to drinking, and he called Lila and me "my two little eggs". Whenever he was on duty, the sisters tried to be nice to us. Between ourselves, we called them, after the evil sisters in *Macbeth*, Goneril and Regan.

The camp warden assigned me two two-hour shifts by the phone, one in the morning, one in the afternoon. The telephone was on a small table outside the door of the office where all the members of the camp's management hung out together. They had no idea that I could hear everything they talked about.

The camp physician requested that I be permitted to act as his stand-in nurse. In a white gown and white lace-up shoes I almost began to believe in my "calling" and exploited it for the benefit of prisoners threatened with deportation to Ricse, the worst prison camp in Hungary. On a rubber dummy and, later, on the poor patients themselves, I learned how to give subcutaneous and intramuscular injections, and after consulting the doctor and with the acquiescence of those in peril I would give them either injections or pills that sent their temperatures sky-high and made their hearts pound. As an undertaking it was risky, illegal, but then so were the circumstances under which it was all being played out.

The doctor was a lacklustre, middle-aged bachelor from Zagreb. The only striking feature about him was his bushy, shaggy, sandy moustache. He seemed to be enclosed inside a glass bubble full of somewhat bitter sighs over squandered opportunities. He probably put up with me because I ignored his testiness. After our morning consultation, we would sit together as he tucked into his favourite food: bread with meticulously sliced cheese and apple. He gave me precise instructions as to which patients were to receive what medication, writing it all out, to be on the safe side, on an old typewriter, his sole possession salvaged from Zagreb.

In the camp, being a girl endowed with good looks and a pleasant voice meant being able, after a fashion, to make the otherwise drab days slightly more agreeable. Under the watchful gaze of one of the agents, we were allowed to hold dances to music from a gramophone, and I used to sing hit songs.

One of the agents, who differed from his colleagues by his decent behaviour and cultivated appearance, was quite taken with my voice. He came over to me and invited me to his table. He had thick, greying hair and fine hands with long, slender fingers and very clean nails. He asked if I was a singer and where I was from and expressed his regret that I was locked up and excluded from normal life. As time passed, I became something like his standby confessor and whenever he was on duty he would have me along for a chat. He told me about his failed marriage. He confided that he had trained for the Catholic priesthood but had gradually realized he probably wasn't cut out for celibacy. And because he had no use for double standards, he had quit the seminary.

"And now you're surprised I'm with the police, right? You have to appreciate that in Hungary a 'padre who's done a bunk' has no hope of landing a job with a salary that would feed a family. Behaving decently is possible anywhere, but in my job in particular, decency is a relative term," he said. We talked about art and politics. Our views differed, but he treated even that as a vitalizing factor in his life.

The agents used to get bored and then get drunk with the top prisoners. They often woke me in the night and asked me to sing for them. When I declined to play the buffoon for a bunch of drunks, they would mock me and drag me out of bed. Though none of them tried anything on sexually. For that purpose they had two specialists in the camp. One of them, a well-fed, fubsy forty-something, triumphantly, with everyone present, showed me her marzipan thighs with blue blotches. The 'padre who'd done a bunk' never took part in these "orgies".

What lives on in my memory most forcefully is the atmosphere, the moods and the tunes on the gramophone that we danced to. Also heads pressed tight to the radio listening to the muffled or half-jammed news on the BBC. And the names of Russian cities, Kiev, Orol, Kursk, Gomel. Disillusion or fervour. Mady wearing a man's hat on her monthly visit. A surprising meeting with my Aunt Ilonka from a town annexed by Hungary. She brought us some chocolates and fruit, and her appearance and actions so reminded me of my mum. Beethoven's Seventh and Schubert's Unfinished. Huge bundles of second-hand clothes stored in the basement. My first experimental conversation, on a soft mound of unsorted second-hand and not very clean clothes, with a young man who was the son of the former owner of the largest dry-cleaner's in Vienna. His name was Edi Smetana, he had hair the colour of wheat and glasses that gave him the unwarranted appearance of an intellectual. And one other unexpected visitor, a young man we didn't know. He didn't say who'd sent him, only that he'd been given the job of liaison between his group outside and us two. He assured us he would always know where we were and that he would be supporting us however possible.

So many different people from so many countries and environments, so many odd happenings, so many meetings and partings, so many clever people and so many ordinary ones, the courageous and the timorous, and so many madmen, genuine or faking it in the hope of being let out, all jumbled together in my mind in one multicoloured ball of wool with endless knots in it.

I can remember the walls and the barbed wire. The grey flurry beyond the windows, snowflakes and the smell of a Christmas tree being burnt in the grounds of the hospital that was separated from the camp by a wire fence. We would stand at the fence, watching the patients, doctors and nurses. They would move in and out of the buildings unimpeded and disappear through the doors of the various pavilions. A red mitten left behind in the white snow seemed more real than the life we were living. When, following an attempt to escape, they put a stop to our rare outings and having visitors, we would talk to people we knew through the mesh of the wire fence, which only had spikes along its top edge.

We got on well with many of the people inside the camp, but our most special friends were two sisters of our own age. After four months of camp routine, we four decided to attempt to escape. Our liaison supplied us with pliers, a file, a skeleton key, a screwdriver and other useful small tools. The arrangement was that at night, while everyone was asleep, we would creep out in twos to what had been the school toilets, a room with a green door, where the locks were broken and all the taps kept dripping. Next to the store-room where the cleaning things were stored was a larger room used for other storage. That was where we were meant to hide. At half past one we were to clamber through a hole in the fence into the grounds of the hospital. There our liaison would be waiting for us, a night nurse who was in the know. She would hide us inside the hospital and phone a number unknown to us. All else was in the hands of our mysterious saviours.

As we were standing outside the school, which was partly concealed by the fence, and had begun getting out our bags of tools, which we had divided among us and were carrying hidden beneath our clothes on strings round our necks, we suddenly heard shouting and screaming, doors banging and the shrill voice of the camp deputy's wife. "Mira, Lila, Ulla, Mara... They're not in their beds! Where are they? They've run off! Start a search! Get up, you lazy lot and start looking for them!"

With their hair in curlers and in their nightdresses, the two sisters came running out and banged on the door of the sleeping agent. After the first outcry and before all the lights went on and the woken sleepers began straggling out into the grounds, we managed to slip back into the store and hide behind some mattresses and pieces of surplus furniture. We were found there by our sleepy, good-natured detective Holub. He hauled us out into the light, led us out into the grounds to join the worked-up sisters and told them: "What miserable wretches you are! Why couldn't you keep quiet and sleep? Do you want some disciplinary measures taken? I shan't be taking any!"

Holub was as good as his word. No one at the camp was punished by losing their days out, having visitors banned or getting reduced portions of meat.

But there were those who did not forget our attempted escape. At the first opportunity they had us transported to Ricse.

15

The Ricse internment camp lay in among some Hungarian villages, close to the Slovakian frontier. The red-brick barracks were in two sections. One held interned men, the other women. The land on which they'd been built hadn't been paved over, but reinforced with sand and gravel. In summertime it was overgrown with grass and after heavy rain great puddles formed.

We were guarded by policemen in blue uniforms under the command of a tall, taciturn sergeant, a Ruthenian whose expressionless, severe facial features looked as if carved from stone. He came from Subcarpathian Ruthenia and could speak Czech. He was flinty to the point of brutality. The commandant, an idle, vain, well-fed, high-ranking police officer, showed up at the camp only rarely. On ceremonial occasions he would wear a pale-blue uniform in which he looked like some character from a Kálmán or Lehár operetta. He had a portrait of himself done by Bobby, one of the fairly numerous professional artists who had fled or were deported from central Europe or Yugoslavia. Lilly, Bobby's girlfriend and also a painter, designed clothes for the commandant's wife.

Most of the lodgings had two rooms. After the medical examination, when we were being divided up into the huts, we four friends chose one of the front rooms with four bunks. The room was at the same time the access point for the three prisoners in the back room. The fact of our being allowed to stay together was some compensation for the unpleasantness of being constantly disturbed.

Despite the strict regime, the commandant desired some entertainment, which was organized by Livia, a tall, slim, pretentious, egocentric young woman from Belgrade who couldn't tolerate any potential competition. Her mother, who held fast to the slowly fading elegance of a former *grande dame*, supported her in all that she did. They didn't like the fact that I'd become a member of the professionally managed music and drama company. Our shows were attended by the commandant and his wife, the local landowners and their families and other local worthies, and by policemen and prisoners. Internees who could play a musical instrument, sing, dance or act didn't have to work and weren't subject to the limitations imposed by the camp regulations. When other girls refused, for reasons unknown, to lend me their pants for my imitation of Marlene Dietrich, Danica, a Croat, let on that Livia had warned the other girls about possible infection with a sexually transmitted disease, because in Budapest I'd been a prostitute, evidence of which was my bleached hair, which was growing back, my general appearance and my "sexy" voice. The malicious gossip was put a stop to by the doctor. He called a meeting and announced that, having examined us all, he knew I was not only not infectious, but was even *virgo intacta*. I felt that second part of his defence was a breach of my privacy.

One day, the Ruthenian sergeant called me in and informed me I'd been chosen for some gardening. At my urgent request, he allowed Ulla, Lila and Mara to go with us. At six o'clock every morning he would stand in the yard outside our hut and call out our names in a loud voice. With him in the lead we would then march out through the gate into the road and then along the road to Ricse village.

To me it was like walking through a mirror of my own childhood and I felt like Alice in Wonderland. Whitewashed houses with tiny front gardens, where sunflowers reared their yellow smiling heads on long necks high up over the low fences. The dame's violets, marigolds, dahlias and begonias were just like back home. The clatter of hay wagons. The cracking of whips. Hens and geese along house fronts and on the dusty road strewn with ears of corn. Open stable doors. The familiar smell of manure. Fruit-laden trees in people's gardens. Ripe apples lying in the grass. Spotted pigs. Harvest time. Men and women in the fields. Stacks of straw.

We were there to pick black, red and white currants and gooseberries. We weeded vegetable plots, pulled up carrots, radishes and kohlrabi, cut cabbages and lettuces, and I, at the Ruthenian's request, sang whatever came to mind by way of Slovak, Czech or Russian folksongs, but also songs by Voskovec and Werich and others from E. F. Burian's Liberated Theatre. The Ruthenian never spoke, but at odd moments an unrevealing smile glimmered on his motionless face. I did wonder what past and what thoughts were lurking behind it, and I thought of Ivan Olbracht's books about Subcarpathian Ruthenia.

With some of the thirty pengő sent us each month by our unknown benefactors we would buy jam, bread, sunflower oil and eggs at the village shop, and also cigarettes, which were strictly banned inside the camp. The Ruthenian would wait for us outside. He asked no questions and did not check our purchases. With egg whites and jam we used to make a pale-yellow or pink mousse. We thought it the best treat in the world along with bread dipped in sunflower oil. Among the prisoners there were those who envied us, and when Márton, the vilest and most deeply loathed of the policemen, caught us smoking, he bawled me out and threatened me with the blockhouse. However, he didn't carry out his threat; as a result, camp rumour now had it that I slept with the policemen. This came as no surprise. For every misdemeanour, and that included smoking, prisoners would be locked up in the blockhouse, a narrow, rectangular, grey, concrete structure, inside which you could only stand up. The punishment lasted at least three hours and at most six. When the sun beat down on its concrete walls, the prisoners inside would faint, and when The Ruthenian opened the door they would tumble out onto the ground, unconscious. For people with a heart problem, the blockhouse was a death penalty.

I watched as several of the internees visibly aged. Many vanished from life and from my memory. But there are some whom I shall never forget. They include an Austrian dancer with snakelike movements of her arms and hands, some piano virtuosi, violinists, a world-renowned lady cellist from Salzburg,[4] and a tall, bony young woman from Vienna, dismissive and introverted, but with a great talent for and a wide knowledge of music. She was a wonderful player of all instruments, including the accordion, which no one else even touched. I still remember the faces of Lilly and Bobby, who painted our scenery. And I have a clear vision of many of our audience and can still hear their acclaim and their criticisms. Very few of their stories would culminate in a happy ending.

Every day we would rehearse for two hours in the morning and two in the afternoon. I attended the rehearsals by permission of the Ruthenian. They were done to piano accompaniment, with perfumed make-up and a medley of colours. The professionals stretched the amateurs and achieved some minor miracles. We played chamber music and sang songs by Schubert. At the commandant's behest we put on the operetta *Summer in Tyrol*. If ever I happen to hear someone sing "*Im weissen Rössl am*

Wolfgangsee", I see before me Pepi, the thin, short-sighted accountant from Vienna, who sang it beautifully. Props would be got together by Bobby, with the commandant's approval.

The company was our pocket of air in a sinking ship. My own contribution was some Judy Garland songs in Hungarian. In a dinner jacket and cardboard top hat, I sang: "*Ich tanze mit dir in den Himmel hinein, in den siebenten Himmel der Liebe*"[5], while a Croat girl, Mina, who was dressed in pink tulle, was doing dance steps with me. After we finished, we would both leave through the large, red, heart-shaped door painted by Bobby with its windows looking onto Paradise and then come back out again to take a bow and receive the applause and cries of "Da capo!". The commandant would be smiling benignly; he gave me a wink and whispered something to his female companion. After such kitsch he also sat through Schubert's *Death and the Maiden* quartet. Our brief moment of euphoria was curtailed by the realization that nothing lasts forever.

On 10 July 1943, British and Canadian troops landed in Sicily. The doctor, who listened secretly to the BBC, told us the good news. On 25 July, certain officers of Mussolini's who were close to the royal court were placed under arrest. Marshal Badoglio formed a new government and asked Eisenhower for peace talks. The zesty name "Badoglio" bounced around the camp like a ball and triggered hopes for our early liberation.

In that brief intermezzo, which was brimming with illusions, the camp was graced by a visit from the papal nuncio. In his red cassock and red gloves, he stood in the middle of the camp, while around him, at a respectful distance, the prisoners received his blessing. Some of them stepped out of line, threw themselves on their knees before him and kissed the edge of his red vestment. This trivial, equivocal act on the part of Pius XII was of minimal significance in relation to all that he had let pass as an all-powerful spiritual leader and human being. Several Polish prisoners were released, Badoglio capitulated, the Germans took charge and the war went on. As did our days at Ricse. But with even greater savagery. October saw an epidemic of dysentery hit the camp. All the prisoners had a fever and the whole camp reeked of excrement. We grew weak and lethargic. The oldest suffered the worst. They gave us opium, but it didn't do much good. Lying abed in the room next to ours was Marta, a lady of fifty or so, of whom we were all fond. A former literature teacher, she discussed world literature with us, taught us to recognize the constellations, and helped those who were depressed or lovelorn. She also gave us much practical advice. She taught me to sew by hand, and so I began to convert mere rags into useful things to wear. Marta suffered the worst because she had a weak heart.

In the middle of this outbreak, which was so humiliating to us all, they brought three wagonloads of willow twigs into the camp and ordered us to strip them. The police drove the prisoners out into the yard and threatened those who could scarcely rise with the blockhouse. The Ruthenian and three policemen checked all the rooms and found Marta on her bunk.

"Get up! Get up! Don't think you'll get away with lazing about, you trollop!" he shouted, shoving her about and threatening her with his baton.

Hearing him cursing, I went back inside and told him: "If you don't let her stay where she is, she's going to die."

"Let her then, the lazy old cow, and if you don't stop interfering, I'll clobber you with this! Ugh, it doesn't half stink here, stinks everywhere!"

I left the room filled with rage and a feeling of powerlessness and joined my fellow prisoners, who were laboriously, and with frequent breaks, stripping the bark from the willow twigs. When I returned from work, I discovered that the Ruthenian had allowed Marta to remain in bed.

16

By the end of February 1944 Mara and Ulla were no longer with us. Following an intervention by some influential relatives they'd been released from the camp. Lilly's and Bobby's departure was taken care of by the commandant, whose portrait they'd done many times. Of my closest friends only Mara's classmate Nadya was left. Lila and I were transported back to Budapest.

Szabolcs was in the grip of uncertainty, commotion, confusion, disorder and a foreboding of unpleasant changes to come. The camp was in a state of collapse. Nothing was as it had been. Houses were collapsing with the growing number of Russian air raids. The Hungarian fascist leader and his *Nyilas*, which was akin to the SS, gained greater influence over parliament and its clampdown on alien elements. The detectives distanced themselves from us, some of them becoming downright aggressive and brazen. I was again ordered to man the phone outside the office, where I could hear every word.

Vincze, the most arrogant of the detectives, never paid me any attention. He only ever spoke to me once, and that was to tell me off over something or other. I overheard one of his acquaintances, the daughter of one very rich Budapest household, complaining to him about her lover, a handsome internee who'd owned a factory in Bratislava: "The villain's cheating on me. He's always cheated on me and I've always known who with. But at least he's got taste! Right now he's cheating on me with that little whore who mans the phone. I'm sure he's sleeping with her, the bitch! You have to do something about her!"

Vincze had the accused brought to him and the cursing and

accusations came through the door louder and louder. "I'll shoot you if you so much as look one more time at that scruffy tart!"

"You're being paranoid, Kató," her friend Vincze said calmly. "Jealousy's making an idiot of you. If you don't apologise to the girl, who is, incidentally, entirely innocent, and has certainly heard every word of your inarticulate yammering, I shall have no more to do with you!"

The next day, Kató came to our hut, apologized and asked if there was anything she could help me with.

"No, there isn't!" I said, and I could read in her bright-red face the rage that sprang from her forced and fruitless humiliation. In the uneasy atmosphere of the camp the whole affair struck me as embarrassingly ridiculous. Yet that scene didn't mark the end of this farcical melodrama. In the final act, the grievously sore Kató, armed with a revolver, stole into the hospital ward where her lover was lying with a broken leg and shot him in the left shoulder.

"And this life of ease really is coming to a close. What you're about to be served up is going to taste quite different from what we've been feeding you with so generously till now!" Vincze said to me as he passed me in the corridor, and I sensed that his words were no mere malevolent aside. They contained a hint of relish at the prospect of something rather nasty, a prognostication that was already becoming a reality.

When the usual agents were joined in the camp by some Arrow Cross men, *Nyilas*, it was obvious that things were bad and that we were about to be hauled off somewhere. Lila hid beneath a low, wide divan in the caretaker's room, and Nadya helped me crawl down to the bottom of a large chest filled with duvets and quilts. I shall never forget the feeling of naked, powerless ignominy when the Arrow Cross men began removing the wadded bedding piece by piece and laughing right in my face. I felt like a snail being dragged forcibly out of its shell and, thus exposed to a sinister arbitrariness, I had to keep a firm grip on myself and not risk the consequences of spitting in their faces. After they'd found Lila as well, they shoved us out into the yard to join the rest of the internees, who were already lined up and waiting by the open gate.

17

That the place they carted us off to was Kistarcsa I learned only years after the war was over. The trucks went along the streets of the rather pretty town, as we'd known it, though now it seemed hostile and like a wicked stepmother, and stopped outside an austere building with countless vacant, uncurtained windows. Darkness glared at us from within. The women were housed on the third floor, the men on the fourth, in what had been the classrooms of a school. Some rooms still had blackboards with traces of chalk. The only thing left in our classroom was a large, old brown cupboard.

We were to sleep on bare mattresses under dark-grey blankets. There was frost in the air. We felt it on our daily, one-hour constitutional round the school playground. During one such walk I got talking to a tall, fair-haired young man. His name was Igor. You could tell that his status as a prisoner was of recent date. He wore a tailor-made suit and kept the collar of his belted, wool-lined cotton coat turned up round his neck. Sometimes he wore, under his coat, warm sweaters knitted in tasteful colours. The saying goes that "clothes make the man". But in the uncertainties of the waiting-room atmosphere, between hoping and despair, amid jitters and trepidation, it wasn't – any more than at other times and now even less – clothes that mattered, but the person wearing them.

"You're cold. I'll give you a sweater, or maybe two. If it's too big, pick it apart and knit yourself a new one. At least that'll help pass the time," Igor told me.

"How can I knit without needles?"

"I've got a cousin in Budapest who's permitted to visit me. I'll get her to bring some."

On our walks Igor told me about his girlfriend, Eva, interned somewhere in Poland, at a camp that unconfirmed reports said was called Auschwitz. At its research institute Eva did botanical drawings. She wrote about that in a letter to her parents, smuggled out for her by a Slovak guard. She wrote that she was all right. She reported to her parents on health matters of dead family members. She also named notorious local thugs and murderers: "Imagine my surprise when I discovered just how many of those heading the research institute resembled them," the letter said. It wasn't hard to imagine that conditions at Oświęcim [Auschwitz] were at best blurry. When Eva's parents asked the guard how the girls who'd been deported were living, he replied that they were doing absolutely fine, going about in fur coats and leather top boots.

"If you happen to end up in Auschwitz and bump into Eva, do tell her I haven't forgotten her. Promise!" Igor begged me as he handed me a sweater and some knitting needles.

The sweater was a mix of olive-green, beige, rust-coloured and light-brown wool. I unravelled it and began to knit.

Lila, Nadya and I made an attempt to escape. At the end of the corridor was a toilet. From there a staircase led down to a door with a padlock. With the aid of our hidden tools we managed to file through it. We came out into a yard surrounded by high walls. This was at night, but by the light of the moon we detected a large locked gate set in one of the walls. Its huge lock was of solid iron. We were loath to give up without trying, so we got to work on it. We struggled, filing and sawing, taking turns, but all to no avail. The whole time I had this feeling that the invincible lock was looking back at us poor things with sheer pity. Tired and sweaty, we went back up the stairs in our stockinged feet, through the door with its filed-through bolt, then tip-toed along the cold corridor back into the classroom full of mattresses.

At six in the morning we were woken by an alarm going off. Standing in the doorway was an agitated male prisoner from the fourth floor. "If you've got anything the Nyilas mustn't find, hide it right now. They're swarming all over the building. It appears someone tried to escape in the night!" he warned and disappeared. We removed our bags of tools from our necks and tossed them behind the old brown cupboard. Some of the women started having a go at us: "Are you mad? Do you want to get us all into trouble?" "Dumb bitches! Only thinking of themselves!" "I'll kill you if you don't shut up!" one young woman threatened them.

No one told on us and the Nyilas left once it became clear that the prisoner numbers were unchanged.

I went on knitting my woollen jumper. I finished it the evening before we were transported off. But throughout the knitting process an inner voice had kept telling me: "You'll never get to wear this jumper!" And I didn't wear it even once. The bag containing it disappeared in the mountain of luggage unloaded onto the platform at Auschwitz.

My sister was caught trying to cross the border illegally and was interned in the Slovakian camp Nováky. From here she escaped with a group of prisoners, who, after overpowering the guards went to the mountains and joined the partisans.

A group of prisoners in Risce. Lila is the third from the left, I am second from the right.

BOOK 3

DARKNESS. PAGES FROM A RETROSPECTIVE DIARY

I

We're being transported in cattle trucks. This is our fourth day on the road. People of different ages. Adults and children. Czechs, Slovaks, Germans, Austrians and Yugoslavs. Fugitives and foreigners plucked from prisons and internment camps, picked up on the street or hauled from hideouts that have been betrayed.

Whenever the train stops at a station, we get given water. Guards come rushing out of their squad rooms, armed with submachine-guns. The crashing of doors flung open and slammed shut. Swearing. The noise of commands being barked. Much banging. Constantly under guard, we empty out our overflowing cans in the station toilets. The straw on the truck floor is filthy. The crowded space stinks of urine, sweat and faeces. People brawling from fear, insecurity and enforced physical proximity.

In the perpetual half-light of the truck something starts to wail. A child crying. Words of consolation. Cuddling. Soothing. The pitch-dark nights are disturbed by sudden shouts, by sighs and by snoring. Whenever we get the chance, Lila and I push up against the barred window.

At stations, it's like any ordinary day. Baskets hanging from platform canopies. We can visualize them filled with red geraniums. Trains coming and going. Passengers sitting around in waiting rooms or on benches. Do they register us? Can they see us? Do they try to dispel any unpleasant, pointlessly troubling thoughts? Do any of them see us the way we saw the transport at Trebišov – stars that have faded, but are still managing to shine.

Cemeteries, villages, churches, roads, avenues of trees. Meadows grazed by cows, horses, sheep. A cat asleep on a window ledge. A black dog blocking someone's doorway. Time is rushing backwards. Nadya, Vera and we two sisters are talking in a whisper about possible ways to escape.

A screech of brakes. The train comes to a sudden halt. The engine is quietly panting and then blows its ear-splitting whistle. Buffers clatter up against one another. The trucks are uncoupled. A blinding light shines into our darkness and cuts at our eyes. Men in striped, blue-grey prison uniforms help empty the trucks. They reek of chlorine. About their mouths they have scabs coated in white ointment. "They smell of death," I whisper to Lila. She looks at me and nods.

The train is in a siding. Any corpses are being dragged out of the trucks and tossed onto the ground. All the luggage is piled up in a heap. The mountain of suitcases, rucksacks, bags and boxes just grows and grows.

Standing legs apart on the platform are some SS-men in their tailored uniforms, their caps with a prominent shield-shaped badge, wearing glistening jackboots and dishing out orders to the prisoners. They have Alsatians with beautifully groomed, silky fur sitting at their feet. Dogs and masters alike radiate controlled vigilance.

By the loading bay there are some lorries. Their green-uniformed drivers are sitting motionless at their wheels like waxworks. I glance at my fellow-passengers. Their faces pale and lined, filthy, resigned, defiant, frightened. We all look old before our time, decrepit and forlorn next to the clean, upright, arrogantly stand-offish SS-men. They order us to form lines. Men in one, women in another. Silence! Follow orders! We are facing an unknown future. We have no idea what's happening to us and to what end.

"Those who are exhausted, in need of sleep, sick, elderly, old and mothers with children can board the lorries. Go ahead, please, don't worry, just climb aboard. You'll all meet up at the other end," says one officer with a chilly civility.

Next in line behind me is Hertha from Magdeburg. Short of stature, she looks like a ball – she's wearing eight sets of clothes. "Thing is, you never know what might come in handy when," she whispers, then goes on jubilantly: "See how right I was. Like I've told you before, we Germans are a civilized nation."

One of the fellows in prison uniform speaks quietly, but insistently: "Quick, quick, give the kids to the old folk, come on, hurry up! Faster! Trust me!"

The resentful, frightened and bewildered women clasp their children even more firmly to their bosoms, their legs, their bodies.

Vera, Nadya, Lila and I, four good friends, instinctively stand erect, trying to give the impression that we are fit young people capable of working, and demonstrating as much by showing no need to clamber up onto the back of some lorry.

"*Marsch! Eins, zwei, eins, zwei!*" comes the order. The lines move forward. They walk as best they can, in marching order, and proceed through a cast-iron gateway. In the arch above the gate it says in letters of iron: "*Arbeit macht frei.*"

I didn't know that we were on the marshy plain not far from Cracow, where the rivers Vistula and Sola meet, and that, passing through that round-topped iron gateway, we'd just entered the

Auschwitz concentration camp. All I could see was an area of sombre two-storey barrack huts, an area surrounded by two lines of electrified barbed-wire fence bearing the warning sign: *Vorsicht! Hochspannung! Lebensgefahr!* And terrifying, sky-scraping lookout towers from which SS-men pointed submachine guns towards all points of the compass. It was early April, but here frost was in command, and I had a feeling of a desperate, invisible, ice-cold wind getting right through to my very soul.

The simultaneity of past and future

Forty-five years later, when I saw in Die Zeit an article about mass murder, above which they had a wispy graphic image of the gate into Auschwitz and, beyond it, the geometrical lines of barracks, almost opaque on the porous paper, I wrote:

Why does it feel as if I'm hearing but a dull echo
as if the living "I" was never here
in these flat, uninviting places
beneath this indifferent heaven
that looks unseeing through the dead lines of fences
in the impervious void
beyond this gate
where from out of the cranial cavity of faded history
comes crawling a mute crab
before vanishing backwards
in future forgetfulness.

But the black-and-white outline of the gateway stirred within me the notion of THE GREAT UNSPOKEN. It stared out at me like a feculent mess of undigested and falsified reality, default humanity, contrivance and uninterest. A great unspoken concealed within words spoken, in the veiling of the revealed, in responses freed of all responsibility, in a repetition of what is being repeated all over the world.

How can one comprehend the incomprehensible, monstrous reality of perfectly planned extermination? It is only in my nightmares that I go back there, I see it, feel it, smell it, I take fright at it, understand and all my senses sound an alarm.

How can I ever be reconciled to the possibility of some future contagion that will weaken or destroy the ability to feel shame and *outrage at any overstepping of the bounds of common decency and truth, or to the fact that pure chance and instinct alone had helped me survive the constant snares of a gigantean enterprise of murder, its precise timing, and the countless associated crematoria, the prescribed turnover of gas chambers, and the meticulously functioning timetables of transports from every corner of Europe, paid for by the victims themselves?*

How can I grasp that I did escape from the running dogs of an absolutely dehumanized technology, remotely controlled by civil servants, captains of industry, politicians, banks, generals, doctors and lawyers, and employed and overseen by SS-men and compliant, duped or primitive, beggarly human small fry?

How is it that I am alive and can gaze at that faded picture in the paper and catch the distant echo of a setting where, in the shade of chimneys, a skeletal, wretched, toilworn workforce perished, having become a resource for the production of mattresses stuffed with their hair, a supply of gold for the teeth of others, and of bones and skin for the manufacture of soap, of bodies for medical experiments, and of clothing, footwear, spectacles and every kind of prosthesis whisked off to the Third Reich?

The ashes from crematoria used to be tipped into the Vistula, spread on fields and, having been rid of incombustible debris and mixed with gravel, used in road-building. Today I know that dehumanization in various permutations, even those less extreme but functioning to perfection, is an attribute of every kind of dictatorship.

2

Two days passed. We spent them in some imponderable space. I see the girls and women waiting with me inside that space as mere hazy blotches. What I can sense and well recall is the all-pervading stench. Maybe also because it invariably smote my nose whenever I found myself in one or other of the countries behind the Iron Curtain. Chlorine, cheap, foul-smelling cleaning fluids and in them something that always clings fast to hardship and unfreedom.

They took away all our personal belongings. Watches, jewellery, handkerchiefs, toothbrushes, all those oddments that get forgotten or hidden in pockets: bits of paper, receipts, photos, theatre, cinema or tram tickets. They were all tossed into a huge basket. It was there that then lay our stolen, abandoned identities. The final bits and bobs went with our clothes. We had to strip naked. I was embarrassed, though it did occur to me that it could be in my favour that I was young and slim. I could forgive myself that brief moment of smugness; it passed very quickly. The guards in SS uniforms and the men in prison attire came and went, opening and slamming doors with an expression of being concerned with more important matters. Our shared impersonal nakedness languished in a strange place charged with vulnerability and indifference. For the guards and their prisoner-henchmen we weren't women. They watched us, but paid no heed to us. They talked among themselves, but their words meant something different from the sense that we would have accorded them. They exchanged looks that were inscrutable. Their smiles inspired fear while making it easier to bear at the same time. I could sense that everything inside me was fighting back against being seen as a mere object. I withdrew inside myself, began to sheathe myself within a shell and hide away in a visceral invisibility where I might preserve my individuality and self-respect.

"What are we actually waiting here for?" one of the girls asked.

"We're actually waiting for a response from Berlin," mockingly replied one of the guards. "They'll tell us what sort of transport you are and what we're to do with you!"

"Will we be waiting long?"

The guard shrugged: "As long as it takes... We don't have room for you yet. A hut has to be made vacant first!" he said, exchanging a knowing glance with one prisoner, who had, sewn on the left breast of his uniform, a red triangle with a number above it.

We were led off to a larger, warmer room. They let us sit down on the heated concrete floor and some bench-like concrete projections. Only after a time did we learn that we were waiting for a response from Berlin in the attic of one of the crematoria.

In through the door came trundling a group of female convicts wearing clean, made-to-measure uniforms. They looked fit and neat and we began to hope that what lay ahead might not be that bad after all. I seemed to recall someone saying in the train on the way here that there was an assembly camp called Auschwitz and that soap was manufactured there. Maybe we were also going to be involved in making soap.

The female convicts ordered us to stand, then led us off into large, cold room, doused us in some strong-smelling, stinging liquid disinfectant, shaved off all our body hair and closely cropped the hair on our heads, somewhat unevenly. Some of the girls began to cry when they saw the shorn heads and their own hair tossed casually onto the pile in one corner.

"Quit hollerin'! You've been given an exemption. Count your blessings you don't have to wear white kerchiefs on your clean-shaven bonces!" one of the female convicts bellowed. Later on we learned that we were the first unusually non-homogeneous transport from Hungary with no Hungarians among our number and that that had led to some dithering on the part of the administration, which was otherwise used to working to a strict plan and systematically. The convicts worked efficiently, quickly, mechanically, with no hint of affability. They took from cupboards and drawers dresses, stockings, underwear and shoes. They tossed each of us a bundle of things. Mine contained a blue-and-grey dance frock, its lower edge trimmed back at an angle, covered in stains of various colours. Stockings of different colours and lengths. One shoe high-heeled, the other low. I protested and asked if I might not have a pair that matched.

"Shut up!" the convict came back at me. "You've got what you're getting."

"But your uniform's clean and orderly!"

"Who do you think you are? When you've been here as long as I have, you'll be grateful for being allowed to breathe! And that goes for the rest of you. Follow my orders and keep your mouths shut if you don't want to snuff it on the spot!"

We had to line up. Six prisoners to a line. Weary, exhausted, terrified, sleep-deprived, we glanced at one another then immediately looked away. We looked like scarecrows. I just managed to register that Lila's pretty face had, despite this depraved attempt to disfigure it, not changed at all, while I sensed that my own was, as ever, mirroring my internal state and showing signs of age.

"Forward, march! One, two... *Los! Marsch!*"

Nobody explained where we were actually marching to. I was in a daze, torn from any kind of context, freezing cold and hungry. I learned later that in my one high-heeled and one low-heeled shoes I had walked the three kilometres from the main camp at Oświęcim (Auschwitz) to Brzezinka, Oświęcim II (Auschwitz II–Birkenau). In the cool of early morning the camp felt grey and bleak, and so it remained. A gloomy flat area, where railway tracks merged beneath a gateway crowned with a tall watchtower. Next to that was the building that housed reception, and, beyond that, endless rows of wooden barrack huts. Along the pathways between them I could see the inmates, some pushing wheelbarrows, others hauling rocks. Many were just skin and bone. And a sorry sight they looked. They stirred compassion, but also revulsion and horror. They were like insects with burnt wings. Crane flies or midges with their legs pulled off. Flies caught in a cobweb. "You're not going to look any different!" flashed through my mind. "No! No you won't! Stop it!" I told myself in response. Several of the skeletons had seeping wounds on their feet. "Phlegmon," someone behind me diagnosed. "We call the ones that look like corpses *Muselmänner*," said one of the more experienced women prisoners, who'd come to inspect the new arrivals. It transpired that we knew her from the grammar school in Mikuláš.

"Watch out! Here comes the Sauna-Kapo. She's German. With a green triangle. That means she's in gaol for either murder or some other serious crime," she explained.

"*Los... Los... Schweinehunde... Mistbienen... Dreckkäfer! Stehen bleiben!*" All the new ones to step forward – yelled the Sauna-Kapo in a coarse, gravelly voice, then she cracked her whip.

We were to stand for roll-call. Our first such muster. We were starving. We stood there in the mud, waiting and freezing. Anyone not standing up straight got a whip stroke. Anyone who groaned got two.

"*Maul halten, ihr Dreckkäfer,*" the Sauna-Kapo rasped.

A group of female prisoners is carrying pots full of food. Here and there someone spots them and makes straight for them. They ignore the bludgeoning that's their reward and dip their empty tins, or even their bare hands, into the pots, trying as fast as possible to steal a drop of soup and down it at lightning speed.

Each of us newcomers is given a tin plate and a spoon. "Take good care of these," we are cautioned by the female convict who introduced herself as the person in charge of the block where we were going to be housed. "If you lose them or let someone steal them, you'll be eating with your bare hands!"

They fill our assigned plates with a liquid they call *Suppe*. Steam rises from it. At last, some warm food for our cold, empty stomachs. We eagerly dip our spoons into the soup, pour it into our mouths and immediately spit it back out. The *Suppe* is made of unwashed beet leaves and tastes much as the waste from a hospital infectious diseases ward might taste.

"Have you got bits of grit in yours as well?" Lila asks.

"Don't I just!" I reply, thinking how consoling, no matter how catastrophic, it is that there are two of us.

"You have to eat! Eat it, never mind how revolting you find it, otherwise you'll die!" says our acquaintance from Mikuláš.

"*Ist die Baracke schon ausgemistet, Unterscharführer?*" [Has the hut been cleaned out?] the Sauna-Kapo shouts to the SS-man standing on the path in front of one of the prison blocks.

"*Alles Ungeziefer vergast!* [All the vermin gassed!]" the SS-man reports.

3

They file us into the cleaned-out hut. I understand the expressions "cleaned-out" and "gassed" literally. The block wardress assigns us two-tier bunks inside spaces separated by wooden partitions and resembling animal pens. She yells, swears, hassles us, hounds us and keeps barking out orders. She has not one soothing word for us.

Fatigue and shock have left me so exhausted that I fall asleep. I'm lying with five fellow prisoners on one of the bunks. The order "Get up!" wakes me.

I crawl out from the cluster of grumpy, confused, bug-bitten sleepers. I get up, but don't fully wake up. I'm wearing the same clothes as yesterday. The same shoes. Nothing has changed and everything is different. I am and I am not. I feel unreal and clammily filthy. I go outside. I don't know that's not permitted. I don't know where and whether I'm allowed to have a wash. It's early morning. The sun is up. On a square patch of bare earth, pale, naked creatures looking like flour maggots are crawling. "They're the ones who survived the typhus epidemic," explains

Fenia, the Polish "official" who runs our primitive, overcrowded habitation, once a stable. Fenia doesn't shout, doesn't swear, doesn't let on that I'd been outside without permission. She does tell me how she lost her family in the Warsaw ghetto.

We are interrupted by the gross, gravelly voice of the block wardress: "*Appell!*" she bellows, and since her prisoners don't understand, she drives them all out of the block and herds us like a sheepdog to the *Appellplatz* – the muster area in front of the hut. There, on a bare patch of land without a single blade of grass, she orders us to form lines. "Line up! Line up!" she hollers in German from the depths of her raucous throat, ravaged by her constant bellowing.

We try to stand up straight. Anyone who moves will ruin the impression of military discipline; anyone who pokes their head out of line gets a bash with a broomstick. Those who make so bold as to protest are silenced with a barrage of such bashes. We're waiting for a female SS person. The block wardress will report the number of new prisoners to her. The SS-woman, hair spick and span, clean as a whistle and bright as a button after a good night's sleep, in shiny black jack boots and a uniform that sits perfectly on her, will check, using her whip handle, that the report is correct. On the camp roadway, a buckish SS-man is waiting for her. As he takes her hand, I am overcome by a brief, but keen sense of incomprehensible injustice.

Somewhere nearby, the now familiar gross, raucous voice chimes up: *Los! Los! Schweinehunde! Mistbienen! Dreckkäfer! Ihr kennt mich noch nicht, aber ihr werdet mich noch kennen lernen!* [Get a move on, you bastards, scumbags, shitheads, you don't know me yet, but you will.]

I register that despite my eternal fatigue, despite being relocated into a topsy-turvy world, I am still taking in everything going on around me with precision and lucidity. Later, all happenings were to spill out into a kind of patience-saturated twilight, where the horror of reality had become blurred and pain diluted. Misty ahead, misty behind. Yet without any conscious effort on my part, every impression passed through this benevolent mist to sink deep into my memory.

Having gone back inside our block, we were assigned our permanent berths. The wardress gave a speech and we had to stand to attention. "My name is Eta," she told us, "and I've been here since 1942. I didn't elect to be made wardress, but, believe me, I mean everything I say. So if you don't listen and you fail to obey my orders, you will yourselves be responsible for the consequences of your lack of discipline. If you do act to order, everything will be a lot easier and the SS won't come here so often. Anyone daring to break the camp rules or start mouthing off will be out of luck!"

"Amen!" said Vera, a friend of Nadya's, who'd been put in a different block, before adding: "When did you join the SS?"

The block wardress stood briefly, mouth agape, then with the whip that had never left her hand she began lashing out left and right at her charges. "I'll kill you, I'll kill you!" she screamed in her hysterical, hoarse voice, but without even touching Vera. In the days that followed, Lila and I also achieved special status.

"That's because you're from Slovakia, like me," Eta explained her decision. And while I had nothing against Eta's "patriotism", I couldn't refrain from asking why she was so brutal and why she beat her fellow prisoners with such fury and lack of remorse.

"You've only been here a couple of days and already you think you know everything. The old established values mean nothing here. You don't know what *you'd* be like if you'd been here as long as I have, if *you'd* seen and been through all the things I've seen and been through, and if *you* had bottled up inside you all the same impotent rage and frenzy. Here there's never time for any explaining, debating or theorizing. Here you're on the very edge between life and death every second of the day! And I sold my soul to the devil in the illusory hope of survival, though also because I'd promised my mum I'd keep an eye on her little darling, my younger sister, Rena. I know, I know, coming from me that sounds like sentimental evasion, but I made that promise when the normal was still normal. Now all words are just shit! Now just go and leave me alone!"

Eta's sister, the beautiful Rena, worked in the political section. Whenever she showed up in our block, the women would hide under their bunks. Everybody was terrified of that sadist and it was a fluke that she hadn't killed anyone yet.

"Look at her! That beast is to blame for my being here. While the deportations were happening, I had a chance to escape, but I stuck firmly by my poor little, innocent sister!" Eta would complain after Rena's visits. But that was only later, after our camp had settled into a groove and when I had, following the escape of Rudo Vrba and Fred Wetzler, felt a measure of respect for Eta. The miraculous flight of the two prisoners, who had worked in the political section, right next to the gas chambers and crematoria, keeping a record of every death, aware of the number and the grotesque manner of the murders that went on and the enormous rate of the associated thievery, raised an alarm in the camp that lasted for three days. Edita, Fred's friend and Eta's deputy, was allowed, as an official, to make short visits to the main camp, where she was able to see Fred, if only for a brief moment. When she learned of his escape she began complaining vociferously: "He left me here, the traitor! How could he do that to me? But I'll show him!"

"What'll you show him? What a silly goose you are?" Eta sneered at her. "You should be thankful he's escaped from this hellhole! You should be glorying in their miraculous achievement. Nobody believed escape from Auschwitz was possible! If they manage to cross the mountains into Slovakia, they'll tell the world what goes on here!"

I don't know if I've been here four days or even a whole week by now. Time seems to have slipped off the calendar. Here a different order and different laws apply. Irrational, but also quite concrete. I already know some of them. I know that the management of each block consists of the wardress, a *Blockälteste*, her deputy, two typists and two *Stubendiensts* (who keep the place tidy). The *Stubendienst* Fenia, the nice, blue-eyed Polish woman, was the kind of person that nothing can corrupt.

In each berth, six of us sleep on a thin, filthy, louse-ridden mattress. We're not allowed out of the block unsupervised, and everything, including visits to the latrine, takes place collectively. Anyone who dares empty their bowels on their own initiative comes back screaming and with faeces dribbling down their legs, driven along by a Kapo (a higher-ranking official – actually a prisoner directly subordinate to the SS). "Try that on again and you'll go straight to the gas chamber, you shitbag!"

During their early weeks, prisoners were ruled by fear, anger, loss of self-respect, disdain, envy and confusion. Out of this mishmash, groups having a common background and shared attitudes crystallized. It might be said that there was a kind of truce, broken only by outbursts of spite and petty theft, but overarched by prisoner loyalty. The self-preservation instinct shaped one's actions, and established ethical standards and ways of thinking gave it direction. Even before we'd been put on the political card index, we were put to work. We carried heavy rocks from one end of the camp to the other and back. I went barefoot, because I couldn't walk in my unpaired shoes. Fenia gave me some clogs. They were too small and gave me blisters on my heels and toes.

Lila's friend Maja heard of our arrival and came to see us. She was head of her block and so could move around freely. We told her we were there under false names and begged her not to betray us. She promised to help us get some clothes and blankets. The very next day she brought us some skirts, jumpers, blouses, clogs and warm blankets, as "organized" in the so-called *Effektkammer*, where prisoners sorted clothing from robbed or gassed transportees.

"In here you mustn't steal," Maja explained to us. "If they catch you, you pay with your life. Most stolen things get exchanged for bread. Even here, in this mad world, clothing maketh the man. Decently dressed, washed with banned stolen soap, your teeth cleaned with a banned stolen toothbrush, you'll become camp people with a slightly better chance of survival. Bedraggled, scrawny Muselmänner are doomed men and sacrificial victims. But all of us here are doomed, destined for eternity at any moment. They can send any of us to the gas chamber. Death here is planned, and the plan is carried out with Teutonic precision. Come with me, I'll show you where the death factories are!"

Maja led us out onto the track. What she was now pointing to, tall chimneys rearing up into the air, we'd noticed before. They were billowing dense black smoke and spreading their peculiar, unpleasant smell over the entire camp.

"That's the smell of the burning flesh, bones and hair of people who've been killed in the gas chambers and burned in the crematoria. All those who arrived with you and had accepted the offer of being brought on lorries have ended up like this. They've exterminated millions of people like this."

I wanted to ask Maja to stop, but then I realized that her silence wouldn't help me escape the nightmarish reality of the camp.

"And I thought they were bakeries, baking bread perhaps," I said, with abject astonishment at my own simplicity.

"They tell people to strip," Maja went on implacably. "Once naked, they hand out towels and soap and drive them into the 'bathhouse'. They lock the door behind them and then crystals of Zyklon B, shower down into the room, packed as it is with naked men, women and children, change into gas. If there's not enough of it you can hear the crying and shouting and wheezing of the victims as they slowly choke to death. Prisoners who empty the gas chambers and clean them up are called a *Sonderkommando*. I won't describe the things they see in the course of that particular forced labour; all I will say is that they, too, will be gassed and burned in due course and that they know as much in advance. If the capacity of the crematoria isn't sufficient, they even burn corpses out in the open air. The members of one Greek Sonderkommando leapt of their own accord into the flames of a fire that was consuming their countrymen."

Maja looked round at us and fell silent. "Forgive me," she said, "I had to tell you. You need to learn to live and to exploit every opportunity, however unlikely, to slip through the net. Here we simply can't think and act in the old way. Me too, I'm not the Maja you once knew. I can't claim to be a good person. Many of us, having seen what we've seen and being still alive, have become to a greater or lesser extent dehumanized."

I took her words in and everything about "the old way" of doing things began drifting off beyond the soot-stained horizon. Something inside me had collapsed and my self-preservation instinct was starting to close its inside shutters. Noises, voices and shouting only got through them as if coming from a distance, muffled and dimmed, dulling the awareness of my own possible demise. It was only in the post-war decades that my nightmares came stocked from my subconscious with absurd, but thoroughly realistic details and associations stemming from the fathomless horrors that, back in the concentration camp, I'd had to suppress in the name of life.

4

We've become ciphers. They've registered us under code-names.

Ordnung muss sein! Alive or dead, we're all recorded calligraphically on snow-white cards in the camp's filing cabinet. The Third Reich will last for a thousand years and its descendants will be able to study the history and heroic acts of their forebears.

Numbers were tattooed on our left forearms by a German prisoner, Frieda, from the political section. With precision, with great care and with her pointed chin stuck out. With her watery blue eyes set in her pale face and gleaming as she savoured the professionalism of her labours, she followed each move of her hands as she dipped her pen in blue ink and pricked dot after dot into us to form five-digit numbers and a small triangle. The numerals said nothing as to the actual numbers of prisoners. After each hundred thousand the numbering started over again.

To indicate what category of prisoner we were, our uniforms had cloth triangles stitched onto them.

A red triangle denoted a political prisoner.
A green triangle: Criminal, thug or murderer.
Black: An antisocial element. For skivers, prostitutes.
Pink: Homosexual.
Purple: Jehovah's Witness.
The Star of David in a red and yellow triangle: Jew.

The Jehovah's Witnesses were so firmly convinced of the eternal truth of their faith that they weren't afraid of death. One woman, not from our block, was the only person to protest against being numbered and she called the wrath of the Almighty down on anyone who tried to force her. It was a mystery to us that she wasn't immediately sent to the gas chamber. To the SS-woman, who had only shown up at roll-calls, but now even entered our hut on odd occasions, and who declared with a cool savagery: "You'll go up in smoke!" she retorted: "Me today, you tomorrow!" and the woman made a hasty backwards retreat. As three officials finally managed to hold her down and tattoo her number on her, she struggled like mad and threatened them with eternal damnation.

The top ranks of the SS, who lived in posh houses close by the camp, used Jehovah's Witnesses as cooks, maids, gardeners or craftsmen. The Witnesses observed all of the Ten Commandments. They didn't tell lies. They didn't run away. They didn't gossip. They served their Jehovah everywhere and at all times. They knew that once the apocalypse was over they were guaranteed a place in paradise.

People who were convinced of "the eternal truth of their faith" included Communists from the USSR and all the European countries under German occupation. Lila and I were two such. We imagined, indeed believed, that being a Communist meant integrity, humanity and justice and a duty, even under inhumane conditions, to offer help, to support the weak and be an example to all others. That faith can move mountains we had heard as children and it bore us along into the fairy-tale, autosuggestively functioning world of a hope that cured all.

German political prisoners, who had survived years in various concentration camps, included trade-unionists, Social Democrats, Communists and erstwhile volunteers who'd fought for the Spanish Republic, and, being Aryans (the Jews among them were not treated as political prisoners), they managed after a time to win a degree of trust among the upper ranks of the SS. As camp officials and Kapos they achieved slightly better living conditions within the camp hierarchy. Many did whatever they could for their comrades, though there were also those who frankly abused their privileged status at the expense of others. The "final solution to the Jewish question" proceeded steadily according to plan.

I was loath to admit that the Communists included certain narrow-minded, puritanical, intolerant and suspicious types, dogmatists who, even there in the camp, treated all non-Communists as inferior beings and future traitors. Instinctively this appalled me, but I believed that by distancing myself from them I was merely exhibiting my personal dislike and perhaps an echo of my "petty-bourgeois upbringing", the noxious consequences of which I had to uproot, and I put my faith in those things that I deemed positive and indispensable to the future of mankind. And not only that: even within myself I detected signs of dogmatism and saw solidarity with my comrades as the only mental weapon against Nazism.

Working in the political section was a privilege. Its lead prisoner was a star. Hollywood had its stars, and so did Auschwitz. Only rarely did this star put in an appearance among us "pawns". She was swathed in the mythical aura of Greta Garbo. Well-dressed, neat, and with a thick main of long blonde hair, red-painted nails and high-heeled shoes, she looked like an anachronism entitled to mirror herself in a well-concealed looking glass accessible to her and her alone. She was the boss's favourite, the boss being the highest ranking female SS person and the manageress of Birkenau, because she had successfully remodelled the filing system, introducing a new, efficient and well-ordered way of recording those who'd been gassed and those who'd died of typhus, dysentery, malaria, poisoning, starvation and exhaustion, committed suicide on the barbed wire fences, breathed their last during medical experiments, after benzine injections, beatings, being torn to shreds by Alsatians, shot "trying to escape", hanged or by other means of liquidation. There was even a place in the system for those who'd only died on the way to the camp, in one of the transports. In due course even this star stopped shining. She knew too much about the ways and means of murder and the monstrous numbers of the dead. Her own disappearance was veiled in mystery. No one knew where she'd gone. Rumour had it that she'd been taken away to a different camp, where she'd been gassed.

We learned that selection meant choosing which prisoners

were to be gassed, that losing one's spectacles meant death, that a toothbrush was a treasure, that a lemon or carrot was a miracle and that various items could only be acquired by life-threatening theft, known in camp slang as "organizing".

Within the absurd framework of the daily death risk it was dangerous to be: late middle-aged, old or under fourteen, ill, pregnant, or to identify with the view of us held by our executioners and so lose our self-respect, hope and the will to survive.

Today, after so many years, I am still amazed that in that hell filled with all manner of prisoners imperilled by death or by their own instinct of self-preservation, the dehumanizing machine of Nazism failed to match even more victims to their own image.

5

We rise while it's still dark. When the sun comes up, it's not for us. From dawn till dusk our days are contaminated by an indescribable odour that springs from various different sources and they're filled with kicks and blows, humiliation, sadism and bleak despair.

"Get up! Get up!"

This short sharp shout cuts into a brief deep sleep. It's three in the morning. Long before daybreak, densely packed bodies roll over one another off the bunks and head for the washrooms. A shower of lashes from a whip lands on bare backs. They're being doled out by "latrine queen" Ursula, a wizened, dark, evil virago. She looks like a snarling animal, eaten up with forced compliance and hounded into a corner. She's Polish and thirty-something, with a red triangle and a low prison number. We are many, but the taps are few. You're supposed to be clean, but they don't let you wash. Those who don't manage in the time available will be punished. They hurry us back to the block. We drink what they're pleased to call coffee. It's nasty liquid of uncertain provenance, but it's warm at least, thank God. To go with it they give us part of our daily bread ration, a dark chunk of baked dough mixed with sawdust. It has a blob of margarine on it and a dollop of red, probably carrot, jam. A clatter of tin plates and spoons. Arguments and squabbling over bread. The women scrabble feverishly around for their clogs. During the short night they had them under their heads and now they're gone. The block staff go along thumping everyone. Those who get thumped scream, blubber, gripe and generally wreck the smooth progress of the morning routine. They're holding up the roll call. The barracks personnel seek out the sick, who have crawled under their bunks. They drag them outside even though they're buckling at the knees. The prisoners all have to stand in lines drawn up as if with a ruler. They must not, in their groggy, sorry state, spoil the impression of a disciplined compliance. They must stand erect, in silence, and wait. Not moving their heads. Keeping their feet firmly in line. Not shivering. Paralyzed. For maybe an hour, maybe two, until such time as the SS *Aufseherin* arrives and counts us.

We're all louse-ridden. We have lice in our hair and all over our bodies. Our berths are full of fleas and bedbugs. Many of us have got scabies. Many of the terminally ill work just to avoid being sent to the *Revier* (the camp infirmary), from which few ever return to the block. Those who die while working are carried back to the camp slung across tree trunks or hefty branches.

Having returned to our block we're given *Suppe*. That's the sum total of our "lunch" and we count ourselves lucky if it contains the odd bit of potato peel. But one constant ingredient of it is bromine, of which the main feature is its never-changing, disgusting unsavouriness.

Our hut has now had assigned to it a contingent of Hungarian women and girls. Their shaven heads are poorly covered with white, handkerchief-size scarves. A knob beneath the chin and the tip sticking up and out from the top of their heads. It gives them a look of humiliating, thoroughly wretched uniformity. They don't know what's happening to them, they're helpless and seething. They won't take orders. They're being sulkily obstinate. The block wardress and Stubendiensts push and shove them. Swear at them. Keep hitting them.

"You're not at home now! Shut up! Just form lines unless you want to die like dogs and spoil things for others!"

Finally the *Aufseherin* [wardress] shows up. The first rays of the sun have climbed above the horizon. The gleam from them is reflected in the woman's SS boots. She gives them an elegant flick of her whip. She's had her hair done by her own hairdresser, chosen from among the prisoners. The block wardress reports the number of prisoners. She calls out their numbers and each number has to reply with a loud, distinct *"Hier!"* Two of the numbers fail to respond. They must be found! The roll-call is abandoned until they're found and get into line. The assembly ground resounds to the disquiet and shouting: *"Schweinehunde! Dreckschweine! Mistbienen!* [Swinish bitches! Shitty swines! Dung beetles!]"

The SS-woman keeps impatiently flicking her boots with her whip and swishes it about in the air. The chimneys are belching black smoke, which climbs heavenwards as it does every morning and throughout every day.

Two women were hauled out of the block. They were found hiding under the bunks, tight up against the wall. They're at death's door. All skin and bone. They've lost their headscarves. Their shaved heads look like turnips. Their teeth are bared like a snarling dog's. They can't close their mouths. The very proximity of death forces them half-open. They are feverish and their eyes are desiccating inside their deep sockets. The staff try in vain to get them to their feet, and when they fall down again they get beaten with clubs. The SS-woman goes over to them and kicks them in the head. She stamps on them with ever greater fury. The roll call is taking up a lot of time. The *Häftlinge* [prisoners] are enraged. Those two are practically dead. Eventually the SS-woman stops. We get counted a second time, our numbers are called, including the numbers of the two dead women.

For work purposes we're split into groups – squads or *Arbeitskolonnen*. Doing outdoor jobs beyond the camp. Demolishing houses. Making roads. Carting rocks. A handful are set to work sorting out the remains of the gassed Hungarians. The groups working in the gas chambers and crematoria consist only of men. Everything that is played out here has a kind of hole in the bottom, like the jugs of the Danaïdes, and has to be constantly refilled with the same contents.

Lila and I have been assigned to a squad that is to construct a railway line. It's been raining since morning. We're freezing cold, soaked to the skin. They took all our civilian clothes from us and dressed us in belted, blue-grey uniforms. Beneath them we're naked. The sole of one of my clogs is split. We flounder through mud among sharp stones and large sodden clods. We dig, we load onto barrows, using heavy spades we shift the soggy earth. What descends on us from the heavens is despair, fatigue, gloom and the airborne raucous, interminable shrieking of the chargehands of slavery: "*Vorwärts! Los! Los! Vorwärts! Weitermachen!*"

The noise of the blows and the shouting reaches crazy heights in proportion to how close the SS-men are. I feel as if the only living parts of my frozen body are my splitting head and the injured feet inside my mud-squelching clogs. The monotony of forced labour is invaded now and then by unwelcome fears: Let's just hope we don't fall ill! Let's hope we don't get typhus or malaria in this bog they call Auschwitz! Let's hope we don't get sent to the infirmary!

Only rarely and by some kind of miracle does a "patient" in the infirmary recover before the date set for a mass gassing of the sick. The infirmary is the last port of call for those who would rather labour with a high temperature than let themselves be laid out on one of the double bunks occupied by people suffering from typhus, dysentery, malaria, or with festering wounds on their bodies, legs or their faces where, through gaps in their rotting flesh, you can see their bared gums and teeth. Bandages are made of toilet paper. Pus and faeces dribble down from the top onto the bottom bunk. The dead are borne by the "corpse-bearing squad" to the crematoria on barrows. Any baby born in the infirmary is either drowned or strangled so that Dr Mengele doesn't need to send a mother and her babe-in-arms to the gas chamber together.

Mengele is aided by Ena, a beautiful medical student from Prague, who helps the sick to the very best of her ability. Two of the female doctors requisitioned to the infirmary come from Mikuláš. One is on the verge of breakdown. The other, Magda, is holding on. Everyone knows she's lesbian, but whereas what in a small town was a source of outrage, censure and malicious gossip is here, in Birkenau, taken as a matter of course. Magda brings consolation to the dying and the terminally ill, and she and Ena together try to "organize" medications from the luggage taken off transports and from the SS clinic in the main camp, Auschwitz I.

From Magda I've learned how the female Jews from Mikuláš who'd been taken on the first Jewish transport out of Slovakia in 1942 had died.

The athlete and climber Ruth had been put in the punishment squad for "disobedience"; all the prisoners in that squad had a red patch stitched onto the top left of their back. When the starving Ruth wanted to pick a dandelion growing beside the road and stepped out of line to get it, an SS man shot her in the back, through the red patch and so right in her heart. Hertha and Erika had died of typhus. Eva, a girl with red hair and freckles, had been one of my favourites in Mikuláš. Because Mum had forbidden me to be friends with her, I used to go and see her in secret, to Vrbica, where she lived in one of the white cottages that had gardens running right down to the Váh. She wasn't good at school and she wasn't pretty, yet she reminded me of the typical heroines of novels for girls with their boy-like qualities of courage, fearlessness, resourcefulness and independence. She used to look after her brother and her father. She cooked for them, bottled vegetables from their garden and grilled the fish that her father used to catch in the Váh. When she felt peckish, she would take a preserved one from a jar, hold it above her mouth and munch it with evident relish, piecemeal from head to tail fin. Using a little gadget, she would roll her father cigarettes out of cheap tobacco, climb trees like a squirrel and she was the best runner in our whole school.

"Eva's mother plays cards, hanging around in hotels for days on end, smoking like a chimney, completely neglecting her disabled husband and failing to bring up their two wayward kids," Mum said to explain her ban. And when I protested and boldly objected that Eva didn't play cards or smoke, she tried to explain that Eva's environment was simply no fit place for a young person. Here in the camp all that was a thing of the past. The most important things now were solidarity, the self-preservation instinct and awareness of one's own worth. Eva had all of that. She was the most tenacious, most vigorous, intelligent and resourceful inmate in her block. She helped her fellow-prisoners and they admired and loved her for it. Because she was a great runner she got given the job of "courier" and she so successfully bewitched the SS-men with her physical and mental faculties that they let her live and called her by the affectionate Slovak diminutive Evička. However she failed to bewitch death. She contracted typhoid fever, wasted away and changed into the very thing she had fought against: she became a Muselmann. They took her to block 25 where the sick destined for the gas chamber were assembled. The block was surrounded by a wall and the day before her scheduled gassing she managed to climb over it and drag herself to the block where her old companions were. She died in their midst. After her, the women from Mikuláš began dying, one after the other, of starvation or exhaustion, in the gas chambers, on the barbed-wire fences or from sheer loss of hope.

One rainy day after the arrival of the transport from Hungary, Lila and Vera successfully became the owners of a lemon. They decided to give it to Marta, who had tuberculosis. She lived in a different block, one their dorm wardresses refused to grant Lila and Vera permission to enter. Having failed to send them away, she summoned the block wardress Zuzana.

"Get lost!" the mannequin-like block wardress ordered them; she was one of those who identified to perfection with their role as a privileged convict with an important role to play.

"We want to give Marta a lemon. She needs vitamin C. Even you must recognize that much!" said Lila.

"Shut up! I'm the one who decides who needs C vitamins. I'll report you to Stenia, you miserable, impudent piece of shit!"

"So, are you going to let us in to see Marta or not?"

"Who do you think you are, you Schweinehunde! Don't you know who you're talking to here?"

"How could I not know! A vile convict in a concentration camp," Lila replied and when the grossly offended block wardress started lashing out at Lila and Vera, who gave her all they'd got in return, she fell in a mud-filled puddle and was left in a posture that was quite undignified and deplorably ignominious for a person of her high standing.

6

The *Lagerälteste* Stenia (our most highly ranked prison official, a Volksdeutsche from Poland) suddenly, for some unknown and incomprehensible reasons, showed an interest in me. It happened on one of those countless, endless, unpleasant days when it drizzled from morning till night, sending hundreds of tiny needles through our uniforms into our bodies and dripping constantly from our hair and faces. We were just pushing some tubs filled with heavy rocks along a stretch of railway track.

"*Los! Los! Schneller! Schneller!*" yelled the overseer when she spotted Stenia, who was known to have sent hundreds to the gas chambers and to be the mistress of a certain high-ranking SS officer. The tall, slim Stenia in her black waterproof cape stopped in front of us, stood legs apart in her highly polished riding boots and stared with unflinching scorn at our group of mud-spattered and soaking-wet slaves doing our level best to keep the tubs moving. When the *Sturmbannführer* came by she turned her pretty head to smile at him, and he smiled back. She followed him with her gaze and once he'd left she let fire again: "You shitty, idle creatures... *Los... Los...* Faster, faster! You've a job to do, so do it! And not at a snail's pace!"

We cracked on, running back and forth, loading, pushing, unloading, when suddenly into the wet, crazy, almost insensate bustle like a knife jabbed an order from Stenia: "Come here! You! Yes, you!"

She pointed a finger at me.

"Drop that and follow me!" she said and I, filled with foreboding, abandoned my shovel and followed her down a muddy track towards the wooden shack that was the SS-men's refuge during foul weather. She opened the door and ordered me inside. "Don't just stand there like a lemon. Sit on the bench. Do you want a cigarette?"

I gawped at her, uncomprehending.

"D'you want a cigarette or don't you?" She retrieved a pack from her pocket, took out two cigarettes, stuck one between my lips, lit hers and mine, joined me on the bench and for a while we just sat there in silence, smoking, puffing out rings of blue smoke as I struggled to make any sense of Stenia's actions.

"What's your name?"

"Mira."

"What do you reckon, Mira, when will the war be over?"

I was frightened. I knew that Stenia was unpredictable and that my answer would seal my fate.

"Nobody knows how the war will go following Stalingrad," I replied.

"Tell me the truth: do you think the Germans will lose?"

"I don't know."

"Are you afraid of dying?"

"Not something I think about," I said. Then Stenia did something so unexpected that it all suddenly felt like in a dreamworld: she removed her raincoat and handed it to me. "Here! Take this and come and see me sometime."

She opened the door, departed, and I, wearing an oversized coat that seemed to have sponged up my amazement at Stenia's unpredictability, went back along the muddy track to my work team. My fellow-prisoners stared at me, their eyes filled with distrust and suspicion. "You fink! You traitor!" I read in their looks. I quite understood. Something had happened of a kind that didn't usually happen in camps, but since it had, why me? They didn't believe me. How and why could the inhuman Stenia become human even for a second? That it could have been from a sudden rush of fear for her own fate crossed no one's mind. After a quite unpleasant break things did return to normal.

Following Lila's clash with Zuzana I decided to go and see Stenia. She had her own flat in one of the barracks. She was sitting in a huge, comfortable easy chair, reading a hefty magazine. I spotted that it contained some colour photographs. Inside the camp you couldn't have in your possession even a single scrap of paper with writing on it, let alone an entire magazine. I began: "Hello. It's me, Mira, if you haven't forgotten me," and I waited for her to look my way. She didn't. She went on reading. Over her shoulder she just gave the room servant the order: "Give her some bread and cheese!"

The woman cut a thick slice of fresh white bread and spread it with soft curd cheese.

"Eat that and go away!" said Stenia, still with her back to me and immersed in her magazine. I relished the strong-smelling, quite heavenly treat, felt like a beggar and just had time to register that Stenia was actually reading a "novel for women".

Zuzana had complained to Stenia about Lila and Stenia came to our block. Impudence directed at a block wardress was often a death warrant. I tried to have a word with her, but Stenia's response was an angry growl: "Cut it out!"

"But Stenia, please, Lila's my sister!"

Stenia stamped her foot: "You vermin! The trouble you lot cause!"

She turned to Lila and yelled: "Apologize! Ask for forgiveness!"

"All right, sorry, forgive me," said Lila to the visibly disappointed Zuzana, and we all heaved a sigh of relief.

Approaching beneath a filthy, smoke-filled sky sprinkled with flimsy clouds is an SS man. His face is like a round loaf of white bread with a crinkly crust. He announces that he's looking for any prisoners capable of writing elegantly in block capitals, and because I am one such I put my hand up, at which he sends me to do the cards for the card index of the latest transport from Hungary.

We leave the block. At a marching pace. Left, right... Left, right, following the long barbed-wire fences. Fence after fence, all of them electrified. We're on a grey track, though maybe it's even black, and maybe tracks aren't even tracks any longer. The tracks are lined with huts. All side by side in long rows, constructed for new inmates in new "housing estates", with new officials chosen or volunteering from among the prisoners. Everyone knows that some of the wardresses steal some of the supplies intended for the prisoners, which gives them a contingent chance of surviving longer.

The deportees from Hungary include many children and some fairly young girls. I fill the cards in with all the relevant data. I'm recording milestones in lives long and short. My god, I'm thinking, how tragicomical is this bureaucratic normality within the perverse, unbelievably effective operation of the abnormality that is mass murder. Or is its effectiveness perhaps merely a by-product of thoroughness?

In Hungarian, I tell a number of twelve- and thirteen-year-old girls that I'll put them down as older. "And if anyone asks how old you are, say sixteen."

They look at me wide-eyed. I can see the uncertainty, fear and suspicion rising inside them. Why? What for? And who am I, actually, in prison uniform with a star and a number? Naturally, they view their youth as a guarantee of protection and I advise them to make out that they're older. I can't tell them they'll otherwise be sent to the gas chamber with their mothers and older women. I mustn't create panic. They might hurl themselves at me out of fear and the inconceivability of the whys and wherefores underpinning my advice. I record data with a sense that among the "new ones" there is a new hostility towards me.

Every day sees the arrival of more transports and every day and every night thick black smoke billows up from the chimneys. The B II B *Familienlager* has been joined by some elderly people from Theresienstadt, and I've been sent to sign them in. The camp in question is seen as a miraculous exception. Its inmates didn't have their hair cropped. Czech families are permitted to stay together, keep the contents of their luggage and wear their own clothes. Children in the *Familienlager* go to school, do exercises, put on plays, perform concerts and their elders only ever work on the upkeep of "their own" pathways and huts. But even here a quarter of the four thousand prisoners died, and later, in 1944, they were all sent to the gas chamber. Very few indeed survived, by some miracle.

It was getting dark when we entered the *Familienlager*. Standing outside one of the blocks was a group of old men and women. They had numbers tattooed on the sallow, spotty skin of their bare forearms. Old bones enveloped in paper-thin, wrinkled skin. A bunch of white-haired old men and women, well past the point of no return. Someone switched a lamp on and in its pool of light, lying on a thin layer of grimy snow, were those for whom even crawling had proven too much.

We spent the whole night registering these people, recording each one's name, date of birth, newly tattooed number, religion, education and employment history, and chatting to them as far as circumstances permitted.

"Next!" I said for the fiftieth time. Outside it was getting light. Standing before me was a thin, very clean little creature wearing a black velvet hat, beneath which its hair was tied in a bun. I took down her name and number.

"Please note that I'm an aristocrat and that my husband was a high-ranking officer in the German army, decorated with an Iron Cross for bravery in the Great War."

"If ever there was an absurdity, then this is it," flashed through my sleepy, drained mind, but everything was much more complicated where the hopeful afflicted were concerned, and so greatly simplified for their implacable persecutors. Man proposes and Hitler disposes. And God? Where has He got to? How could He be watching what's been going on? Or could it have been us, the people whom He had created in His own image, and entered us thereby, who have sullied that image, mired it, mangled it? In the camp I heard all kinds of answers to this existential question. Not one of them struck me as acceptable. Might people simply not know God yet? But why should I, an agnostic, be bothering at all with such issues? I ask myself about them, but I find no answers.

Outside they're busily tattooing the forearms of the dead. From inside the block comes the wailing noise of those who've gone mad. One of them is begging heaven for help with words trumpeted out through the hole in the bottom of an enamel mug.

At the Ricse camp for Hungarians, Nadya, an intelligent, sensitive young woman, always in love with someone but never loved by anyone, being rather unattractive, had pursued me constantly with such comments as: "Nothing will ever come of you. You're only interested in men."

At Auschwitz, Nadya's dislike of me became a thing of the past. And not only because all contact between men and women was strictly forbidden. I began to understand her better on account of one thing that could, no matter how briefly, revive my anaesthetized ability to feel pain, which was the thought that I might die a virgin. One day, Nadya revealed an unbelievable secret to us: in the *Effektkammer* she had lost her virginity to a Dutch prisoner in a dip among the tall piles of clothes from all over Europe. Neither of them could have cared less that their misdemeanour was one of those punishable by instant death.

Whenever I had to go past piles of dumped corpses, it was as if a wind was rising inside me and seeking, in vain and in confusion, an exit from a chamber of horrors with seven locks on the door. This was the most inhumane dehumanization of mankind, man's bitterest and most overwhelming defeat. I wished that the fertility symbols on the stalk-like slain, with the residual roundness of breasts and scrotum, might become united in their final separation, then rise and fly like birds across the barbed-wire fence. The disconsolate loneliness of the dead found a home inside me and it has not left me to this day. My pupils began slowly to wander and seek concealment beneath my heavy eyelids.

Those prisoners who worked out in the fields or in outposts of the main camp were bearers of news and messages. From them we learned that some friends of ours had contrived for us to be transferred from Birkenau to Rajsko, a few kilometres to the south-west of Auschwitz proper, where the chances of survival were rather better. Before being relocated, we had to be examined by Dr Mengele. I was scared because I knew that the slightest hint of a rash could mean the death sentence and I had three tiny red spots on one thigh. The fact that they kept coming and going had forced me to exploit my inventiveness and self-preservation instinct to the full. At all costs I had to avoid being deloused, when prisoners were examined closely from foot to toe. I loathed myself for the price it cost me to buy enough time to disappear for the duration of the examination. I was kept in hiding by the most repulsive and most loathsome block wardress in Birkenau. I pretended to be her friend and she sent for delousing one of the "reliable" inmates of her block in my stead. At a delousing ritual the only thing that mattered was the numbers involved, and matters were helped by the checks being carried out by convicts. However, this time the check was carried out by the angel of death himself, Dr Josef Mengele, notorious for his choice of the prisoners to be killed, for his experiments on men, women and children, especially twins, and for his services and utter devotion to the murderous Nazi regime.

When, naked and with my heart pounding I entered Mengele's "consulting room", he was just telling Ena a joke and she was laughing her head off. Ena's melodious response stirred in him a degree of lofty benevolence; he glanced at my little red spots and asked: "What about this? Shall we take a closer look?"

"I wouldn't bother; it looks like a flea bite," said Ena, and I knew she was taking advantage of Mengele's momentary bonhomie.

"All right, then, let's say I believe you," the doctor remarked and signed the release as he had done for Lila the day before.

Released from my fears, I went out into the road, still puzzled that Mengele addressed Ena in formal terms. But that needn't have come as a surprise. After all, the SS officers who had waited on the platform for arriving transports had sent people to their death with all the courtesy at their disposal.

7

Like the sand in an hourglass

From the outset I was like a machine. My face as if wooden. I took in my new environment, its movements, colours, words, commands, differences, shades, all as if being played out behind thick glass. Everything being tossed about inside me like waves in a tempest kept crashing into a stone wall of involuntary isolation. I was like a wax figure that couldn't raise a smile, not even so much as a grimace. Tanya, a Russian in the horticulture workforce to which Lila and I were attached on our arrival at Rajsko, tried her best to shake me out of my catatonic state, which was no fun for those around me either. She would tickle me or chase me around the field if Scharführer Schmidt or Unterscharführer Lothar were nowhere around.

"Smile... Show us you know how to laugh," she coaxed me, and when I failed to respond in any way to her attempts to revitalize me, she hit me with a spade.

"All right, cry, for hell's sake, you idiot!" she yelled, and when I failed to cry, she hit me again.

The Auschwitz outpost at Rajsko was split between horticulture and plant breeding, the commander of which, *Obersturmbannführer* Joachim Caesar, selected specialists for his militarily important division from all over Europe: biologists, botanists, chemists, engineers and draftsmen, all of them prisoners. He hoped that they would help him achieve a positive outcome from his experiment to extract rubber from a small relative of the dandelion, *Taraxacum kok-saghyz*. The process for making ersatz rubber had been bought by Caesar from a Russian scientist, who would come from time to time, surrounded by high-ranking military figures, to be shown round the experimental area, which was full of brick-lined squares housing the young rubber dandelion plants. I've no idea why his face, the one time I saw him, in a brown suit, appeared yellowy-green; maybe that was how I imagined the face of a traitor.

For the furtherance of an early positive outcome to his undertaking, Caesar saw to it that his "*Häftlings*" had a better life out of it all: they received better food, were given regular medical check-ups, slept on beds with pink woollen blankets and ate in a canteen equipped with nice crockery and cutlery. In an annexe next to the two main blocks there were two showers and a laundry room with a massive cauldron in which the girls could wash their lingerie and cook "organized" vegetables, wrapped in bits of old white sheets. The working hours in the Pflanzenzucht (plant-breeding section) were shorter than in the horticulture section and the prisoners who worked in it enjoyed a higher social standing.

Conditions in the Pflanzenzucht section did, however, affect life in the horticulture section. There, too, in its two huts, we had pink blankets and ate in the canteen. In the interests of keeping the peace between the Russian and Polish women, the latter had their own premises. The Russian women and prisoners of all other nations were housed together.

They used to wake us at four a.m. Roll call was the same as at Birkenau. Once that was over they split us up into work units. With shovels, spades, rakes and other tools perched on our shoulders, we would march, headed by our forewomen, into the fields singing *"Auf der Heide wächst ein kleines Blümelein und das heißt Erika."* The refrain from this German marching song, "hai-li... hai-la... hai-lo", evoked in me an image of the fustiness of army barracks.

At Rajsko, as elsewhere before, we were driven forward by the constant bellowing of orders:

"Los! Los! Schneller... Schneller... Weitermachen!" Get on with it, Get on with it, you lazy bitches... "Lazy" was an *epithet constans* in the rhetoric of concentration camps.

When the SS were not around, the Ukrainian women used to sing folk songs, the sad-sweet melancholy of which seeped through my armour plating to remain with me forever. Not even long years of manifold and far-reaching changes have erased the tune and words of this one:

> *Poviy vitre na Ukrajinu*
> *de pokynu ja divchinu*
> *de pokynu karije ochi*
> *poviy vitre do piv nochi*

Blow now, wind, towards Ukraine,
I left my girl there, oh, the pain!
I left behind those brown eyes bright,
blow now, wind, until midnight!

The greatest drag of all was having to carry wet manure on stretchers across great expanses of ploughland whatever the weather. The physical effort, whether because things were going too slow or too fast, often drove either the front or the back stretcher-bearer mad. The manure was heavy, the ground waterlogged, soggy lumps of earth kept sticking to their clogs and we were so weak that each successive motion seemed hopelessly arduous. Only by a supreme effort of will, as it seemed to us, and by tensing the enfeebled sinews in our shoulders and forearms did we manage, despite feeling that they had slackened almost to a standstill, to force them to persevere. They knew they had to.

The difference in the social standing of the two sections of the camp was mirrored in the kinds of punishment meted out to their occupants. For a transgression in horticulture the culprit was sent back to Auschwitz. For one in Pflanzenzucht the punishment was a temporary stint in the fields.

The horticulture section had two commandants. Its administration was in the hands of Oberscharführer Grell. We saw him only rarely and what little we knew about him we gathered from his secretary, Genia, a tall, extraordinarily beautiful Polish Jewess.

Once – it must have been sometime in November 1944 – Genia told us that in a fit of conscience Grell had ripped off his SS stripes. She had won his trust and told him how her parents and the rest of her family perished, and she'd described growing up in a cultured and academic environment and the horrendous conditions in Poland following the German assault on it, and she'd asked him if he was deaf and blind, or merely a Nazi.

"And get this, he didn't even fly off the handle! He told me he'd never thought about it, that he'd known nothing about it, that he'd merely been doing his duty, but that now he was starting to see what was happening through my eyes."

We listened to her and thought it pretty obvious that Grell had fallen in love with her and that his not knowing about anything had been a lie; one of the girls remarked with a hint of sarcasm that there was more rejoicing in heaven over a single repentant sinner than over ten of the righteous.

One day in December, Genia didn't come in from work. She and Oberscharführer Grell simply vanished. Someone did see them on a sleigh drawn by two horses, but where they were going nobody knew.

The second commandant in the horticulture section was a Sudeten German, a former teacher, SS-Scharführer Schmidt. Unimpeded, he ruled over us, the fields, the fruit and vegetable beds and two huge greenhouses. They were for growing grapes, tomatoes, paprikas, cucumbers and flowers. Only men worked in them, mostly Poles and Austrians. We used to meet them whenever we were tasked to join them.

In the early days of his career in the SS, Schmidt used to boast of the sheer numbers of "vermin" that he had personally eliminated from his particular National Socialist patch, and he would harass, bully and beat prisoners left, right and centre. He used to kick them and call them the most vulgar names imaginable. As long as he remained convinced that Hitler was going to win he acted like a sadist. His worst treatment went on male prisoners, especially when there were some women he fancied to witness it. But as his faith in the Thousand-year Reich began to falter, he picked out a cluster of beautiful girls – Aryan and non-Aryan – with hair of every shade from platinum-blond to raven-black. Lila was one of his dark-haired favourites. He arranged for tailors in the main camp to produce uniforms with made-to-measure jackets for them. He would take them on outings to Auschwitz. He would stroll about with them in full view of the barracks that housed his SS colleagues, as proud as a sheikh of his exclusive harem. He thought he could impress the ladies by ordering male prisoners to doff their caps to them, lean forward and stick their bums out so he could give them a good kicking. After each kick they had to shout: "*Danke, Herr Scharführer!*", then hold that pose as they listened to the string of invective to which he treated them: they were impotent gimps, shitty pigs and stinking Muselmänner. At scenes like these I used to feel an unforgivable twinge of unconscionable disdain for male humans who would, without resisting, let this vile SS-man so humiliate and torment them. This was born of my stupid misconception, which asserted itself even within a concentration camp, of how a "regular guy" should act, a product of my reading, prematurely, all those "novels for women and girls", and, regrettably, not only them.

8

On our way to work we used to pass a massive compost heap. On its rounded top, high up beneath the heavens, men like scarecrows, all skin and bone, wearing camp uniforms, would be working away, turning the brownish mass over with shovels and their bare hands, jettisoning any undesirable trash. They looked so diaphanous and fragile that any slightly stronger gust of wind might pick them up, toss them in the air like fallen leaves and blow them about like it did the vapours rising from the brown mass of compost. At unguarded moments we tossed some "organized" vegetables up onto the heap. On landing, the heavy cabbage heads threw up a little cloud of brown dust.

One day there was, standing among the flimsy skeletons in their grey-blue prison uniforms, a young man in civilian clothes. He struck me as symbolic of a "Once upon a time" landscape of yesteryear where love had once blossomed. He had a dense mane of light-brown hair, broad shoulders and narrow hips. Having thanked us for the carrots, his smile revealed his white teeth. Two weeks later the young man was nowhere to be seen at the compost heap. To my question as to what had become of him, one of the compost separators replied:

"Here it's the young, athletic newcomers who are the first to die!"

I was woken in the night by the sound of my own weeping. I cried every night for about a month and only fell asleep as dawn approached. The girls noted my red eyes and other signs of exhaustion and kept asking if I was ailing. I just shook my head and carried on with the camp routine, saying nothing about how I felt as if I'd just come out of a narcotic stupor, or that I was aching all over and Tanya needn't tickle me or hit me with a shovel any more. Slowly my speech returned and I was able to communicate once more with the girls who shared my incarceration. I talked about personal matters, politics, philosophy and literature, I began teaching them languages and singing their songs with them. But my attitude to the male prisoners in the greenhouses changed only slowly.

Between the sexes, platonic relationships would emerge, even at a distance, possibly precisely because of that environment of segregation, as echoes of an indomitable will to live. The relationships would be manifest in the small gifts that girls, temporarily assigned to jobs in the greenhouses, took there with them. And one of the Austrian men had the girls bring a parcel back for me. It contained some flour, margarine, freshly picked tomatoes, a red pepper, an onion and a ring plaited from strands of different coloured hair. It was a precious gift, but it left me feeling repelled and half-minded to send it back.

"You're weird! What an idiot! If you won't accept such a wonderful gift, you can let us have it!" a pretty Polish blonde, Halina, told me. She took the ring and tried it on her middle finger. She examined it with obvious delight as she turned it this way and that. In the laundry cauldron, Emanuelle, a maternal, kind-hearted Frenchwoman, used the Austrian's goodies to cook us up an excellent meal, which even I enjoyed.

Food was a frequent topic of conversation. At every opportunity we would cook fictitious European specialities of every kind with detailed accounts of the time needed to boil, bake or steam them, the actual contents, the quality of the raw materials used, and any spices or other special ingredients to enhance the flavour. I best remember Melita's "Bosnian stew", which consisted of many different kinds of vegetables and meat, the only dish she would have loved to make for us and probably the only one she knew how to make, which was why she repeated the recipe so often. We cherished the hope that one day, after the war was over and we could meet up, we'd be able to treat our friends to our respective national dishes. These discussions would make interesting subject matter for an international concentration-camp cookery book.

Those who did meet up after the war were, however, very few in number.

9

Rajsko dwelt in a spirit of relatively benevolent neutrality and solidarity. That applied to women and girls of every nationality and confession: Polish, Czech, Slovak, Yugoslav, Russian, French, German, Hungarian or Dutch, believers and non-believers alike. The actual degree of tolerance depended on the circumstances and the dispositions of the various individuals and groups. Certain traditional preconceptions and misconceptions were diluted only slightly by our common lot. The one thing that was shared throughout was our attitude to the main enemy. Out of it we erected a temple to which we all resorted and which was home to icons of the resistance and the martyrs tortured to death in prison, a veritable cult.

One of the icons of the Pflanzenzucht was Ruženka from Moravská Ostrava. She had been transferred to the camp from the prison where she'd been held for illegal activities. Her husband, a Communist trade-unionist, was awaiting his verdict somewhere in the Reich. Adored and waited on by her acolytes, she would sit on a top bunk and condescendingly accept the fruit and vegetables the girls brought her from the gardens, and she would invariably remind them, like a prim old schoolmarm, how steadfast members of the Communist Party should conduct themselves. Her pale, freckled features and aqueous blue eyes radiated her suppressed contentment and a kind of triumph of affliction. I myself felt conscience-stricken and guilty, because I was disinclined to come bearing gifts to her, though I did recognize her courage and deserts. The trouble was that she reminded me too much of my Mikuláš classmate Mária, who had once leapt onto the platform and shouted: "Don't forget, lads, you are Catholics and your actions and uniforms show you to be acting in a good cause!" I also had an image of a certain pair of hugely bigoted twins, just as pale and freckled as Ruženka; my eyes had met theirs the day anti-Jewish legislation was brought in. They had worn the same smug, even malevolent expression. When I mentioned my ambivalent, irrational and unwarranted attitude to Lila she reprehended me for my injustice towards a person who deserved my respect.

I knew that my stalwart, self-reliant sister had a tendency to idealize and romanticize things and ascribe remarkable qualities to people she'd taken a liking to. That couldn't stop me feeling excessively sober, suspicious and insensitive by comparison.

Lila's idealizing tendency was accompanied by a desire to protect the sick and the frail, animals and humans. She'd been like that since childhood and she was the first of us sisters to know what she wanted to become. She used to say that when she grew up, she would be a doctor.

The sick and the frail at Rajsko that Lila had taken charge of included Stanka, a fragile eighteen-year-old Polish girl with a weak heart. She came from an elite family of big names in Polish culture, all now in prison. Occupying the sole bed in the camp infirmary, she was being looked after by her compatriots. They saw it as their patriotic duty to watch over her and protect her from any detrimental and irksome intrusions. It took Stanka's own tears for Lila to be permitted to sit on her bed and chat to her. "Leave her alone! Lila's my friend!" she would berate her Polish friends, who tried to get her to dedicate her affections only to those who truly deserved it.

The youngest, smallest and one very bright Polish girl in our work team had won the nickname Piccolo. With her platinum-blonde hair, large blue eyes and little rosy cheeks she looked like a china doll. I couldn't fathom why her Polish fellow-inmates often made fun of her, taunting her by saying she was useless at work, no good at handling a spade or rake, in short that she was cack-handed. Piccolo's response was to grit her teeth in silence and keep her aggressive wariness in check.

This was all explained to me by another of the Polish girls, the fair-haired, doleful-eyed Hanka.

"Tell me, Hanka, what on earth has Piccolo done to deserve such resentment?" I asked her.

"Nothing!" Hanka replied. "I'm a good Catholic, like all the other Polish women here, and I believe we're all children of the one God our Lord. But Piccolo is Jewish. It was only thanks to her fair hair and blue eyes that she, alone of her family, managed to save her life by pretending to be a Christian Pole. The Germans gave her a red triangle and treat her as a political prisoner. Some of the girls resent that and think she doesn't deserve it, because it was Jews who killed Jesus. Nobody's going to turn her in, but they do mean to show they know who and what she is."

I was about to ask if they'd prefer to have Piccolo sent to the gas chamber, but held my tongue, having seen and sensed that Hanka was a kind person and any such question might be hurtful to her.

It was summertime. Harvest time. The air filled with the fragrance of ripening and reaping. I don't know if I was actually inhaling the sweet scent or if that was just a childhood memory. Spread out across the long, wide fields, we worked from early morning to late evening in the stifling heat with not a hint of a breeze. Close to the road was a field of ripe sunflowers. Their heavy heads drooped from their long, stout stems. From the recently repaired road came the smell of fresh asphalt. And the road was a constant stream of motorbikes, cars and army vehicles, their wheels shooting tiny bits of gravel in every direction. The old trees in what had once been Polish gardens cast their smooth, dark shadows across the grey, grainy surface of the road. My head was filled with the twittering of sparrows. I was working alone in a dense sea of sunflowers, slicing off the tired, brown-eyed heads from their compliant necks with a small, sharp knife. At the end of the working day the female chargehands used to collect the knives into baskets. I felt as if I'd been emptied out into one of the last, drowsy, straggling days of August. Only the thought that the SS had stolen from us summertime, the trees, the rain, love and liberty, that they had usurped all rights to a road dappled with the shadows of leaves and the ripe fruit that bent the branches low, briefly inspired me with intense moments of orphanhood. Amid the rustling spikes of corn at my back every movement was an echo of its own unreality. I felt as if unshackled light years were floating over my head.

To my left, a watchtower reared up into the sky, on it a guard nursing his gun. I thought I was hallucinating when I caught the sound of him singing and couldn't believe my ears after it dawned on me that the song, which he was now singing for the third time running, was the Jewish lullaby that my paternal grandmother had sung to me one summer: "Sing, sing, my little heart of gold, close those eyes that are so dear to me." You must be dreaming, I told myself, but I didn't have any more time to reflect on my state of mind: I had glanced up to find the soldier approaching. When he reached me he began by explaining he was Volksdeutsch from Romania.

"Where did you get that song you were singing," I asked.

"I used to hear it in my home village. I was taught it by a Jewish girl I'd fallen in love with," he replied, and suddenly a conversation of this kind between prisoner and guard struck me as like a scene from a Surrealist drama.

"I'd much rather get away from here, but I'd need to get hold of some civilian clothes. Could you get hold of some for me?"

"Me? How? And where from?"

"Auschwitz. I've heard you folk can get hold of anything!"

"You heard wrong."

"I'm only here for a short while. They're taking whatever they can away. Old, sick, young, foreigners, all are getting packed off to the eastern front."

"And you don't fancy that?"

"Certainly not. And please, do whatever you can about those clothes," he said, then he turned and left.

I watched him go and saw how slouched down he was, and out of my sense of the unreality of it all suddenly sprang an image of the world and the people in it like the sand in an hourglass. Now we're up, now we're down... And vice versa.

We were gathering in the harvest and Auschwitz's own crop was also reaching its peak. Day and night the crematoria belched their black fumes. We could smell it even from out in the fields, and as dusk fell we saw in the sky, in the glow of a giant bonfire, the shadows of children's corpses skewered on pitchforks. For want of capacity, they were burning dead children out in the open.

10

By their friendship, encouragement and example, girls of various nationalities helped ensure that, despite my frequently clouded, misty sense of it, my own identity did not evaporate completely.

A Polish girl, Marysza, who was ten years older and whom we always called by the diminutive Maruszka, had grown up in a university environment, in Warsaw. She had worked in the Pflanzenzucht, but because she'd been caught smoking, they'd punished her by putting her in the horticulture section for three weeks. She was a relaxed, tolerant young woman, who could switch easily between languages and surprised people by how much she knew about art, politics and science. She acted with a natural, graceful dignity and, like most of the other Polish women, with an indomitable self-assurance that could even get the better of SS-men as they oscillated between admiration and loathing. Maruszka worked alongside me and she knew how to bring me to my senses thanks to her instant appreciation of my mental state.

Her own "programme" resided in conscience, social justice, common sense, emotional intelligence, curiosity and universality.

"In politics, abstractions are often dangerous because they can obliterate the magic that makes an individual a unique, independently minded being. I don't believe anyone should be declared an enemy or an agent of 'evil' merely because they come from a well-to-do family and so be tarred with such labels as bourgeois, parasite, begetter of injustice the world over, or on the contrary that any poor and perhaps even ignorant individual should be described as the sole personification of 'good'. In politics the 'good' needn't know anything as long as they know how to obey and fall into line."

Maruszka's melodious voice was so soothing. I didn't know that her words were becoming etched on my memory and that after many years and experiences they would be a perfect match for my own view of the history of human thought and action.

"I get goose bumps whenever I hear intellectuals of a certain type, who mostly lack a sense of humour or any self-knowledge, calling themselves representatives of the common people. Many of them don't have a clue about the life of those they generalize as 'the common people'. That term is riddled with sentimentality, nationalism, fanatical exaltation, an arrogant exclusivity and romanticism. Chauvinists and demagogues also claim to be serving the people as they manipulate the masses: *Ein Volk, ein Reich, ein Führer!*

"To accord 'the common people', or the masses, one common identity and the noble, historic, mission of being *the* instrument of progress, is, I believe, a gross simplification. To make the masses – in the name of science and what they call the epistemology of objective reality – the sole dispensers of destiny strikes me as highly irrational. Some promote this because they genuinely believe it's the only way to eliminate social injustice and inequality, while others just exploit naivety, hope, suffering, poverty, humiliation and even envy to win political power for themselves."

I listened to Maruszka as if in a dream and forgot about what she'd been saying just as dreams get forgotten the following morning. Her words might as well have been tales from the One

Thousand and One Nights. They served only to postpone the date of our physical and mental demise.

When I asked her how it could be that even here, in a concentration camp, among prisoners afflicted by a common fate, anti-Semitism was still rife, she replied: "Some people feel complacent for being seen as better than others. Their views are reinforced by the fact of being less under threat simply for not being Jews. People imbibe anti-Semitism with their mother's milk. I was brought up as a Roman Catholic believer. I went to church and believed every word the priests uttered: 'His blood be upon them and upon their children...' they preached as the duty ordained by God to persecute Jews. The Lord God formed the light and created the darkness. Since the dawn of time Jews have been children of the darkness, children of its ruler, Satan, and his synagogue. And the poor and ignorant, faced with a lifetime of drudgery, see their salvation in the love of Jesus and redemption by him, and so they hate those said to have killed him, who allegedly also want to corrupt the entire world and rule over it. People can't live without a belief and hope. You have your own belief, but promise me you'll read Rosa Luxemburg's appraisal of Lenin's blindness to the danger that threatens the Soviet system because it falls short on democracy."

One day Maruszka asked me: "Do you know what POW is? You don't! But then you're hardly likely to have come across it. It was a secret military body set up by Marshal Józef Piłsudski to target Austria-Hungary and Germany. It was abolished as early as 1921. One of my uncles, a devoted Communist, emigrated to the USSR. In 1933 he was charged with spying, just for being a member of a non-existent 'agency of sabotage', the POW, and executed along with many more Polish Communists. He wasn't the only member of my family to be falsely accused by the Soviets and condemned to death."

As I listened to Maruszka she was kneeling down among the

succulent leaves of our sugar beet, having a smoke. I was miles away, imagining I was seeing long lines of railway carriages on their way to somewhere or other and the smoke of the engine dispersing somewhere above Nicovô Hill by Liptovský Mikuláš, leaving us children messages by Red Indian smoke signals. I was very fond of Maruszka. I liked her self-possession, her sense of humour and her indulgence of the conviction that I held to as the only, non-illusory way to escape the woes of human history.

At a muffled trot, a sleek chestnut horse flew past along the road, hitched to a britzka with rubber wheels. Holding the reins was a young SS-woman whose hair was a perfect match to her horse's.

"*Flora, Flora, dyevushky, posmotrite... Flora!* [It's Flora, girls, look!]" squealed Shura, who was standing not far from me.

Two or three Russian girls looked up and waved. I was reminded that somewhere, ages before, I'd read that a kind of interdependency can grow up between prisoner and gaoler but despite that I turned to Shura and asked: "How come you find that SS bird so appealing?"

"You're too new here. You don't know her. She doesn't beat people anymore!" Shura snapped back and stuck her tongue out at me.

I wondered whether Shura perhaps knew something of which I had no inkling, and never in my wildest dreams had it occurred to me that she was simply inured to submissiveness, and that not beating others, even though the system entitles you to do so, is a sign of quite exceptional magnanimity. As I imagined it, the dictatorship of the proletariat was no ordinary dictatorship, but an epideictic "historical necessity", and just like the term "revolution", it radiated the everlasting light of the rising sun. Communist rhetoric left me with a sense of exceptionality, it fascinated and impressed me with its theoretical "wisdom" whose ultimate discovery by the world at large would put it to the test. Maruszka's words did nothing to alter my romantic ideas. They were coming at me from some other, previously undiscovered planet.

The film director Wanda Jakubowska confirmed me in my impressions. She was older than I and would talk about international solidarity, the socialist future, a world without wars, oppression and the exploitation of man by man, and about Nazism as the final stage of capitalist imperialism, of which concentration camps were the consequence.

"It behoves us Communists to be honourable and humane and to be bearers of hope. Hope is what keeps you alive and it's with hope that we have to survive and establish a new world with a new kind of people."

I very much hoped that Wanda's longing for a better world would materialize.

At this point I must move forward to 1972 in Denmark. Following one of my lectures, I was approached by a journalist from Poland, by then a people's democracy, who invited me for a coffee and a chat. I asked him if he knew anything about the lady who directed the film "The Auschwitz concentration camp for women", Wanda Jakubowska.[1]

"Wanda Jakubowska? She was written off ages ago," he replied in a tone of utter scorn.

"What? She's not doing films anymore?"

"No, but that's not the worst of it. The worst thing is that she's become 'judaized'."

I glanced at him outraged and bewildered.

"Am I to gather that Polish popular-democratic journalism has started using Nazi racist terminology?" I broke the anger-charged silence after a brief pause. But then my Danish friends took over. I withdrew from the discussion and left.

A few years later, during a trip to Poland with a group of Danish writers, I found Wanda's number and phoned her.

"I haven't forgotten you, Mirka," she said, her frail voice cracking. "I'm glad you've called, but don't come here. I don't want to see anybody. I'm old, worn out, and even hope has abandoned me."

II

My attitude to the Russian girls was a mixture of trust and disillusion, but I'd read the Russian classics, and Maxim Gorky, and there were those millions of the women's countrymen who'd fallen fighting the Third Reich, and all of this lent them a vast protection zone bounded by nothing but the earth and the sky above. Most of the Russian and Ukrainian girls bore little resemblance to my image of "the New Soviet man". With but five or six exceptions they were ignorant, almost primitive young peasant women. I sought to explain this to myself as being due to the relatively short time that had passed since the Revolution and civil war, and to this new and bloody war, which had seen them hauled off by foreign troops into slavery in Nazi Germany, and I sought comfort in the conviction that one day they would all rise to the intellectual level of Nina.

Nina slept in the middle bed under mine. She had a literature MA, knew the poems of Yesenin and Mayakovsky by heart and would treat us to exciting talks on the life and works of Pushkin and Lermontov. Even the Polish girls from the Pflanzenzucht, with their historically conditioned, negative attitude to Russia, respected Nina and begged her to give them talks and recitations as well.

One day, the severe *Oberaufseherin*, Commandant Bormann, came to check out the camp. She had her grey-brown hair mercilessly constricted in a bun and her spare, scrawny frame concealed beneath her uniform, making her look to me like the woman in charge of some old-world institution for the correction of fallen women. She was there to discover if we'd been stealing vegetables. Under Nina's mattress she found lumps of soil, a thick layer of dust, a carrot, an onion and a mouse's nest. The discovery meant the end of Nina's popularity with several of the Polish Pflanzenzucht girls and snipped the thread of their temporary indulgence. I admired the Russian girls whose lodging I shared on account of their vitality, their powerful instinct for self-preservation, their ingenuity and the great ways in which they handled emergencies. When they needed some gloves, they made knitting needles out of wood: where they found it and where they got hold of the little knives they used to carve it we could only try to guess. They stole cellulose from the medical stores and spun it, and they unpicked old clothes, reducing them to threads that they then wound into balls. The mittens they made had amazingly pretty patterns.

In October and November 1944 there was a long period when they put no salt in our food. The frosts came early and the Russian girls brought salt back from work in hankies made from rags and twisted into cornets. The salt had an odd, reddish hue and the girls would exchange small quantities of it for bread, soap and items from the Polish girls' food packs. I didn't know that it was the salt used for spreading on roads so that the horses pulling cartloads of cabbages and cauliflowers could make it safely to the SS kitchens in the main camp.

The Russian girls gave one another nicknames. Tall, corpulent Lyala, who was hardly ever dispirited, would take aggrieved and distressed inmates into her gentle embrace, was called Mama Lyala-golubchik [little dove], and to me she was the very embodiment of all-embracing Mother Russia. But the fact that not everything was quite so clear-cut as I would have liked became clear the time Lyala yelled madly at one Hungarian Jewish lass: "You Jew-bitch, pity Hitler never completed his and our task! Pity he didn't do a sweep of the whole of Russia and muck all the Jews out!" I stood there like a pillar of salt. *Idus Martii*, I thought, and had a sudden image of my sickly Latin teacher, Mr Černocký, back at the grammar school in Mikuláš, giving us a fiery lecture on Caesar and his killer, Brutus. Like for like, image for image.

Aggressive little Lyubka, a tiny thing with a pointy nose set in a face like a little dog's, who always sat on her bed with her legs crossed, snarling, snapping and cursing at all and sundry, had the nickname Volchok (little wolf) Lyubka.

Lyuba-White-Night got her name from her fair hair, big bright, blue eyes, pink cheeks and silky complexion. She was tenderness incarnate, treating everyone with the same kindness. She loved folk tales, which she saw as symbolical reminders of our lot: "You can see how such tales foretell everything, how well they embrace folk wisdom and our own experience of life. Just think of 'The Salt Prince', where salt comes out as more precious than gold," said Lyuba-White-Night after they began serving us unsalted food.

Gypsy-girl Shura, a tall, raw-boned woman with a dark, pockmarked, horsey face, had straggling, curly, black hair tied in a plait that hung all the way down her back. In her deep, raucous voice she would spit out expletives left, right and centre, tossing her plait right and left as if to drive away bothersome insects.

Tigress Tonya looked like a wooden statue cut from a thick tree stump by a fairly inept carver. In fits of rage she would scratch, bite, kick and hit out at all and sundry with arms and legs as straight as a die. "Tonka can't help herself," the doctor explained to us. "She's psychotic."

Dunya the Bitch was a malicious, blonde Cossack woman, broad in the beam and with thick, sturdy legs. Several times a day she would hurl herself to the ground, out in the field or between the vegetable plots, and thrash about this way and that, screaming: "A man! A man! Oh, dear God, send me a man!" For all her great bulk and weight this odd biddy had the voice of an angel. I can just hear her singing *Sinii platochok* [The little blue kerchief]. Each time she wound up with "There's never a night when, little kerchief of mine..." I sensed that somewhere, in some little depression deep inside that huge mound of flesh, was a wellspring of love.

As Dunya sang we would all join in. The SS didn't object to our singing while we worked because we then worked better and faster. Even Roska the Saviour sang along, pausing from her endless tying and untying of knots in her sweat-soaked hankie. Roska was a mystic of a religion that was her own invention.

"One day, my brother Vanka and I were sitting in the hayloft, just having a chat. Then suddenly I saw, right there before me, an angel with its wings outstretched and a halo. I asked Vanka if he'd also seen the angel and he said he had, but that he hadn't dared ask me the same question in case I thought he'd gone mad. Now he's somewhere at the front and I don't know if he's still alive or not. If he does survive and returns home, and if I do too, we're duty-bound to make good the oath we swore, to save Russia through our faith, because if Russia doesn't change, she'll be damned to eternity," Roska told us.

The enigmatic Guitar-Genya had somehow got hold of a guitar, nobody knew where from, and she would sing to it in a voice as wispy as Dunya's was bright. It glowed like coals while being as remote as Genya herself. She never said a word and only ever communicated with us through her singing. Rumour had it that at night her bed was empty, that she kept secret rendezvous with one of the guards, and that he had taken care of the abortion after she fell pregnant by him. We wondered if that was even conceivable and what Genya had had to do in return. However, no one knew anything for certain; this was all guesswork and probably no more than gossip. Genya remained veiled in her own perplexing taciturnity.

Lena was the latest to join our hut. She looked like a filthy, mangy cat with dry, messy hair, and her slanting, narrow green eyes would watch us suspiciously out of her pale, hard face. Lila and I spotted her standing in the canteen doorway and invited her to join our table, and because she reminded us of a character out of Gorky's *The Lower Depths* we felt obliged to make her a member of our group. She proved to be unreliable and a thief, and after one of the other women told us that she used to walk the streets of Kyiv, she got the nickname Harlot-Lena. One night I woke up and discovered something sticky dripping on me from Lena's top bunk. It was her blood. She refused to be examined and would go to work with her trousers packed with rags she'd got from who knows where. One day, when she failed to get up, she was found to have bled to death.

There were plenty more Russian girls. Tanya, who'd tried to perk me up after my arrival at Rajsko. Natasha, a beautiful lass with thick auburn tresses, lofty and inaccessible, as if surrounded by a transparent bulwark as defence against all contact with the horrors of the concentration camp, the disdain and the brutality. I have forgotten many of their names, but they all stirred in me curiosity, a natural affection, sympathy and in all cases partnership, because it was in these girls that I placed all my hopes and my youthful craving for an end to the killing, the muteness and the apathy of the wider world.

12

Kapo Angela, a Volksdeutsche from Carinthia, spoke German and Slovene with equal fluency. She was a moody, idle, slovenly, corpulent woman given to laughing very loud and merrily. This produced little dimples in her chubby pink cheeks and set her enormous breasts bobbing beneath her long, wide, floppy jumper. She left the job of overseeing our work to the group leaders. One day, as summer was giving way to autumn, she announced that we were to receive a visit from the Red Cross.

"If anyone asks you, just say everything's fine, and I hope you all get my message."

They dressed us in freshly laundered uniforms with white collars and lined us up on a vacant potato field in front of the two reps from the Red Cross, who had first inspected the barracks, all freshly scrubbed and cleaned right down to the last speck of dust. The pink blankets on our bunks and the severe order of our lodgings can't fail to have struck them as rather like the dorm of some minor girls' college. No one asked any questions and the visitation concluded with a well-rehearsed bit of play-acting: one of Schmidt's favourite Polish girls, whose sole asset was to be the epitome of Teutonic Aryan beauty, came cycling along the nearby path, wearing a broad smile and with her blonde pony-tail blowing about behind her. She gave Schmidt a passing nod, which he reciprocated with a smile. At that moment I did wonder if the two Red Cross gentlemen could also detect the smell of burning flesh drifting across the fields from the chimneys of Birkenau.

We laboured from dawn till dusk under the command of Unterscharführer Lothar, who reminded me of a turkey. He had an un-Aryan, long, bent nose, a stoop and bow-legs, and his spiky Adam's apple bobbed about on the long neck that poked above the collar of his uniform like a flower stalk. Whenever he thought our work wasn't brisk enough, he would swear at us, drive us on and keep prodding us with his rifle butt. If ever he cleared off for half an hour, we heaved a sigh of relief, took a rest, sang songs or extended our knowledge of the languages of Europe. Years after the war, when, as a student in Prague, I was accused of "cosmopolitanism", I did wonder if my alleged cosmopolitanism hadn't been born in a concentration camp field in the shadow of gas chambers.

Autumn brought with it some nasty weather and the first signs of disintegration. Some Jewish members of a *Sonderkommando* mined one of the crematoria and blew it sky-high. The swirling smoke and the whiff of the explosives even reached us out in the fields. I can still see Schmidt standing transfixed between two onion beds. With his mouth agape and revealing a consternation born of utter disbelief, he was staring at the flames billowing from the temple of his confession and listening to the sound of explosions. A little while later he caught my sister Lila having a smoke and, perhaps to mask his state of shock, he slapped her across the face. When she failed to show any response he asked her: "How come you're not crying, Lili? You ought to be crying!"

"Can't be bothered," Lila replied.

"While I was still teaching and a pupil did something against the rules, I would cuff him. I was always strict, but fair."

We couldn't fathom why this SS character was actually being polite to Lila and doing so much explaining, but Lila was one of his chosen ones and he himself was quite shaken by the completely unexpected, bewildering event.

"Your line in pedagogy doesn't impress me!" said Lila, and Schmidt turned without another word and left.

We were not prepared for a hard winter. We froze in our flimsy dresses and the snow kept on coming. The growing, hardening layer of it buried the cabbages, Brussels sprouts and cauliflowers. My clogs had holes in them and that Bormann woman was harsher than the cold itself. She ranted and raved following her failure to reform us by application of Herr Schmidt's pedagogical system – promising that we'd be given some meat once a week if we stopped stealing greens. However, to us vegetables mattered more than meat. Girls who'd been caught stealing had to spend a whole winter's night standing outside their hut, while some were transported to Auschwitz.

The Pflanzenzucht girls complained about the Bormann woman to Obersturmbannführer Caesar and, with reports from the battlefields being apparently so dispiriting, he saw to it that she was removed from Rajsko. The camp acquired a new Oberaufseherin, a blonde, chubby SS-woman of around thirty-five, whose first move was to choose from among the prisoners a masseuse and a hairdresser, whom she would always take with her when she went for a sleigh ride.

Milka, one of my Polish friends, applied for me to be allowed to assist her in the stables, thereby saving me from falling ill. Inside the stables it was warm and cosy. The sound of the horses snorting, the stamp of their feet on the straw-covered floor, the rustle of haulm, the warmth emanating from the horses' bodies and the softness of their mouths, the freedom to bury one's face in a horse's mane, to sense the animals' trust, groom them with a curry comb, pick their hooves clean – all that lent me a feeling of home, from which I was wrenched whenever I was needed in the fields.

The wind used to blow the fumes and a dusting of snow off the compost heap. I would be freezing cold in my broken clogs, the frost got behind my finger nails, the days were filled with grey-white hours of agony, and I had my work cut out to prevent the scattered seeds of despair from germinating and taking over completely.

Unterscharführer Lothar made a bonfire, but if any of us dared to go near, he would start shrieking and hitting us with his rifle. In one of his turkey-like eyes he had a red stye. Angela came out to the field to join us; she was wearing a thick pink jumper, a long pink scarf wound round her neck and long black trousers tucked into her top boots. Looking like a fat hen, she gave the

Unterscharführer a wink and started openly flirting with him. She asked if she could help by tossing more branches onto his fire.

"*Halt, oder ich schiesse!* [Stop, or I'll shoot!]" he called out with a grin that laid bare his yellow equine teeth.

"*Ach mein Gott, er scheisst* [Oh my god, he's shitting]," cried Angela with a belly laugh.

"*Mensch, bist du doch ein freches Frauenzimmer!* [Gosh, you're some cheeky wench]," he hollered back.

"*Ja, ich bin ein Frauenzimmer, aber bist du ein Mann?* [Yes, I'm a wench, but are you a man?]," came Angela's challenging reply.

And suddenly they weren't there, so we girls crept over to the fire to put a bit of warmth in our hands. However, that only made the pain behind our nails even worse.

Angela was groaning behind the snow-coated raspberry patch and the white dusting began to fall from it.

"*Mensch!* Mind your gun, it might go off!" Angela squeaked.

"*Ja, mein Schatz*, if you carry on like that, it jolly well will!"

The Unterscharführer popped his head up above the bushes to check, then bellowed: "*Los, los! Weitermachen!* [Quick, get on with your work!]

The bonfire died, the cinders were still smoking, then even the last ember turned to ash.

13

I was so relieved to have returned to the stable that I barely noticed how sad Milka was.

"The thing is, Mirka, my family lives not far from here. And now, with Christmas approaching, it's as if they were a million miles away," she said. "I'd love to see them and spend the festive season with them. I'm thinking more and more about escaping and at the first opportunity I'm going to have a go. I'll take you with me if you want."

I was very fond of Milka. She was kind to both people and animals.

Angela banged at the door and summoned us to a cabin to do some pea-podding. The wooden cabin had a stove inside. One of the girls was just scraping frozen snow from its tiny windows. One of the older Polish women – we called her Tetuška, Auntie – was stoking the stove with some logs. The dry wood crackled in the feedbox and Auntie remarked that to her ears it sounded as if the Infant Jesus was turning over in the manger and suggested that we sing a carol.

"*Ja, ja,*" Angela cried, "Let's sing Silent Night." Afterwards, Angela came over to me and asked: "*Hast du Schulen?* [What school did you go to?]"

"*Gymnasium... Ist das gut genug?* [Grammar school, is that good enough?]"

"*Fein, fein,* so you can write. Can you write German?"

"Sure."

"So you can write me a Liebesbrief."

"You want me to profess my love for you?"

Angela's roaring laughter ended in a coughing fit. "Not for me. For Unterscharführer Lothar, because I can't."

"How should I address him? And what do you want me to write?"

"This: *Geliebter Lothar, mein Schatz, mein Kätzchen* [My beloved treasure, my pussy-cat]... Come on, you've been to grammar school, so you ought to know how to write about love. *Ach, die Liebe, die Liebe...*" she giggled. "And d'you know what: Write and tell him my brother was a partisan and they executed him."

"But Angela, they could send you to Auschwitz for that!"

"They won't send me anywhere. The whole thing's just a bit of tomfoolery. I don't have a brother nor do I know anyone else they executed, but heroism calls for respect, even when the heroism is the enemy's. Put down what I said and then add that Christmas is coming, a festival of love, and that I love him etc. etc...." said Angela, handing me a sheet of white paper and a fountain pen.

And while the women and girls were shelling peas, stoking the stove and singing carols, I was sitting alone over a sheet of paper with a vision of the bowlegged, grotesque and evil Unterscharführer Lothar. Writing him a love letter was beyond my powers, despite my seeing the whole situation as an absurd joke. But I had to write to him, and so I found a solution. I wrote a letter to the dead boy from the compost heap.

I showed the letter to Angela. "Is this more or less what you were thinking of?"

"More or less... but it's all *ganz egal* [It makes little odds]."

Outside, snow was falling thick and fast.

Schmidt opened the cabin door, shook the snow from his epaulettes, stepped inside, leaned against the wall, watched us for a moment in silence and suddenly, as if having taken the time to make up his mind, spoke: "It looks like we're going to have to join forces and move to the eastern front. Our Führer needs us all right now. But before I leave you I just want to say that everything that has happened here was by orders from the top, and that I wish you all a merry Christmas."

After the door closed behind him Auntie said: "And we you – underneath some Russian Christmas candles."

14

Notes

Even in the most totalitarian of regimes, governed by the strictest of rules and in total control even of private lives, chance and coincidence reign as side effects of mankind's unpredictability, the weather, the character of individuals, instincts, intuition or the delayed execution of measures dictated from on high. There are gaps and lapses in time which you either fall into, or out of which you might find an exit from some sudden jeopardy. In a concentration camp, where speedy or protracted manslaughter was an item on the government's agenda, certain rules applicable to certain types of prisoner could be inferred.

Prisoners' ability to shake off the terrible burden of the initial shock depended on the kind of life they had lived before internment. Those who found themselves in a concentration camp for political reasons – whether they were Aryans or not – and whose philosophy of life gave them hope, faith and conviction that added force to their integrity, had always had to reckon that underground resistance or simply being different would cost them their lives or their incarceration.

Those who had been locked away for "antisocial behaviour", criminality, thuggery or murder took malicious delight in the knowledge that they were sharing life inside a camp with the very people who had caused them to be put through the legal system: politicians, lawyers and judges. That bolstered their self-assurance and sense of superiority because here their crimes were not the exception, but the rule, legitimized by the establishment and the law.

People accustomed to submission and to acting obediently and unquestioningly on the orders of the establishment within any political system (even the Nazi one) could never grasp the why and the wherefore of their presence in a concentration camp. Many grasped at the straw that was awareness of their former social standing, never doubting the workings of the law and believing that what had befallen them must be due to some misunderstanding. Their attitude and the impotence arising from it engendered the scorn directed at them not only by their fellow-prisoners, but also by the SS. Having eventually realized the sheer absurdity of their position, they either gave in, died or began collaborating with their gaolers.

All Jews knew that they were being persecuted for being Jews and that, as such, they were treated as inferior human material unworthy of being kept alive. The fact that this was nothing new to history did not temper their despair. The believers among them argued with God and their own doubts, but having faith at least offered them some consolation and the hope expressed in the prayer with which they went to their death: "My God, my God, why hast Thou forsaken me? So often hast Thou left us to the flames and not once have we denied Thee."

Many Jewish inmates, believers and non-believers, to whom the Star of David in the red-and-yellow triangle on their prison uniforms brought only suffering and death, saw in the crimes committed against them, the humiliation and disgrace of their brutish tormenters.

15

And the snow kept falling and falling out of the grey heavens above. It settled on us, on the ground, on the barracks, on the villas and gardens misappropriated by the SS, it gave the trunks and branches of trees a profile, and it buried all the previously untouched crops in the fields. Angela came to me and handed me her long, pink, woollen scarf.

"Here, that's for the Liebesbrief!" she said, and she glanced down at my clogs. "My God! They're utterly useless, woman! You'll get frostbite and that'll be the end of you!" she commented, then she turned and left.

Beneath the thick layer of ice-coated snow various kinds of cabbages were waiting for us. They had to be scrabbled clear, their heads chopped off, loaded onto carts and transported to the SS kitchens at the main camp, Auschwitz I. I hacked away with my bare hands. I had to scrape away the snow surrounding the stumps with my stiff blue fingers and stack head after head onto mounting piles. Suddenly something glinted before my very eyes with all the colours of the rainbow. I bent down towards the object that had suddenly appeared beneath the green-and-white head of a cauliflower. It was a ring set with tiny diamonds. I picked it up and hid it in my jacket pocket. I looked about me, but no one was paying me any attention. I told no one about my find. Angela's shawl kept me warm, though I had dreadful frostbite and my feet were like icicles. I remembered what Angela had said about my utterly useless clogs and it occurred to me that my find, somewhat superfluous in a prison camp, might yet prove useful. And then I heard wheels crunching through the snow and the warm snuffling of horses.

We loaded the cabbages onto the cart and while the SS man wasn't looking I went up to the carter, an elderly German political prisoner, and in a whisper asked him if he might be able to swap the diamond ring for some shoes for me. He stuffed the ring in his pocket and promised to try, though there was no guarantee of anything. A few days later he brought me some boots with thick wooden soles, apologising for having failed to secure any leather ones. Neither he, nor I guessed that he had found me the very best.

Not only was Scharführer Schmidt being despatched to the eastern front, but so too was Unterscharführer Lothar. Weighed down with rucksacks and rifles, they struggled through the deep, frozen snow and waved back to the prisoners gazing after them from behind the barbed-wire fence. That these two great devotees of the Nazi Idea really fancied dying for the Reich could not be detected even remotely from their general posture or their gait. All we saw were two wretched, stooping figures who'd been growing thinner by the day and the seats of whose trousers were drooping down to their calves. They slowly dragged one foot after another along the snow-covered camp roadway.

"The mills of God grind slowly, but surely!" remarked Halina from the Pflanzenzucht.

"We're not out of the woods yet!" said Lyala.

I told no one I felt no Schadenfreude. Analyzing my own lack of response, odd as it was even to me, I concluded that with their backs to me, so I couldn't see their faces, they were to me a generalization of the fate of mankind. This was my eternal

Strindbergian duality, as expressed in a line from one of his plays: "Those poor people!", though his plays had plenty of cruel, evil characters. And maybe that was why.

Changes were happening all around us. The SS guards were replaced by young Volksdeutsch and some older men, who looked pathetic and ludicrous in uniforms that were too big or too small for them.

One day, after I'd walked past the electrified wire fence that surrounded the living quarters, I was addressed by a fairly young man barely out of his teens, wearing a German uniform, speaking Slovak: "Can you understand me?"

When I replied that I could, he asked if I could get hold of two onions for him, or at least one, because they were being given very little food and their hut wasn't even heated. Meeting a young speaker of Slovak behind a hostile, life-threatening fence stirred in me a notion of the irony and vicissitude of history. Now up, now down, and vice versa, in every possible permutation, even the most inconceivable.

"If you like I can let you have this newspaper. But you have to read between the lines," said the young Slovak in the uniform of the SS.

And thus did I discover that everything was falling apart and that the Thousand-Year Reich was coming to an end. I took the guard a stolen onion, but in great secrecy, lest any of my fellow-prisoners accuse me of collaboration and sympathizing with the enemy.

Suddenly, out of the blue, the Allies started bombing Auschwitz. Someone told me they'd seen a booted but bare-bottomed SS man flying through the air along with the latrine.

"Serve 'em right! But why's it taken so long?" remarked Tanya, expressing thereby the general reaction of the prisoners.

"The Soviets' katyushas will sing 'em the one and only real carol!" said Lyala, whose Weltanschauung had undergone another change.

The camp was rife with rumours: The front was quite close. All the prisoners were to be evacuated. The sick were to be incinerated along with the barracks. The gas chambers and crematoria would be blown up. All evidence of the atrocities committed by the Nazis in the concentration camps had to be obliterated without trace.

But it was too late for all that. We were informed that we were to be given rations of sugar, bread and margarine and that we would be transferred to a different camp. Since I was standing in the doorway when two SS women came in with a basket full of rations, the block wardress ordered me to distribute them. I'd only done half of them when I was suddenly attacked by four girls I didn't know. I was still wondering where they'd sprung from when they began hitting, kicking and scratching me like wildcats; they grabbed the basket from my hands and vanished into a crowd of desperately weeping women and girls. The SS men drove us out onto the road and any attempt to make up for the lost rations was in vain. Whether this was in late 1944 or early January 1945 I no longer recall.

It seemed inconceivable to be in Prague and see the quivering shadows of leaves on the park paths in May 1945.

With resistance fighters in homemade uniforms. Their car was almost a status symbol due to lack of petrol.

With Russian soldiers and Czech children in Brevnov - a suburb of Prague.

August 1945. Smile at the photographer.

One of the roads in the Liptov valley that I cycled on for pleasure and later on an illegal errand. In 1945, nature experiences became part of my struggle to return to life.

BOOK 4

A LONG, SLOW DAWNING

I

We must have been preceded along the road by numerous convoys carrying other evacuated prisoners: the dead and dying were lying in the roadside ditches and on the road itself, along which we were being propelled by our guards. The sick, skeletal and those incapable of moving and marching at the pace dictated by the SS men fleeing from the advancing Russians, were either shot or left lying where their last ounce of strength had deposited them. From where they lay, moaning helplessly, they reached out their arms like aquatic plants towards the marching column of prisoners. Those with enough strength left to cry out were silenced by submachine guns. The silence that followed each burst of gunfire was broken only by the crunch of snow being trampled by hundreds of shoes.

Striding alongside the endless, wide, compact regiments of concentration campers, who looked like salvage from a rubbish dump, were their guards, male and female. In their billowing black capes they looked like angels of death in a Brueghel-esque winter landscape.

"*Schneller! Schneller!*" the SS men bawled, shooting at those who failed to respond to their commands. My boots with their thick wooden soles were a blessing. In the bitter cold and the relentlessly falling snow they marched along as if with a will of their own.

We passed through villages and small towns. The locals kept to the pavements, carrying baskets or shopping bags, mostly old men and women, some accompanied by children. Wearing winter coats, the women wrapped in thick woollen shawls, bonnets or headscarves drawn down across their foreheads, with misted eyes they watched the huge, snaking stream that was flooding the roadway. Children who'd been asking awkward questions were pushed ahead by their mothers.

After nightfall they allowed us to rest in the shed of a large farmstead. Starving, freezing and worn out, we burrowed into the straw as deep as we could.

"Don't take your shoes off," Auntie warned us. "You'll never get your shoes back on your swollen feet!" Those who ignored her advice bitterly regretted it.

In the gloom of the shed we chatted in undertones. The Polish girls ate some of the provisions left over from their parcels. Milka brought me some bread and a bit of bacon. Just as I sank my teeth into it, someone behind me whispered in my ear: "Give me my bread and margarine!" I looked round and saw a pair of shining eyes and the lips that were mechanically repeating the same sentence: "Give me my bread and margarine!"

"You know I don't have anything; they stole everything from me," I protested. But the woman kept on repeating her demand, and several others backed her up. Their voices merged into a rhythmical, muffled chorus: "Give us our bread and margarine!"

Out of the corner sprang an SS woman, who shouted: "*Maul*

halten or I'll shoot. I've got enough bullets to go round. *Ihr Dreckkäfer! Ihr Schweine! Maul halten!*"

As daylight dawned, they ordered us to rise. The hay began to rustle and turned into a mass of straggling heaps of life. Not one of us had had a decent night's sleep. We were exhausted and several of the women were ill. Lack of sleep turned the onward march into unimaginable agony – most notably for those who'd taken their shoes off and were now having to pull them back on their sore and swollen feet as fast as they could.

"*Los! Los! Schneller! Schneller!*" the SS men bellowed. They were wielding pitchforks, raising them high and jabbing them as deep as they could into the undulating hay. Only two of the women managed to escape. One was Tetuška [Auntie] and the other a Jewish girl from Slovakia. Auntie took her home to a village nearby.

Milka had also managed to escape. She'd come to me in the night to say how sorry she was she couldn't take me with her. Her two Polish friends wouldn't hear of it. "They're afraid because you're not our sort and people in our town don't like people like you. I hope you're not cross with me," she said as we parted.

And the march went on. "*Los! Los! Los!*" the SS men bellowed, troubled by news that the Russian front was getting ever closer. For the sake of a little extra warmth we took turns at being in the middle or at the edge of the lines. Not everyone was willing to give up their relatively warmer position. One little Frenchwoman, a chemist from the Pflanzenzucht, wailed aloud: "Don't let me die! Help me! Let me lean on you! Humanity needs me! My research will benefit everyone. Help! Hold me up!"

We did help to keep her upright, dragging her along behind us, although, given the wretched state we were all in, we found her lamentations an appalling overestimation of her importance.

Then suddenly, from behind my back, I heard a voice: "Give me my bread and margarine! Give me my bread and margarine!"

Persistent, repetitive, in a low tone so the SS men wouldn't hear. One of the Polish women began reciting the Lord's Prayer, then others joined in: "Give us this day our daily bread... Give us our bread and our margarine! And forgive us our trespasses! Give us our bread and our margarine! As we forgive them... and our margarine...!" And the SS men didn't shout, they didn't shoot, they didn't break in on the monotonous, crazy, ever louder fugue of our common prayer.

In the evening, when they allowed us a brief rest in a snow-covered field, I felt not only the sting of the frost, but also the inertia that precedes falling ill. There were moments when my eyes misted over and everything seemed to be vanishing into the far distance. All I can remember is them ordering us aboard some open freight train trucks, the engine blowing its whistle, the train moving off, the snow coming down on us out of the sky, us all pressing together for that bit of extra warmth, and me wishing I didn't have to rely on the animal warmth of other people's bodies. And this was played out as if in a dream.

It wasn't a long journey. We had to get off the train and continue on foot along roads covered by ever more snow. The SS women in their black capes were no longer with us. We were now being guarded by just some men with submachine guns, and I began miraculously to emerge from my private mist.

Quite unexpectedly, our transport and guards passed under the command of an officer of the Wehrmacht who lacked any SS insignia. He was a tall, good-looking man wearing a freshly ironed uniform, who treated us nicely and was ready to help us to the best of his ability. The impression he made was of the kind of man whom, before the war, we would have described as a "cultured German". He marched with us along the snow-covered, bumpy roads with a Romanian prisoner, Dora, as his constant companion. At night, we slept in sheds, Dora with the officer. She clung to him like a leech. Despite the revulsion that we felt towards her, we begged her to ask the officer to get a fly sheet for us to give us at least some protection from the snow and the cold in the open railway truck. We got it. Before boarding, the officer warned us there was going to be an inspection. "It would be best if you leave your watches, any jewellery and other valuables with me. I'll let you have them back after the inspection," he said.

I was amazed at how many of the women and girls still possessed prohibited objects and at their readiness to hand them over to the man. He took them, put them in his pockets and went off with Dora.

No inspection showed up. The only person who did show up was Dora. Alone. The officer had vanished, never to be seen again. Without his protection, she was exposed to contempt and ridicule, though we hadn't forgotten, and remained duly grateful, that she had arranged that fly sheet for us. However, even under that we were freezing cold in the overloaded railway truck, and the icy wind chilled us to the bone. Beneath the fly sheet there was a lot of arguing over space, food and even the chance to lie down for a moment and stretch out after long hours spent in a sitting position. The dismay of the prisoners robbed of their last mementos of home spread to the rest of us. Though some did evince a certain *Schadenfreude*. We were all progressively more spent and irritable and a real fight might have broken out if the train's brakes hadn't squealed and the train itself hadn't come to a halt. The sudden silence was broken by the thunder of anti-aircraft fire. We peeped out from under our canopy. It was night time. The train had stopped in a siding. We could hear the whizzing and deafening explosions of bombs. Our truck shook with the shock waves. We heard whining, wailing and weeping coming from the adjacent truck. "We're not going to start yammering! We're not cowards!" said Nina, and the quiet that followed her words was broken only by the suppressed murmur of Roska's praying. The frightened Piccolo lay her head against Nina's shoulder. Nina winced and shook her off with an expression of scorn and disgust.

"Air raid! There's a fire! Everything's on fire all round us!" one of the girls screamed.

"I can just see myself splattered on the walls. It's probably the Brits, or our lot. What an irony of fate if we get killed by our own!" said Lyala.

When sirens announced the end of the raid, the guards ordered us to remain in the trucks. It was morning before they chased us out of them. The station had taken a total hammering. Everywhere lay bits of concrete, bricks, iron and smoldering sleepers. Smoke rising from the ruins was spreading out across the landscape. Only the transport full of prisoners and their guards had remained untouched in the railway siding.

We continued along long stretches of unknown roads on foot, in cattle trucks, whenever it was possible to join the transports that had brought the wounded from the eastern front. One day, as we were taking a rest in a field beside a main road, there was a low-level bombing raid by allied planes. We waved to them and flung ourselves flat on the ground or into the roadside ditches, and we could see that anything that moved on the road was hit by machine-gun fire and flattened. Things went flying through the air – horses and carts, fleeing Germans, cattle, children and adults with handcarts and backpacks. Bits of bodies everywhere, blood, shattered remains, *Armageddon*. At that instant, the fact that just such a catastrophe could have struck us as well was not nearly so important as the realization that the war was coming to a close.

2

Our march ended at Ravensbrück, next to a high wall, where we were kept standing in the snow for two freezing cold days without food, drink or sleep. Some of the women prisoners, dressed only in flimsy grey-and-blue striped uniforms, stood as if glued to the wall in a catatonic trance. Some Russian and Polish women had had the foresight to get hold of blankets and now sat wrapped in several layers as they rested on the steps of a large building.

"Get lost! You can snuff it for all I care, you piece of Jewish shit!" was the response of Sashka, wrapped tight in four warm blankets, to the sickly little Hungarian, Eva, blue and shaking with cold, who'd begged her to lend her one of the blankets. After they finally made space for us and herded us into the barracks, there were so many of us inside that it was impossible to breathe.

Ravensbrück was run to the same routine as Auschwitz. Here, too, there were those morning and evening roll calls. And here, too, there were crematoria.

"There's no hope of escaping from here," one of the existing residents of Ravensbrück informed me. "The camp's in Mecklenburg and it's surrounded by marshland, lakes and kilometres of electrified barbed-wire fences. And just think, Berlin's not that far away!"

At Ravensbrück I met the guinea-pigs, the Czech and Polish girls and women who had experiments carried out on them involving bacteria that brought them out in festering phlegma. They were injected with the gangrene contracted by German soldiers in the bitter cold of the eastern front. The experiments were intended to bolster the fighting spirit of the Wehrmacht. All the women who'd been mutilated by the loss of one leg, or even just half of one, went about on crutches.

Since we hadn't been split into work teams, we could wander freely about the barrack huts, where we learned – possibly as a consequence of a degree of relaxation brought on by intimations of the approaching end of the war – about the tragedies and the more and less weird stories being told about cruel and hugely jealous women guards and SS women who fell in love with some of their pretty female prisoners. Such stories ended in revenge and murder, and because they were played out inside a concentration camp, the notion that they might become subject matter for penny-dreadfuls, shilling shockers or broadside ballads struck me as obnoxiously frivolous. I set about looking for any friends or people I might know who by some miracle or happenstance were still alive. To my great joy and surprise, I did find three girls from Liptovský Mikuláš: Kata, Juca and Božka. They were woefully thin, translucent even, as if cleansed of all the world's contaminants. I so wished we would all survive until the spring. Only one of them did; the other two died of typhus in March 1945.

At Ravensbrück, I committed my first and only theft during the entire time I spent in the camps. Fenia, who'd been a wardress at our block in Birkenau, had called to me: "Mirka, come with me to see your sister."

She took me by the hand and led me towards one of the multi-storey bunks. On the top level was sitting the pale, beautiful Stanka with two of her Polish friends, holding Lila's hand. It wasn't hard to figure out that the Polish women who'd been assigned to the SS kitchens had given their countrywomen some food, with which they were now feeding themselves and their protégée. But they'd given nothing to Lila. I couldn't bear to see my sister excluded from this "communion", this most elementary law of humanity, and ran out and dived at a cauldron full of potatoes that two women prisoners were carrying past. They tried to drive me away, hitting me with clubs, but I did manage to steal four potatoes. I tossed two up to Lila and ate two myself.

One day, at roll call, I spotted a group of boys from the Jugendlager being led by two black-caped SS women. They were walking twelve abreast, dressed in long grey robes and cowls. When they were ordered to stand to attention I noticed that the only sign of life in their pale, emaciated, juvenile faces was their eyes, which gleamed with a sneer of loathing. They had undergone "re-education", so they now knew that the only road to survival was via theft, mendacity, fighting and mistrust. I was shaken by a feeling that these eyes were watching me with Schadenfreude at the prospect that I, too, would soon be dead.

I remember how we were led out onto the road to be evacuated and how everything ahead and all round me went fuzzy. My head felt heavy and I was moving like an automaton. I don't recall how I wound upon a bunk with a splitting headache and feeling utterly starved. Two girls were sitting on the adjacent bunk picking bits of meat from a tin. "Yippee... Goulash... Beef... Veal... Pork... Lamb... Horsemeat... Bosnian stew, Melita's Bosnian stew," someone was writing on a partially obscured, black panel. The girls were sliding the meat between their bared teeth and I could see them moving, hear them chewing, and I gazed at the sharp shiny edge of the open tin over which the meat was crawling like maggots, ever so slowly, as if the girls were trying to prolong the treat to get at me. With each bit of meat they ate something juicy and green... Crunch... Crunch...

"Hey, she's watching us!" said one of the girls and she handed me a tiny piece of cabbage. I had neither the strength, nor the desire to eat it.

Then suddenly there, next to my bunk, was Ena, the Czech medic from the Auschwitz infirmary, the one who'd saved me from Dr Mengele's death sentence, and she told me to open my mouth and show her my tongue. "Oh God, another case of typhus. She needs to go to the infirmary."

I don't know how long I was unconscious. I came to on a narrow pallet, where I was lying between women prisoners with typhoid fever. I felt very ill. Twenty times a day I had to go to the lavatory, which was at the far end of a dark, seemingly endless corridor. Not once did I make it in time. I fainted on top of a heap of corpses, the harvest of twenty-four hours. When I came to and hauled myself back, I had faeces dribbling down my legs. I was surrounded by a revolting stench. But each time I was seen to by

Nadya, a Russian girl properly trained as a nurse. She washed me down, supported me and led me back to the tropical heat in the gap between two bodies that reeked of diarrhoea and sweat.

"I think I'm going to die," I told Nadya.

"Rubbish! You'll pull through. Look what I've got for you. It's good for diarrhoea," she said, handing me a piece of raw potato.

Nadya, a Red Army soldier, had been captured by the Germans and sent to work at a German arms factory. She'd been transported to Auschwitz for insubordination. She cared for the sick to the best of her ability, with no medicines or injections. The best medicine was her indomitable willpower and intractability.

(As I think back on Nadya today, I am so glad that she had no inkling of what awaited her, an innocent captive, when she finally got back to her beloved homeland. Neither she, nor I would have believed it possible. The absurdity of unwarranted retribution would have seemed to us like the most disgusting falsehood on the part of an enemy.)

Suddenly I'd had as much as I could take. Of the bodies of strangers, then of the feverish buckets of sweat, the fleas, the feeling sick, the faeces. I crawled off the bunk, sat down on the cold stone floor and leaned back against the wall, intending to stay there till eternity. When a Hungarian nurse ordered me back into my gap, I told her I'd rather peg out.

"Just you wait. When I die I'll come and get you!" I told her. My voice seemed to be coming from somewhere far away and my head was getting heavier and heavier.

The doctor checked my heart and lungs with her stethoscope and said, "Wouldn't you just believe it! This one's got pneumonia as well! Get her a bunk."

The sick women and girls were dying like flies. Even the pair I'd been lying between on the pallet. One hanged herself with a sheet. I've no idea how long I was sick. All I remember was that, quite suddenly, things about me began to brighten. Nadya sat down beside me on the pallet with the greeting: "Welcome back!"

"We all thought you were going to die," said the girl on the pallet next to mine.

I tried to sit up, but was too weak.

"You'll be sitting up by tomorrow. For now close your eyes and sleep. I'll sing you a lullaby," said Nadya and she launched into a song from a Maxim Gorky film:

> *Mesto na Kame,*
> *kde nevieme sami,*
> *mesto na Kame,*
> *matičke rieke.*
>
> *Leží za horami,*
> *skryté za lesami,*
> *mesto na Kame,*
> *v diaľnej diaľave.*
>
> *City on the Kama,*
> *where we don't know,*
> *city on the Kama,*
> *the mother of rivers.*
>
> *It lies beyond the mountains,*
> *hidden beyond the forests,*
> *the city on the Kama,*
> *so far, far away.*

The following day, Nadya brought me some vegetable soup, which Lila had swapped for her whole day's bread ration. They wouldn't let Lila herself go any further than the window. I ate a few spoonfuls of this precious dish. Nadya stood me on some borrowed kitchen scales: I weighed 35 kilos.

3

Sickness, changes, and the rapid sequence of unfolding events impaired my perception of time. My memory has preserved some things with clarity and precision, while others are no more than smells, moods, colours or scattered fragments.

I left the infirmary crawling on all fours. Lila and Vera helped me back to the hut where we were lodged.

It was still freezing outside.

I was extremely feeble and what recollections I have of my time at Ravensbrück only surface from my subconscious in snippets. I can see one SS woman, the camp boss, sitting on horseback, hopping off it, jumping over a fence on it, giving Vera, sitting closest to her, a slap across the face, jumping over the fence, hopping onto her horse and disappearing. I can remember the camp was called Malchow[1] and I knew we were evacuated from it and ordered to march goodness knows where to.

We made good use of the confusion that arose with an allied air raid. Four of us lay down in a corpse-filled ditch by the road. I lay there, waiting, then realized I'd become stronger. After the marchers had all passed, we ripped open the fronts of our prison uniforms. Beneath them we had several layers of the jumpers and skirts that we'd "organized" before the evacuation from Rajsko. After my bout of typhoid my hair had fallen out, and now it was sprouting back in ragged tufts. I covered it over with the headscarf given to me by Nadya. The fact that we'd mastered German in early childhood made it easier for us to mingle with fugitive Germans. Mostly we proceeded on foot, with occasional lifts on tractors or horse-drawn carts, and one stretch on a train crammed full of bombed-out families. We avoided any towns, sticking to fields and footpaths, and survived on whatever we could find in the fields. We slept on straw or hay, in haylofts and sheds. For our own safety's sake we split into two groups. Lila and I remained together. Now and again we would run up against Yugoslav or French POWs, who'd been installed with German peasant farmers or on larger estates.

One day, somewhere in Germany, we broke the lock on an isolated hay barn and spent a whole day and night there. We were woken in the morning by an enraged male voice. "*Schon wieder diese verfluchten Diebe!* [Those wretched thieves again!]" it swore. The barn door opened slowly, squeaking, and in it stood a thin, elderly little chap. He had a cap and badge on his head and a pitchfork in his hands. Before he could launch his attack, I said in German: "*Entschuldigen Sie bitte. Wir haben hier nur geschlafen* [Forgive us, we've only been sleeping here]. *Und wir sind keine Diebe!* [And we're not thieves!] We're fugitives who've been bombed out. When we arrived here, night had already fallen."

The man discovered to his satisfaction that his thieves were two young girls, so I quickly went on: "We were shattered, our legs were aching, and so we took the liberty of opening the barn. Please don't be angry. We really didn't know what to do and we don't even know where we are. Please be so kind as to tell us where we are."

"You're in Saxony, on the Mügeln estate, near the town of the same name. I'm their wagoner and I've come to get some hay for the horses. You can't stay here! If the estate manager finds you, things will turn nasty!"

"Could you help us? Do you need any help on the estate? We'll take on any kind of job!"

"Stay here. I'll see what I can do. I'll send you someone you can ask for advice."

The wagoner grabbed some hay, left and it occurred to us both that we were in a bit of a pickle. But we were past caring and were loath to leave our warm haven. "Who knows what's coming next. But let's just wait and see," said Lila.

The wagoner must have been a kind man because he didn't betray us, even though he hadn't believed our explanation. The assistant he sent to us was a Pole who'd been recruited for farm work in Germany and who introduced himself as Stanisław; he told us he'd been put in charge of the cowshed.

"You've nothing to fear. The wagoner won't tell anyone. Follow me. I'll hide you away then have a word with the estate manager. If you can make do with just getting food as recompense for your work, well there's plenty of work to be done here."

We confessed to Stanisław that we'd been held in a concentration camp and that we were from Slovakia. He hid us in a little room behind the cowshed and gave each of us a mug of milk and a chunk of white bread. That same evening, he brought along two Yugoslav and two French POWs and they brought two roast chickens and some potatoes.

"Go easy! Don't overeat or you'll make yourselves ill," Stanisław warned, and he informed us that he'd told the estate manager that we were German women who'd been bombed out of their homes, that our families had all died during an air raid and that we were fleeing ahead of the advancing Russians. The manager had allowed us to help out on the estate and to continue living in the little room behind the cowshed.

4

Once winter had passed, the town of Mügeln, lost amid the total degradation surrounding it, looked like a grossly idyllicized picture postcard. Dinky white cottages with green shutters, little gardens behind freshly painted lattice fences. Trees budding, spring flowers in little tubs beneath windows. Lace curtains. Freshly scrubbed doorsteps. The odd aeroplane circling over the manor house, stables, fields and barns as if on a sightseeing flight. The thunder of cannon in the far, far distance.

The first to leave were the French POWs. Thereafter, Stanisław, the Yugoslavs Niko and Radko, and a Polish family – father, mother and daughter – who'd spent the entire war living and working on the estate, took care of us. We slept and ate with them in their quarters and the mother saw to our delousing. Every garment that had originated in the camp they burned. They washed and scrubbed us clean. The daughter, Eva, washed our hair three times in a row with paraffin oil. We went to work in clothes that they gave us. We planted seed potatoes and cut rhubarb. The housewives of Mügeln would take armfuls of rhubarb home and bottle some, make more into jam, bake cakes and pies with it and use these goodies competitively to lure the one German deserter in the town. They kept him hidden from Volkssturmführer Weiß in his Tyrolean costume and his white, knee-high socks. The latter accused them of treason and when he threatened to report them and pointed his rifle at them, one lifted up her skirts, turned her back on him and said: "You fight alone to the last man! We're not giving this man up. If you want, you can shoot me in the backside!"

No other utterance would have confirmed me more in my conviction that decisive change was afoot, with the defeat of Hitler and the gradual collapse of Nazi "morale". The women would invite us round for rose-hip tea and cakes at their prettily laid tables. China, silver cutlery, serviettes, all of that from their pre-war essentials. My eyes would roam their walls, spotting the paler squares or rectangles where portraits of the Führer had been taken down; my main concern, however, was to observe the rules of polite behaviour vis-à-vis my hostesses. That likewise brought me to terms with my doubts regarding the motivation of our generous Polish benefactors and their long sojourn in Germany. Their conversations and secret glances also led me to the view that they were perhaps creating an alibi for themselves, just in case. However, in the circumstances I thought such ideas rather graceless suspicions.

One day, as I was forking over the compost heap, the owner of the estate, who was going round checking how the spring jobs were progressing, paused in front of me. He stared at my arms with the rolled-up sleeves and I felt sure he was focussing on my concentration camp number tattooed there, which I'd quite forgotten about.

"You lied to my estate manager. You're not bombed-out Germans. You're escapees from a concentration camp!"

"So, and now you're going to tell the Gestapo?" I asked him.

He remained silent, thinking for a while before replying: "No, I won't, providing you promise to tell the Americans that I helped you and have been kind to you."

I gave him that promise and he left. But that wasn't the end of our communication: to our great surprise the estate manager had us moved into a huge furnished attic in one of the buildings on the estate and re-assigned us to working in the kitchens.

5

Some of what I experienced at Mügeln I am rediscovering, like photos in an album from which most have either fallen out or lie in disarray beneath reminders of other times and places:

It's our time off and Eva and I are strolling about the town. The walls of houses, other walls and kiosks are hung about with posters proclaiming: "*Achtung! Der Feind hört mit!* [Caution! The enemy's listening!]". I see them as a tragicomic anachronism, a backdrop to a war film. Relief and hope, but also the young spring foliage on the trees carry me off to some timeless place. Certain roofs, windows and flagpoles are decked with white tea towels, sheets and table cloths, though some citizens look upon them with disdainful smirks. They're the ones who still believe in *"der endliche Sieg* [the final victory]".

A meadow outside the town, dotted with scattered rocks and yellowy patches grazed bare by sheep. Nearby, a babbling brook. Lying in the grass are some empty food tins. A group of Polish fugitives, father, mother and two daughters, have just eaten the horsemeat they'd contained. The pretty, fair-haired girls and their young mother, all in black – but with white, freshly washed and ironed collars and cuffs. They're sitting on the grass, legs stretched out and bolt upright. They're chatting about the nightlife of pre-war Warsaw, the restaurants, cabarets and dance halls, and looking forward to going back. One of them sings a hit song about a love letter that arrived late. The father, dressed in a black, discreetly striped suit, radiates dignity, not speaking and staring into the distance. Not far away, bombs from allied air raids are falling on the towns of Riesa, Strehla, Oschatz and Döbeln.[2]

As in a clip from an old film, I can see a war invalid, limping – waving a duster, he's running across the yard after his screaming wife in her flannel nightshirt. She's rolled it up to her knees, is running fast and wailing: "*Mein Gott! Mein Gott!* What's to become of us?" And Käthe, one of the scullery maids, is standing beside me at the kitchen window, explaining: "That's Eiche. He was away from home for over a year, never wrote, came back without warning and found his wife with a new-born."

"Not the first, and certainly not the last. *Im Krieg und ohne Krieg* [In war and with no war]," the cook, Frau Metzler, calmly remarked as she took some freshly baked bread rolls out of the oven.

A week after we'd spoken, the owner of the estate came to see us, accompanied by his handsome, fair-haired, twelve-year-old son, Christof. He spoke highly of our grammatically correct German and asked if we'd mind his asking us to recount some of our experiences from the concentration camp.

"Not in the boy's hearing," said Lila.

"But it can't be that bad. Just let him listen, it can't do him any harm," our host said.

In concise and matter-of-fact terms we described the purpose and objectives of the Auschwitz camp and how these aims were arrived at. When we were done, he blurted out in indignation: "No! It's not true. It can't be true!"

"But Father! What do you mean? You know full well that it's true. Even I can remember how the Jews were chased about town, how they were beaten, and how all the Jews in Mügeln simply disappeared when you were chairman of the NSDAP," said Christof.

The owner of the estate gave his son an injured, reproachful look, said not a word to him, took his leave of us and they both went off.

Following that meeting, the boy would come to see us alone. He would sit with us, drinking rose-hip tea, telling us how they were packing up and hoping that the Americans would come, though they were afraid the Russians would get there first. He brought us a gold brooch and ring, and when we declined to accept them, he grew sad and said, "I found them on the steps. They were lying there like bits of rubbish. Grandma's so nervous that she's not paying attention, doesn't notice things are missing. She's packing now and she's got so many, while you haven't got any. Why won't you take them? Are you cross with me for all the bad things we've done to you?"

I was sorry for the lad. He was like all children, and like us, too, a victim of the war. "Of course we're not cross with you," I sought to reassure him. "You were only a baby, and you're still only a little boy. None of it's been your fault."

"Yes, but a little German boy!" said Christof.

A rumour was rife in the town; the Russians were getting closer. The owner of the estate despatched two removal vans full of furniture, pictures and Persian carpets towards the west. The housemaids and farm hands were dashing up and down the stairs inside the manor and bringing out whatever they could. The courtyard was littered with newspapers and wrapping paper and scattered wood shavings.

Mr Schulze, the wagoner, parked his hay cart and the horses in the courtyard and hollered: "*Die Russen kommen!* [The Russians are coming!]" The larger and older part of the family had already departed in cars, leaving the abandoned courtyard now reeking of synthetic fuel.

Whether to their own relief or against their will, the citizens of Mügeln surrendered one by one. Even the ageing Volkssturmführer Weiß hung one of his own white duvet covers from his attic window. It billowed out in the spring breeze like a large under-inflated balloon.

6

We saw our first soldier in Red Army uniform when he strode into our room.

"I've been told there's a couple of girls living here," he said in Russian.

"What you're looking for you won't find here," Lila said in the same language to the tall, burly man with rosy cheeks and a good-natured expression on his face, and with thick, pale-brown whiskers beneath his short, broad nose.

"Now then, stay calm, my little darlings. Nothing to be afraid of! You don't have to do anything you don't want to, so don't get excited and just look what I've got here for you," he said as he removed a big red apple from his pocket as if it were the most precious thing in the world. Before I even had time to ask him where he'd got it from, he cut it in half with his penknife and handed one half to each of us. "So, what do you think of that, then?" We couldn't help laughing and offered him a chair, some tea and the biscuits the cook had given us. In answer to his questions as to who we were, where we were from and how come we spoke Russian, we explained that we were from Slovakia and had learned Russian in a concentration camp. As tit for tat he told us he was Ukrainian and how surprised he'd been to see in Germany, but also in Poland, little towns and villages with neat little houses and gardens and tidy back yards where people seemed to be living a better, nicer life than anything he'd seen at home before the war. Everything was different from what Soviet propaganda had alleged about the wretched, exploited West. He was having second thoughts about going home afterwards. Before he left, we had to swear not to tell on him, because that could cost him his life. One week later, he arrived on a motorbike and sidecar to pick us up and take us into Torgau, where we witnessed the meeting between the Allies and Soviets on a bridge over the Elbe.[3] This promising, historic event lit all the lights in our hope-filled, but still faltering images of what the future held.

Two more Soviet soldiers showed up on horseback. Both had coarse features, the face of one of them riddled with pockmarks. They kept shouting all over the place, using the most primitive Russian swearwords. The kitchen maids fled through the back door and hid. The only German woman who stayed in the kitchen was the estate accountant, a very pious spinster from Prussia. She believed firmly in Almighty God and His protection. Lila, she and I were watching the yelling pair of Soviet horsemen through the window when suddenly young Christof appeared. He approached the soldiers, began stroking the horses and offered his hand to the man with the pockmarks.

"Durak! [Idiot!] Fuck off, you Teuton sonofabitch!" he swore and gave Christof such a kick with his booted foot that the lad went flying and landed face-down.

The lady accountant turned away from the kitchen window and begged us to go out and talk to the soldiers.

"*Eto tolko malchik!* [He's only a little boy]! Shame on you for kicking him like that!"

A flurry of oaths came down upon my head: "Shut your trap, you German whore!"

"We're not German, we're from Czechoslovakia," said Lila.

"*Vriosh*, you're lying, bitch! And how come you speak German, you Belarussian pig?"

I rolled up my sleeve and showed him the number on my forearm. "That's where I learned Russian!"

The other soldier whispered something to the pockmarked one, who ordered us to get lost. I refused! I went over to Christof, who was still on the ground, picked him up and took him back into the kitchen. I washed his scratched and bloodied hands and face and told him to go out by the back door and hide in the manor house. In him I saw the wounded personification of a better future Germany, while also seeking some justification for the lack of understanding and coarseness of the Russian soldiers in the suffering brought about by the inhumanly cruel six years of the war. Lila and I waited in the garden shed at the far end of the large garden until the soldiers left.

When we went back into the kitchen, we found it empty. Equally deserted was the room behind the kitchen, where the two kitchen maids slept, but the furniture and walls were streaked with blood. The accountant lady never resurfaced, and when the kitchen maids came back and carried on with their work as if nothing had happened, they said the Russians had raped her, killed her and dragged her corpse off somewhere. I remember thinking as much, but at the same time was still able to perceive this indefensible, and so frequently repeated, act as one of the specific characteristics and consequences of war.

7

Marshal Zhukov's motorized units took us with them. I rode on a motorbike with a Russian soldier, Dimitriy. Not even the fact that I was sitting on top of a lumpy pile of spoils of war could dampen my spirits at the realization that the war was over and I was on my way home. I asked Dimitriy who those soldiers were who'd arrived first, and just the two of them, on horses, and who had acted with such utter inhumanity.

"They must have been a couple of those jailbirds, released from prison for the duration of the war and assigned to the army," Dimitriy replied.[4]

The troops looked after us. They gave us food. They found us some accommodation and generally saw to it that nothing happened to us.

We travelled through bomb-ravaged Germany. I saw in it a shredded, pulverized reflection of Nazism. Piles of stones and bricks. Weeds growing among the ruins. Scattered remains of human dwellings littering the landscape. Photos of First World War soldiers in a pile of rubbish. Wedding photos in smashed frames. Faces of happy, smiling families on photographic paper. Photos of sportsmen. Of schoolchildren and their teachers. Of old men and women, probably long dead, atop a heap of rubbish. Drawers full of SS men in heroic poses. A lone kitchen chair. A table with only three legs. A cooker. Pots. Helmets and cherry orchards in bloom, untouched by war. And somewhere, in a building close to collapse, someone playing a desperately doleful hit about parting.

Dimitriy was an amiable, kindly man. He would give me the best bits of any food, because he thought I was too thin.

"You're as thin as a lath. If you put on a bit of weight, you'd be a lovely lass!" he used to say. Lila rode on a motorbike with a curly-headed, bearded, Georgian captain, who had a ready laugh that exposed his snow-white teeth. Dimitriy hated "those damn' diabolical Germans". They had cut off his wife's nipples so that she couldn't breast-feed their son and they'd killed his two-year-old daughter. "Most of all I'd like to strangle all those sons of bitches with my own hands!" he would snap.

One afternoon, our two motorbikes veered out of the convoy, braked and halted. The men ordered us to alight and wait under the trees by the roadside while they discussed something. When they were done, Dimitriy came over to us and announced that in return for their liberating us we were duty bound to show our gratitude.

"After six years of indescribable horrors, we'd quite like it if you were to gratify us, as women."

"Shame on you! We've also been through indescribable horrors and deserve to be allowed to show our gratitude in such ways as we ourselves decide!" said Lila.

The soldiers looked at each other, mounted their bikes, started the engines and disappeared round the next bend. Shaken and surprised, we were left standing in the road swathed in swirling clouds of dust and without a clue as to where in Germany we were. We sat down under a tree, not knowing what to do next. Apart from two sets of dusty clothes we had nothing. I don't know how long we'd been sitting there beneath the tree with our heads bowed and feeling abandoned and betrayed, when our silence was suddenly disturbed by the sound of engines. The two motorbikes were coming back. The men braked, stopped and nodded without a word for us to get back on the pillions, which looked like camels' humps. We got on and went on our way.

For a long time Dimitriy said nothing. "But it still irks me, you know. You surely can't still be a virgin," were his opening words.

"And what if I weren't, but as it happens I am!"
"Swear on your life that your hymen's still intact!"
I swore.
"In that case I'll just have to hang on!"

The unit set up camp by a small wood on the bank of the river Elster. The wood and the village nearby bore signs of a recent air raid. Broken and mangled trunks and branches. Bombed-out houses. Just the odd living being creeping around stealthily. Most of the survivors had moved out westwards. Next to a solitary white wall with some of its red brickwork laid bare stood a black grand piano, all covered in dust. One soldier, Yevgeniy, played some Bach suites on it. He had grey, almost silvery eyes, a narrow face and a dimple on his chin. The group of officers always kept close to him. Something about their behaviour made me wonder. I wasn't sure if they admired him, or were keeping a close watch on him.

I asked Dimitriy who and what Yevgeniy was.

He shrugged. "A Soviet soldier!"

Sasha, a young university student from Leningrad, lit a bonfire. As he poked about to get it to burn properly his sleeve slid up to reveal a forearm covered in watches. His eyes met mine and he said, "That's just small compensation for all the stuff the Germans stole from us!"

"Tell me, Sasha, is Yevgeniy a great musician?"

"As you can tell, he knows how to play the piano."

"All right, but they do all treat him differently from the rest. All he himself does is smile and play and play away... What is it about him?"

"Only a fool tells everything he knows," said Sasha.

"Is he under guard or protection?"

"Speech is silver, silence is golden!"

"Cut the proverbs and tell me the truth!"

"Okay, I will, but then keep it to yourself, for your own sake as well! Yevgeniy's political. He's been in prison and a labour camp. I reckon his friends are guarding him from the *politruk*. Yevgeniy's a great artist."

"Will he have to go back to prison after the war?"

"The war's not over yet," said Sasha and, perhaps in order to gloss over his slip of the tongue, he began prodding away at the smouldering embers with a thick stick. As we sat by the dying fire, Sasha never stopped checking the watches on his forearm.

"Give me one!" I said on impulse, then immediately regretted it.

"I can't. I've got relatives all over Russia, and, as you know, my native land spreads far and wide..." Sasha replied and I felt his rebuff like a well-deserved slap in the face.

The following day we continued our journey. It drizzled all day long and puddles began to form in the depressions and potholes along the damaged road. After dusk, the convoy stopped in the little town of Mulda, and three soldiers, one of them Dimitriy, set off to find somewhere for us to spend the night. They chose a small house with a garden and yard. Its sole inhabitants proved to be a man and a woman. Both old.

Dimitriy pointed to us and said, "*Dyevushky tu schlafen!* [Girls to sleep here]."

The old woman craned her neck, stuck out her chin and said in a tone that carried a revealing trace of the vainglory of recent days: "*Nichevo tu schlafen, nur zwei Betten* [No sleeping here, only two beds] and they're where we sleep!"

"I'll give you *nichevo*!" one of the soldiers barked back at the old German woman while the other two set about opening drawers and throwing stuff on the floor: badges with swastikas, large and small portraits of Hitler in silver frames, and a photo of a young man in an SS uniform.

"You damn' Nazi prick. You'll be sleeping outside! And you,

you old hag, here on the floor!" said one of the soldiers, then he pushed the old man out through the door and down the three steps. Outside, the man floundered into a puddle with a plaintive yelp.

"But the war's over," I told the soldier as he began kicking the old German. "Leave him alone! Haven't we all had enough of violence? I won't be sleeping in his bed!"

"Oh, yes, you will! And keep your trap shut or I'll have you done for sympathizing with the enemy."

We slept in freshly made beds. They were Nazis after all, I told myself. And the soldiers, just like us, had had their fill of the ruthlessness and virulent barbarity of Nazi violence. But did that entitle us to act likewise?

The motorized unit set up its headquarters in a large villa somewhere on the German side of the Sudeten Mountains. In the evening, they invited us to a victory celebration and offered us borshch, from which the tipsy chef first had to retrieve his revolver with a wooden spoon and some wailing. The point being that forgetting or losing one's gun, even if only in a soup, could carry the death penalty. However, they were all in a good mood and poked fun at him for overdoing the salt in the borshch with his tears, they filled water glasses with vodka for us and put huge chunks of fatty pork on our plates.

"*Kushaitye, dyevushky, kushaitye* [Eat, girls, eat], the grease will line your intestines and protect you from the effects of the alcohol!" the commandant tried to persuade us after we refused to eat or drink what they were offering us. "Surely you're not going refuse to toast the victory of the Red Army!"

Willy-nilly we had to drink a toast, and not just the once, but again to the Soviet motherland and to the great and glorious, all-victorious Comrade Stalin.

We were sitting outside at a table set in the long grass of the unmowed lawn, which was overgrown with ox-eye daisies. The soldiers picked whole armfuls of them and showered us with them.

Someone switched on the radio.

"*Govorit Praga! Volá Praha!* [Prague calling! Prague is calling for help!]" This was the urgent message of a man's voice, delivered in Russian and Czech. And I felt as if the last remnants of some hidden ice had started to melt in the cracks and crevices of my being.

"There's an uprising in Prague. We leave early tomorrow morning! You must go and get some sleep!" the commandant told us, and he ordered the least drunk of his men to stand guard outside our bedroom. I woke in the middle of the night with excruciating stomach cramps. I felt so ill that I was certain I was going to die. Everything was spinning. Ceiling, walls, the whole world. I crawled to the toilet on all fours. In the morning I was as white as a sheet and as feeble as a fly. I glanced at Lila. She had coped with Russian hospitality much better than I.

On the way across the mountains we slipped more than once off the pillions, which were overburdened with the spoils of war. One of the girls being transported with us fell off her pillion and broke a leg. "Good thing it's only a leg!" said my new driver, Grigoriy. Lila's guardian angel, and mine too, saw to it that we reached the Prague suburb of Břevnov on 9 May 1945. The citizenry was lining the road. They were holding huge armfuls of flowers, shrieking *Hurrah!* at the top of their voices, crying, throwing their arms round us and they even welcomed us two, unwarrantedly, as liberators. The soldiers set us down in a small park. They had to be on their way, but before they left us, they passed a cap round and then gave us all the money that had been collected. Additionally, they gave us a large suitcase, which we were to open only after they'd left.

8

Two sisters, both of them grammar school teachers, invited us to stay and placed an entire villa at our disposal. After one very long break we could now participate in the routine of everyday civilian life with all the rules of propriety that govern it. The sisters washed and ironed our not entirely clean blouses for us and let us have some of their own as well.

Everything around us still seemed unreal. Buildings, houses, churches, parks untouched by devastating air raids, and everywhere the fresh green of manicured grass. Laughing, carefree girls, dressed for summer, walking dogs in a park. The gently flickering shadows of leaves on sun-warmed footpaths. Even knowing we were in Prague seemed somehow unreal, Prague, the legendary, magical city of Gustav Meyrink, Jan Neruda, Jaroslav Hašek, Franz Kafka, Karel Čapek, Egon Erwin Kisch and many other writers and poets. Equally unreal was seeing, with our own eyes, Prague Castle, the chateaux, cathedrals, gardens, underpasses, narrow streets, flights of steps, the bridges over the Vltava, the lindens and poplars in springtime, and hearkening to the voice of the city, not yet disturbed by traffic.

These first impressions, powerful as they were, were affected by fatigue. They unfolded as on a strip of film. In the glass of one shop window with barely anything behind it, I saw a reflection of myself: the thin, careworn face, the scarf on my head, there to cover my messy hair, still not fully restored after my bout of typhus, my legs housed in shapeless, black, men's trousers and hobnailed Russian top boots and the anorak, which I'd found in the suitcase left us by those Russian soldiers, draped over my nicely washed blouse.

"You look a real sight," I told myself, in part resigned, in part dismayed.

Besides two anoraks, the suitcase had contained two pairs of pink pyjamas, two sets of lingerie, a huge roll of olive-green cotton gabardine, and a flashy red umbrella. I can't think why I imagined the suitcase had some magical properties that we had yet to discover. Like flying us home in the manner of a magic carpet.

After the first two of our ritual lunches, each involving three courses, we had let the last drops of soup drip from our spoons, licked them, and laid them on the table cloth next to our plates. Having noted the puzzled look on our hosts' faces, we glanced, equally puzzled, at each other and at what we'd just done. We apologized, then explained that in the concentration camp a spoon was the only item of cutlery we had and licking it like that was the only way to keep it clean.

The perfumed soap on the wash basin was far too tempting: we took it and automatically put it in our suitcase. When it dawned that we were actually committing theft, we put it back. We promised to take good care that no such action would ever be repeated.

During one of our daily walks around Prague, we got into conversation with a fireman from the fire brigade attached to the Wilson railway station. He offered us accommodation at the fire station. "From here you'll be much closer to any trains leaving for Slovakia. They're still pretty infrequent and irregular, but you might just catch one!" he said.

We spent over a week with the hospitable, attentive firemen. The wife of one of them baked us some buns and got us some thread, needles, a thimble and some scissors. I immediately cut a piece from the gabardine roll and made myself a skirt.

On Wenceslas Square we bumped into an officer from the motorized convoy that had brought us to Prague. He was with a group of resistance fighters dressed in odd bits of uniforms picked up here and there. Two of them took us to Red House, a large commandeered building from which various "clean-up" actions were being organized. The lads had got hold of the car of some "collaborator", which rarely got used because of the petrol shortage and whose actual function was to act as a visible symbol of meritorious engagement in the Prague Uprising. This was a time of genuine, and bogus, freedom-fighters, of disintegration and a start on rebuilding, a time of doers and gold-diggers, volunteers and adventurers, anarchy, rage, revenge and joy, but above all a time of hope.

For a daily ration of hot food we would take a long walk to the military hospital in Střešovice. On one of these treks we were accosted by four Russian girls, friends from Rajsko. Like us, they'd survived the death march, made it to Prague and, hoping to get back home as fast as possible, they'd joined the motorized army group of General Vlasov, who had helped with the liberation of Prague.

In 1943, Andrei Vlasov, a Soviet officer, had organized a million-strong army of Russians who had fought alongside the Germans, but had never been involved in the murder and torture of civilians. In the Soviet Union the Vlasovites were condemned to death for treason.

The olive-coloured gabardine served us as a means of payment. We swapped pieces for lifts in cars that were running short of fuel, we used it to pay for places aboard army trucks or on branch lines whose rails hadn't been sabotaged. In exchange for parts of it we got bacon, bread or fruit. We measured out lengths using the red umbrella, cut them with the scissors from the fire station and thought the whiles of Jánošík,[5] who measured fabric by the distance between oak trees. We held on to the money from the Red Army soldier's cap because we had no idea what lay ahead. By a roundabout route we eventually reached Brno.

Waiting rooms were bursting at the seams with travellers, fugitives, workers returning from their forced labours, and black-marketeers. Russian soldiers came and went in groups large and small. People were afraid of them. Rumour had it that they'd raped women and girls in Brno, stolen anything they could lay their hands on and that the most frequent Russian words were *Davay! Davay!* [roughly: "Come on, hand it over!"]. And that they would happily make do with shoe polish in place of alcohol! I felt so sad, musing on how war turns people into beasts, and yet how without these men risking their lives, and without millions of human sacrifices, we would not now be sitting on a bench in a Brno station, heading for home.

It began to get dark. We sat and waited and, at odd moments, like most of those travelling, snoozed. The ground was covered with paper and other litter. The station's loudspeakers announced that it was not yet known when and if a train would be arriving, but that they would keep us travellers updated.

"I can't wait," Lila announced as she picked up the suitcase. "I'll see if I can find some transport for us in the city."

She was so long coming back that I began to fear for her safety. Time passed, over an hour and a half, and still there was no sign of Lila. She eventually came back, the suitcase covered in mud, breathless and covered in scratches.

"They tried to take it off me! They chased after me and I had to crawl on all fours and drag it through a thorny hedge into someone's garden and then across the fields. I've no idea how I found my way back here!" Lila explained as she struggled to fit in between me and a fat woman who was fast asleep in her rucked-up clothes. "They're trying to rob me! Trying to rob me!" the latter cried agitatedly in her sleep, without waking up.

For dinner we had some bread and black pudding, exchanged for a length of gabardine, then we fell asleep, propped one against the other. We were woken by the voice on the public address system announcing that at six a.m. a train would be leaving in an easterly direction. Sleep-deprived and quite worn out, we did secure places in the overcrowded train, which took us as far as Žilina.

Žilina was not a town that we knew. We left the station and began roaming the streets on the off-chance of meeting someone we knew. Ahead of us were walking two men, no better than sacks of bones. Their shabby, blue-grey, concentration camp uniforms looked as if they'd been hung up on sticks. They were walking slowly and hesitantly, alienated from the world and from their own selves, as if ashamed of what had happened to them. Coming along the pavement towards them were two raffish characters in bright summer suits and two-tone shoes.

"Look at that pair o' scarecrows!" one of them shouted loud enough for all the passers-by to hear them. "We sent so many of 'em off and somehow even more have come back!"

This manifestation of human stupidity and savagery jolted me out of the semi-hypnotic state that had been helping me cope with all the rapid, cataclysmic changes, to move forward, breathe and live, and now it had also laid bare a bit of the shredded, unhealed world into which we were making our way back.

On one of the many unfamiliar streets we almost crashed into a doctor from Mikuláš. This was my first hello from the town that I'd been forced to flee back in the spring of 1942 and to which I was now returning as a free person in early June 1945. I asked the doctor if he knew anything about our parents and siblings. After some hesitation he replied: "Sorry, I don't know anything about them. I haven't been back for such a long time."

His hesitation and the fact that he avoided our eyes as he replied were somewhat disturbing, but I decided to believe him.

We travelled on from Žilina in an army truck that was heading eastward via Mikuláš. The atmosphere aboard was dingy and the silence moody. The soldiers were extremely tired and disinclined to talk. When they set us down by the bridge over the Váh, it was already evening. Before they set off again, one of the soldiers stepped down onto the pavement and gave us his torch as a farewell gift.

9

The once rather splendid iron bridge over the Váh had been replaced by a modest wooden one. Above the river the moon was bright and mirrored on the surface of the narrow side stream between Palúdzka and the road to Ondrašová. Ahead of us, among the masses of broken masonry, we could make out the petrol station and a blossom-laden tree.

We turned left down the street that led past the abattoir to the right and the Catholic cemetery to the left and followed it all the way through Nižný Hušták down to the square. Water lapped and splashed against the banks of the stream. It stank of paraffin oil. Somewhere in the darkness a chain clinked. There were lights on in only very few of the windows. Some were boarded up. The hobnails in the soles of my Russian top boots struck against stones and the sharp, penetrating sounds they made echoed round the houses. We walked along past them, recognizing them, but the darkness held them in its embrace and wouldn't let us go near.

We'd got our parents' last address and a description of it from the doctor in Žilina. It had a spreading tree in the yard. The front door opened at a single touch. I pressed the light switch. It wasn't working. The moonlight struggled in through the dusty window panes and landed on an old divan. That was the sole piece of furniture left. In one of the two rooms of the flat into which our family had been moved after the passing of the racial legislation, there were books and papers scattered all over the floor. In one corner of the other room lay, lit faintly by the moonlight, my father's old trousers and a mangy teddy bear, my youngest sister Gretka's favourite plaything. In one trouser pocket a bunch of keys clinked on being disturbed. We sat down on the divan, deposited the suitcase on the floor, fell silent, began waiting for daybreak, and at some time in the small hours fell asleep.

"They're dead! They're dead! They shot them! They shot all four! Oh, my poor dear orphans!"

The day had dawned. The sun was up. In the open door stood a woman we didn't know. She was wringing her hands, weeping, wailing and screaming: "Oh, dear God! They're dead! They're dead!"

"Stop! Stop it! Go!" I tried to drive her away.

Weeping audibly, the woman ran out through the gate into the street. There she paused and looked round with an uncomprehending, tormented expression on her tearful face. Only later was I to learn that the people shot and buried in a mass grave somewhere near Ružomberok also included her husband.

The following day, Lila left for Bratislava. She wished to avoid any difficult, painful talk about our incomprehensible, irreplaceable loss and to escape from a place filled with echoes of what once had been and no longer was. For many long years we never spoke of what became of our family.

The main square was as I remembered it. There seemed to be a few more trees as well as more benches and blackthorn bushes opposite the County Hall. The Klimeš bookshop, the drugstore, the pharmacy – as before the war. And all the buildings that ran round the square looked the same, though the walls of some of them bore signs of having been shot at. Vyšný and Nižný [Upper and Lower] Hušták had successfully resisted the impact of time and now guarded the reminders of my childhood.

At the Repatriation Office, which had been set up at the north end of Nižný Hušták in a flat where we had once lived, I received a photo ID book and became once again a fully-fledged citizen of the Czechoslovak Republic. In her kitchen, a lady known simply as Alica created some astonishingly inventive, potato-based meals for anyone passing through Mikuláš as they made their way home, but also for any returnees from prisons, concentration camps and partisan groups who had found no surviving relatives. We sat side by side round her table, together enjoying her potato pancakes from a common pool, but despite this togetherness, we all still felt a deep-seated inner isolation.

Alica and her son had survived the war in the mountains. With her had survived her fur coat, the only coat she'd ever owned, because her husband was a gambler, all of whose money had got left behind the closed curtains of the Hotel Europa. She bore her lot with good humour, loved a laugh and did her level best to create a homely atmosphere around us, make us one and keep everyone's spirits up. She had a fine sense of fun and readily made fun of herself as well.

"You've no idea how lucky I've been. If I hadn't had my fur coat, I would have frozen to death in the mountains. Everything has its uses, even an ancient, raggedy, muskrat coat, which no one could be remotely interested in stealing." That there was some deep grief lurking beneath her merriment was known to all of us. The latest history of her extended family was also full of the ruins that follow incendiary attacks.

I felt very sad in our empty, sacked, grim flat with no lights, no furniture and not a single item of kitchenware. I also felt sorry for the people who'd made off with the modest remains of my parents' property in the hope that we wouldn't come back.

In those early days after my return I would sit around beside the river. One late afternoon, as I was sitting beneath the willows and my despondency was merging with the tranquilizing splash of the rippling water, I heard a voice coming from behind me: "Is that you, Iboja?"

I turned and saw it was Kurt, the younger brother of one of the boys in my class at school. We used to call him Krtko [Mole].

"Why are you sitting here alone like this?"

"I can't bear sitting around in an empty flat."

"If you want, you can come and live with me. My sister and

brother-in-law have gone to America. I've got the whole house to myself. Come, I'll take you to our house."

I was so pleased and went off with him. He made us some supper and over it told me how he'd joined the partisans, naming several of his comrades who'd fallen fighting the Germans and also mentioning the death of Dr Goldberg, who used to donate half his wages to the Communist Party. "If ever there was an irony of fate, then his death is it: he was killed by Russians for his leather overcoat."

The nice feeling that came with being able to lay my head on a fluffy pillow and cover myself with a soft, smooth, warm duvet helped me fall asleep. Suddenly I woke, frightened by a hand on my shoulder. With my eyes tight shut I fought tooth and nail.

"Calm down! Don't be scared, it's only me, Krtko."

"What's happened? Why did you wake me?"

"I just fancied a bit of a cuddle," he said and sat down on the bed.

"What's that supposed to mean?"

"Stop pretending! You used to switch boys like socks and you must have slept with at least a dozen of them!"

My dress was down by my feet. I dragged it towards me under the duvet and pulled it on. The whole time, Krtko was sitting on the bed and my anger just soared and soared. I crawled out from under the duvet, stood up and gave him a mighty slap across the face.

"Genuine hospitality demands no service in return!" I said, pushing him firmly off the bed.

"Do you know what people are saying about you and Lila?" he asked, still sitting on the floor behind my back. "They say the only reason you're still alive is because you had sex with SS men!"

On my way across the square, in the silence of the night, to the street leading towards the final dwelling place of my parents and siblings in Nižný Hušták, I kept thinking that Krtko's malicious words were probably born of his injured pride. But if it really was true that the townspeople vilified us in those terms, I would only forgive those of them whose children had been murdered. That's the worst thing that can befall parents. If by way of consolation they sought some explanation for their own irredeemable loss and reasons why we were still alive, I had to explain that, time and time again, we had owed our survival to pure happenstance.

10

My old classmates received me with a bewildered and seemingly apologetic cordiality. There was, however, something about me that bothered them. In my own life, the war had left footprints of unforgettable crimes and so contributed to my greater maturity and maybe to a degree of aloofness. Like them, I was now older, but while they had continued as they were, studying, working, some even starting a family, I, those five years back, had had to break the continuity of the path I'd intended to take. My impression was that either they were imputing to me their own ideas of my attitude to them, or that they had no such ideas at all, or that some simply had an uneasy conscience, given their assertion that they had known nothing. I didn't ask them what that NOTHING was, because I felt – no idea why – sorry for them.

Apart from the damage to buildings and the Aryanization of the shops, the other visible changes to the town were the unfamiliar occupants of familiar houses and flats and the scattered groups of Red Army soldiers. I felt a need to revisit the streets – main streets and back streets – of Mikuláš. I walked up the long Hodža Street, past the meadow where travelling circuses used to pitch up, past the grammar school and onward to the railway station. My mind was on the people who'd lived here during my childhood and teens: the blacksmith whose daughter was insane and who had, to the left of his yard, in the garden reserved for his tenants, some highly perfumed pinky-purple lilacs and among them a swing; the girl in my class who lived in that villa, and that other one from the dressmaker's; the sad girl whose surname was Veselá ["merry"]. I recalled the road I used not to like going down – but only when I got a bad mark for something, so then I used to make a long detour to Vyšný Hušták, round by the council houses at the top end next to the revenue office.

In one of the little streets, close by the Rohonci Gardens,[6] there used to be two crooked little whitewashed cottages with tiny windows that belonged to an old lady. In front of one of them, behind the low, gappy fence, was an ageing, branching elder tree. The cottages had a special meaning for me, a mixture of admiration for their aesthetic quaintness, fellow feeling, and youthful fantasy. When I was very small, they reminded me of folk tales about poor people who eventually, by their own merit and the workings of magic, became rich.

It was near these cottages that, one day in late June, I bumped into Milan. He was walking hand in hand with a young blonde. When he saw me, he looked taken aback and stopped in his tracks. After a brief silent pause he said hello and introduced the girl as his fiancée.

"She's studying medicine. We're colleagues at the faculty and this year we'll both come out fully qualified. You were always a great lass. I hope you survived the war okay!" he said before saying goodbye and walking off with his blonde fiancée.

I followed them with my gaze feeling slightly sorry for myself. Milan suddenly stopped, turned and looked back at me as if to check that I really was me. That put me in mind of that which was never going to be, and that which had been both so close and so far away.

I would run across people who pretended not to see me because I'd been a witness to their enthusiastic execution of the laws and provisions of the fascist Slovak State. Others steered clear of me because they were wearing clothes that had belonged to Jewish friends of mine. Among those, there were even some who'd ransacked our flat and were afraid I might lay claim to the articles stolen. They couldn't have known I wouldn't be doing that, because I would feel such shame on their behalf. I didn't want anything.

From UNRRA, whose local arm was ruled strictly and justly by the kindly, crippled Julko, I received some outerwear and underwear. The stacks of donated clothing didn't include shoes. So I had to go on wearing those Russian hobnailed boots. I had to renew all my personal documents both at County Hall and with the chairman of the tiny, grossly reduced Jewish community, the building contractor Mr Fišer, who'd lost two daughters in a concentration camp. The old-new proprietor of the Hotel Kriváň offered me accommodation in a vacant room at the hotel, to which I moved my ancient divan. The factory owner Mr Haas took me on as his foreign-language correspondent. From him I learned that my sister Dalma was alive and that during the last months of the war, after she returned from the mountains, she had lived at the Lipins' in Palúdzka, where the German *Ortskommando* was. Although the whole village knew who Dalma was and had witnessed her helping to serve the guests at the Lipins' pub, no one had informed on her.

That was kind and brave on the part of the folk in Palúdzka. "But get this, not even the most loyal members of the Guard gave her away when she acted as interpreter at the German military headquarters. Most likely because they already knew that the Germans and they themselves were a lost cause. Dalma left Mikuláš for Bratislava to study drama," Mr Haas told me.

My job at the factory was to be short-lived. I wanted to earn just enough to go to Bratislava, find my two sisters there and go on with Lila to study in Prague.

II

Summertime. Tourists were flocking to the town. They stayed in the hotels or in private flats and went on excursions to the Tatra Mountains. Army officers, new arrivals and locals would all go out promenading. One of the few who'd survived the partisan fighting and was a fringe member of our pre-war circle, was Michal. He was a labour leader in Liptovský Hrádok. He lived with his young wife Rita and their newborn son at his mother's; she had lost her husband and two daughters and went about the house like a shadow. Conversations with Michal were like being read a lecture. He saw himself as a class-conscious Marxist and his discourse was larded with such expressions as "profit", "surplus value", "relationship to the means of production", "class antagonism", "quantity and quality" and above all, "revolutionary change and the dictatorship of the proletariat". The conclusions he drew struck me as distorted, with little in common with my own beliefs at the time, although many of the expressions in his rhetoric also had a place in my own.

"Even the body of a proletarian is a means of production and so has to be employed for their own benefit. Which is why I tell women workers that they can, without scruples, sell their bodies. I've said as much to Rita, but she won't listen." On odd visits, when I found Rita alone, she was invariably in tears.

I found our GP, Dr Hoffmann (who had known all our family and had cured us of all our childhood, and later, ailments) in a damp, dark cellar. They'd put him there because he was of German extraction and because his daughter had married a German. Dr Hoffmann, a kind-hearted and humane individual, treated the poor and the well-to-do with equal responsibility and refused to accept payment from those he knew had little money. I had sought him out with confidence and was horrified at the gloom in which he had to hold surgery and at how he was beginning to resemble his unhealthy, fusty dwelling. He cured me of all the ills that I'd brought with me from the concentration camps and I was terribly sad at being unable to help him or recompense him for what he had meant in the life of our family. He wasn't alone. There were many who were similarly stricken by the mood that prevailed in the post-war period.

Mikuláš struck me as being covered in pollen and open to change from every quarter. Dignitaries were replaced, as were the owners of houses and flats, the malevolent were replaced by the envious, the defeated by the victorious, adherents of the regime by their critics – often one and the same. All of us were, directly or indirectly, involved in the fate of our town. Fascists and their opponents. Those who had acted honourably and those who were exploiting the sins of their fellow-citizens to their own advantage. At the time, all this was of the nature of fleeting, impressionistic images which, however, went deeper than I had imagined and later joined up to give me a more sequential and integrated image of the realities of the day.

12

I don't know how it came about that a group of mostly Vrbica lads appointed themselves as my protectors. They followed me around, watched over me and adopted me as some kind of living mascot. This was all a sort of romantic fantasizing, game-playing and, amid the general post-war uncertainty, a searching for some kind of lynchpin. I caught them spying on me when I had an unannounced visit from a cousin of mine. I surprised them behind the door of my hotel room as they took turns at the keyhole. These young men had been chosen by those in charge of running the town to carry out various public duties. Some had been partisans or at least claimed to have been. They unmasked black-marketeers, carried out house searches and marched any culprits to the police station. Any administrative assistance had to cease when it transpired that their "commander" had been member of the Hlinka Guard [7] and a German agent whom the Germans had parachuted behind the partisan lines and that he had accepted bribes during house searches. My group of protectors duly dissolved itself, though most of them remained my friends.

Those were strange times, filled with sunlight, hope and the sweet scent of acacias, grieving and lazy summer days that passed by without any organized activities. They left me with a feeling that I'd landed on Earth from some other planet, that I'd been sent down to Earth to keep watch and store a close record in my memory of every tremor and every undertone so as to be able at some future date to talk about that time, that summer and the early days of an autumn when the grass that had stalled began to grow from the fresh past.

I would help the humpbacked Emília in the hotel kitchen. She would speak with embittered bewilderment over her beautiful sister's death in the gas chamber while she, an ugly hunchback, had survived every murderous snare of the *Endlösung*. "If death makes choices, then the choices it makes are bad!" she used to say. Meanwhile she would bash lids and ladles against her pans and generally make a lot more noise than was necessary. She worked fast and professionally, a practical person endowed with a generous measure of common sense.

Together we made raspberry ice cream for the hotel guests. My curiosity made me study the latter through the glazed section of the partition that separated the kitchen from the dining room. They were exotic evidence of the return to normality. As we worked, Emília told me how my parents and my two youngest siblings had left for the mountains when the Germans occupied Mikuláš, and that they had hidden the property that they had left, including our bicycles, with some friends in Závažná Poruba,[8] who'd built a special wall to hide it behind. When I went to Poruba to ask those friends for my bike, they wrung their hands and said with either genuine or feigned regret: "Omigod, sweetie! We didn't get to save not one whit of anything! We just couldn't. First it was the Germans, then the Russians and they found everything and made off with it all!" I barely cared whether that was true or not. I was chiefly saddened by the loss of my bike. But Mr Haas lent me his daughter's bicycle. She'd spent the war in England and wasn't back yet.

I went to Vrbica on foot. It was a piece of the past, preserved without a single flaw. The stream, the shadows of leaves on the surface, ducks, geese, the unmade footpath, houses with gardens, the meadows next to the Váh, the familiar fishy smell, voices, fragrances, the bell tower, the mill, everything that had been captured in an internalized image whose protective mantle began to disintegrate at this encounter with the genuine article, and whose contents began to merge with my reviving memory...

I used to cycle up Sirotínska Street past the Protestant orphanage and back down again. In times past, the orphanage had frightened me, because the mere thought that I might become an orphan was the most terrible thing that I could, as a child, imagine. Having now heard from Emília that the lives of some forty Jewish children had been saved at the orphanage, I had a rather less bleak view of the place. I carried on along the Okoličné road to Poruba and Svätý Ján, across the bridge to Okoličné and on as far as Liptovský Hrádok. For days on end I cycled through the villages. I took the Demänovská road, which smelled of pine needles. Through Palúdzka I charged on to Andice, Benice and Paludza and back to Ondrašová, along past hedges of hazel, gardens, inns, fields, hills, along forest paths and tracks gouged out by the wheels of heavy hay carts, along main roads past fields with women digging up potatoes. Pretty wooden cottages, built by the capable hands of their inhabitants, and the sweet smell of hay as in times past. The only real difference was my actual cycling: it was like having a race against my own self. That helped me overcome my sudden eruptions of sorrow. I was known in the town as "the loony cyclist". But to me my wild cycling, my almost ground-touching manoeuvres to avoid other traffic, gave me a reassuring sense of remaining in one piece while also merging with the landscape.

13

I replaced my Russian top boots with some made-to-measure leather shoes. The leather was given me by some friends of my father's, and it sufficed to make some boots as well, and a very elegant, smooth, elongated, brown handbag. I still have it as a memento of those post-war days, of the generosity of my fellow-citizens and of the dramatic fates of individual people, victims of the labyrinthine tangle of the urge for self-preservation, happenstance and emotional shocks. The handbag was made for me by a man whose young wife had survived the concentration camp, gone to join some rich relations in America and come back to Mikuláš to collect her husband and take him to New York.

"Why isn't he glad I've come back? Why is he so miserable? He lies next to me, won't touch me and he stares into the distance looking as afflicted as if he were attending my funeral." She was asking herself that as much as me.

I didn't want to tell her that I knew the cause of her husband's wretchedness. He was conscience-stricken and troubled by his awareness that the truth would be wounding to a dear one who'd been through the horrors of the concentration camp. He was a Jew, as was she, and it was by pure chance that he'd escaped being transported along with the rest of his family. Throughout the war he'd been kept in hiding by a young, beautiful Vrbica woman, and what had begun as human kindness burgeoned into a love that neither compassion, nor the promise of great wealth could overcome. He and his wife divorced and she went back to America. It may sound like a sentimental romance, the worst kind of kitsch, but it wasn't. It was a slice of life that was equally hard for all concerned, because they'd all been snared in a mesh of quirks of fate, one of which is – praise be! – a happy ending.

If ever I happen to take out that still lovely handbag from under the pile of others and open it, I seem to be seeing, on its thin, green, leather lining, three faces. Other faces, filled alternately with hope and disillusion, faces tormented, resigned and marked by waiting in vain, surface before me against a background of rather dusty summer days and remind me of the words of a poem:

> *Životy skladá z kúskov do súvahy*
> *čas, v ktorom sa nič nedeje...*
> *a chabé nádeje*
> *a chabé nádeje*
> *v ňom odšumeli ako holub plachý.*[9]

> *Lives are composed of bits into a balance sheet*
> *by time, in which nothing happens...*
> *and flimsy hopes*
> *and flimsy hopes*
> *have whirred off in it like a timid dove.*

Every day during my stay in Mikuláš I spent several hours lying idle on Sekerka Hill, and, just as during those old times that had aged too quickly, I let my eyes wander after the sailing clouds, the flight of birds and the motion of their wings. Wreaths of smoke left behind by passing trains hailed me like memories of childhood and of what had been, and then that all withdrew briefly in the embrace of the soft grass and drowned in the scent of basil thyme and wild thyme.

What I desperately needed and would have cost more than I could afford, was a winter coat. In Mr Haas's attic there was a huge shelf running the whole length of one wall and on it whole piles of grey woollen blankets. They'd been abandoned by the fleeing Germans. I asked Mr Haas to let me have one. When he refused, on the grounds that the blankets were the property of the state, I went up to the attic when he wasn't in and took one of them with the same feeling as I had during the "organizing" of items from the SS collection points. The parents of a classmate dyed it green for me in their cleaner's shop. I paid to have a coat made from it out of the money I had earned. I wore my coat of "organized" cloth for the next ten years. And when I first went to Denmark on a student exchange in the autumn of 1945, my Mikuláš boots attracted attention for their natural elegance.

That summer, racketeering and the backstreet traffic in hard currencies were the order of the day. The buying and selling of foodstuffs, fabrics, clothing, electrical appliances, kitchenware and goodness knows what else was all done underhand. A group of former resistance fighters deputized for the police in the fight against the black market. The numbers of Russian soldiers, our liberators, on our streets just grew and grew. They would block my way in Vyšný Hušták, stop my bike on the road to Okoličné, ask me why I was riding so crazily, and they would rip off my headscarf to see what I looked like "for real". Officers would invite me to their private quarters, but a firm *No* was enough and things carried on as normal.

I became friends with Martin, a teacher at the Protestant church school. He was a member of the Communist Party and, on long walks in the local woods, valleys and villages, we would discuss politics and the possibility of creating a free world without wars, violence and racism. We both believed sincerely that our dreams would come true, we went to Party meetings together, we were convinced of the science-based truth of dialectical materialism and its ultimate discovery of all the rules of nature that would be taken in hand for the benefit of all mankind. We both liked poetry and read Laco Novomeský and Vítězslav Nezval, we sang the songs of Voskovec and Werich and Burian's Liberated Theatre. Today I know that somewhere in the darkness of the irrational me, I'd been led astray by fireflies, that by the Váh sat Lorelei, singing that since there's a hell, there's also a paradise – *und nach dem Winter kommt wieder ein Mai* [Winter will be followed by another May]. But seven years of personal experience of putting ideology into practice had to pass before I acknowledged this exposure of myself. The following description is a scene from the cabaret of my own life. Or maybe the tragicomedy? One or the other.

I was sitting in the restaurant of the Hotel Kriváň writing, when a Red Army officer wearing a dark-green peaked dress cap asked if he might join me.

"My name is Viktor Gavrilich and I know who you are and what your name is. I saw you at a Party meeting. I have a job to do and am hoping you won't deny me your assistance," he said, taking the seat opposite me.

When I asked him what that job was, he replied that he needed information about people who'd been fascists during the war or who'd collaborated with the fascists.

"Since you know all about me, you must also know that I wasn't here during the war, but spent its entire duration in a concentration camp," I said.

"Yes, I do know all that, but also that you were here when Slovakia became a fascist state. I've got some photos of seven men here and I'd be grateful if you can help me identify them."

"I hate pointing a finger at people and won't identify anyone!" I replied indignantly, and Viktor Gavrilich stopped talking about fascists and began telling me about his wife Masha, his three sons and the terrible things that they'd been through during the siege of Leningrad, and that during his fifty-year lifespan he'd had enough grief for two lives. But after this break he went back to his original topic.

"I'm not going to force you into anything. I'll show you the photos and you can make up your own mind whether your assistance is essential or not. You might as well look at them anyway."

"All right. I can have a look, but I'm making no promises."

"You don't have to. But it's a bit too risky to show you them here, at the table. And walls have ears and I still need to explain certain things to you. This whole thing has to be done behind closed doors," he assured me.

I began to suspect what this man in the green peaked cap with such a grave expression on his weary face and deep wrinkles about his mouth and ears was really after, while I was also conscience-stricken for doubting the credibility of an officer of the Red Army.

"So what do you suggest?" I asked.

"We'll go to your room."

"Not likely!"

"You don't trust me then," he said with reproachful pathos.

So I decided to take him to my room, knowing full well how stupid that was, but telling myself that I was only doing it to reassure myself that my trust in the Soviet Union was not misplaced.

Viktor Gavrilich left the door of my room open. "Anyone's welcome to see what we're doing," he declared.

"Don't my walls have ears?" I hazarded.

He went to the door and glanced out into the corridor.

No one there.

We sat on my ancient divan and Viktor Gavrilich ran off again on the subject of starvation and the multiple deaths of his family and friends in Leningrad. After a brief pause he hinted that now was the moment to look at those photos, but that first we should lock the door. He leapt to his feet, turned the key in the lock, came back, grabbed me, forced me down onto the divan and shrieked: "I love you! I've loved you ever since I first set eyes on you and have thought of nothing else. I want you!"

He hurled himself at me with the full weight of his body and tried to remove my pants. I fought back, defending myself tooth and nail, kicking him and screaming: "What are you doing? You've got a wife and kids! Can't you see the damage you're doing to my faith in the Soviet Union?"

Viktor Gavrilich, who'd probably been through nothing like this in his entire life, gabbled, "I was lying. I have no wife and kids!" and shifted his position so as to get his Party ID card from an inside pocket with his free hand and offer me proof that he was no longer lying. "Look. I'm single and I'm not fifty. Only thirty!"

Only when I started feigning a heart attack, groaning and choking, did he let go of me before crossing to the washbasin, and as he was washing in cold water I managed to open the window and start shouting: "Emília! Help! I'm being raped in room 33!"

Emília came running with a bunch of keys, quite out of breath after climbing the stairs, but Viktor Gavrilich had already opened the door and fled.

"Serve you right, idiot!" said Emília. "What did you expect, taking a soldier to your room, of your own accord!? But you can, if you want, report him to his headquarters. It's the death penalty for things like this!"

I didn't report Viktor Gavrilich. I was merely furious at my own unforgivable stupidity.

14

Martin and I would go for walks around Mikuláš, including parts I thought I'd never seen before. One Sunday morning, with all the church bells ringing, we went further afield. We walked along the Váh. The Gypsy settlement was just as I remembered it. Here the old had been replaced by the old, the threadbare by the threadbare, and everything had merged into the original image of Gypsy life. A number of ragged children followed us across Iľanovo Bridge. We stood on it to watch the Váh flow by. I felt sorry for the islets and bends undone by its regulated flow, which seemed to have wrested its natural playfulness from it. I was reminded how many colours and smells, how great a sense of security and alluring mystique once went with the words "the road to Iľanovo and Ploštín".

We stopped at a village inn. Behind the bar was an elderly woman with a generous crown of black hair flecked with grey. Her face seemed to express smiling Sunday. Through the open door, rays of sunshine lit up the wooden floor. We ordered a glass of stout, went out into the garden and sat on a bench beneath an ancient linden tree. I told Martin how I'd decided to go to university in Prague, but would stop off in Bratislava and seek out my two sisters. He extracted a slim volume from his pocket and gave it to me to remember him by. It was Laco Novomeský's verse collection *Svätý za dedinou* [The saint beyond the village]. To this day, one of the poems in it, *Neskutočný hostinec* [The imaginary inn], summons up for me the aura of late summer in Liptov.

Sme v malom hostinci, v nedeľu predpoludním,
v tom – u nás na rohu – keď ešte nik v ňom nie je,
tu pod stromami prevrátených fliaš
na obrus kvetovaný.

A pozri, hľa, aj okno rozbité
v tých prasklých vláknach jemnej pavučiny;
nohy múch lapených v nich visia čínskym písmom,
ktorému nerozumiem.

Krčmárka – jak by nie? – má plné ruky práce,
poznám ju po zástere:
biela hmla mihoce sa v ľahostajnom slnku,
drozd v čiernom fraku ma v nej obskakuje;
ach, nikdy nie sme sami
v samote s predstavami,
v pustine nájdu krčmu pre tuláka.

„Pán hlavný platiť!
Na obed som mal plný tanier slnka
a večer mliečnu dráhu."

We're in a little inn, it's Sunday morning,
the one – near us, at the corner – when no one else is here yet,
here beneath a covert of bottles overturned
on the floral table-cloth.

And look, see, a broken window as well
amid the snapped threads of a delicate cobweb;
the legs of flies trapped in them hang like Chinese writing
that I don't understand.

The landlady – how could it be otherwise? – is working flat out,
I recognize her by her apron:
a white haze flickering in the impassive sunlight,
in the haze a dress-coated blackbird dances attendance on me;
oh, we're never alone
when alone with our imaginings,
in a wilderness they'll find an inn for the vagrant.

"Waiter, I'd like to pay!
For lunch I had a plateful of sunlight
and this evening a milky way."

Today, whenever I look back at the story of my life, shortened by retrospection, it seems to have been full of such "imaginary inns" and that I had often been a vagrant combing the junkshops of ironic narratives, an idler roaming round vanity fairs, a visitor to the stockroom of mirrors of the twentieth century, now ended, but spilling over into the new, twenty-first, as a swollen river spills out into the sea.

Beneath the mulberry tree – in the yard of the Vyšný Hušták house that had twice been our home, once upstairs with the courtyard gallery, once facing the revenue office, where there was also a print shop, from where the blue-eyed printer from Vrbica would smile up at us as we sat in the kitchen window on the first floor, picking from the tall, branching tree the fresh fruits that bled beneath our finger tips – I bade farewell to the town where I grew up.

15

One cold September day in 1945, outside the General Secretariat of the Communist Party, opposite Prague's Powder Gate, I bumped into Ružena from Rajsko.

"Ruženka! What a surprise! How are you? What are you doing?" I said by way of greeting.

"Labour be honoured, Comrade![10] I'm doing what I've always done – contributing to the victory of the working class, and I hope you're doing likewise! What's that you're wearing? Why are you going about Prague dressed like some petty-bourgeois dame? Dress like a Communist!" Ružena replied before turning away and carrying on down Celetná Street. My eyes followed her purposeful, erect back as I wondered what she imagined "dressing like a Communist" looked like. The one obvious thing was that my black-and-grey chequered, mid-length, woollen coat, extracted from the heap of clothes donated by UNRRA, did not fit her image of it.

In my youth, I was keen to see poverty and injustice eliminated and the rule of social equity and human solidarity take their place, and very briefly, but intensely, and as a symbol of the possible reification of this desire, it seemed to have been met in Liptovský Svätý Mikuláš in August 1937. In the Rohonci Garden, some socialist students from Prague held a rally of solidarity between the intelligentsia and the working class, accompanied by cabaret songs and poetry meant to be a deterrent against Nazism and a celebration of freedom.

Posters intended to draw people in from the mountains, outlying villages and all the surrounding area worked to good effect and peasants and journeymen, workers from the factories and tanneries with their wives and children, students, teachers and civil servants duly showed up in their Sunday best. They all shared home-made bread, bacon, ham, sausages, cheese and hard-boiled eggs brought in baskets. And throughout there was an air of expectation, spirits were high and there was a general gaiety. Brightly coloured balloons, filled to bursting with the insubstantiality and ephemerality of illusions, floated over the dark-red wooden tables and benches and above the treetops. And the students sang songs and recited poems, many of them about love. To this day I can hear the voice of one Prague literature student, his dark curls falling across his forehead, as he delivered Fráňa Šrámek's[11] poem "In the shadow of my long hair, my boy has fallen asleep, should I wake him?" and I can still feel my tingling responsiveness and the wistful, nebulous expectancy that in those vagarious times on the threshold of totalitarianism was gradually transforming us into melancholy rebels. And I can remember how I imagined Prague as a city where everything longed-for, even if remote, was actually quite close.

And now I was living and studying in this city, where the history of Europe resounded in every footstep I took, and where I desired to enrich my restored identity with knowledge of every kind, nourishing it with poetry, literature, music, politics, love and friendships. Now was not the time to attempt to process my recent traumatic experiences, nor was this the place for recalling the ordeals of the past when now the lead roles were taken by hope and the construction of the future. My contradictory feelings, enthusiasms, the suppression of doubts, my current interest in Marx and Kafka, Lenin and Lautréamont, Rilke, Brecht and Orwell, in all the books in the world that were accessible, I had to keep on a tight rein like horses with different pedigrees and sizes hitched to the same cart. And to crown it all, I would sing with great gusto "Left foot forward, no sliding back!"[12] just like all my comrades who, like me, had built up their convictions on "a scientific basis".

Student life was a celebration of every day of liberation. We fertilized and irrigated the days with wine and songs accompanied by whatever instruments were to hand, even a diatonic accordion, with debates, persuasion, winning new adherents and mettlesome proselytizing in people's rooms, corridors, on staircases, all through the night till the break of day. Food was still rationed. One egg a week, though food for the soul was in ample supply.

It was into this atmosphere that some students from Denmark arrived in the summer of 1946. Relaxed, tolerant young men and women, students from faculties of architecture, law and Slavonic studies, among them my future husband. In Czechoslovakia, the only country in Central Europe to have remained a democracy after the war, they wanted to shake off the dust of five years of occupation and see for themselves how "West" and "East" were coming together. They came well supplied with every kind of tinned food, salamis and triangles of cheese. And they were happy to share them with us. Having discovered that our debates were more than just squabbles, they enjoyed to the full the high spirits of Roosevelt Hall. When we asked them what they were taking home with them from their trip they said: "HOPE!"

After the first political trials I changed from being a reliable member of the new society to being an unreliable alien element in a socialist system being cleansed of noxious influences. According to my first personnel file of 1948 I was: "A renaissance woman and well-informed expert in philosophy and six languages, and a loyal Party member." According to my second file of 1952 I'd become: "A bourgeois nationalist, she dresses in a cosmopolitan style – a possible spy who consorts with foreigners." To be my friend was too risky because I was suspected of collaborating with hostile foreign elements. This assessment was the handiwork of Jozef, the (Party) personnel officer at my faculty. He wanted to be rid of me because I knew that he'd been in prison during the war for dirty dealings on the black market, and not, as he maintained, for being in the anti-fascist resistance. This all had very unpleasant consequences for me, and the whole affair was a constant reminder of the frailty, opportunism, cowardice and capriciousness of human nature, though also of the courage and integrity of some individuals. My "one just man" was called Sergei. He came in the night to warn me of a plot whereby the personnel man was enlisting hangers-on and turning them against me with promises of getting them posted abroad. Thanks to Sergei and a handful of other "just men" I did manage to complete my studies and secure an editorial post with Czechoslovak Radio. But there, too, I was under constant surveillance and the tally of my imaginary sins went up by one real one: I failed to shed a tear when Stalin died.

16

Early in 1956 I moved to Denmark. I swapped the Tatras for Øresund and for a long time I could still detect in the sea air the scent of fir needles and dwarf pines, in the clouds I saw outlines of the high peaks of the Tatras and of the ruins of Liptov's castles, and in the blue between the clouds, "there at the foot of the mountains", flowed the Váh. After five years in Denmark I became a Danish writer, a translator of poetry and prose, I worked for Danish Radio, filing reports from Slovakia and Czechia, I gave hundreds of lectures all over Denmark, and after my daughters grew up I began flying to all corners of the world with my husband, who worked for the United Nations.

When, after many years, I saw the Auschwitz Gate again, I didn't go through it. I left that to the TV reporters and cameramen.

I stood in front of the gate in a kind of silent, boundlessly awesome landscape with its own dawn and its own dusk, and from somewhere far, far away, between light and dark, came an echo of a dog yapping, the barking of orders, the swish of a whip, and silence took over once more. Like an outline of the camp drawn with a very fine pencil, this image came to me like a flashback of a black-and-white movie as required for an appreciation of its historic role in a re-issue of an ancient narrative.

It felt as if it had been someone else who, beyond the Auschwitz Gate, had seen, heard and lived through the absurdly megalomanic villainy of it. Yet, it *was* me who'd been held here and who had, luckily, succeeded in transforming an exceedingly abnormal trauma into a fact of life and in living on as the gift of life warrants it. It is only my dreams that refuse to adapt to the time lapse, the relativization afforded by history, and to let oblivion have its way. In my nightmares I am visited by the past in symbolic images and their various permutations:

I am crawling out from under the ground and up a mountain of trash. It's getting dark. Up over some wilting, slippery, rotting cabbage leaves and carrots a train is plodding along, smoke rising, sparks flying. On the slopes of the rubbish heap, in the half-light, flitter flurries of birds. The train gets nearer. The shadow of the huge locomotive grows and blots out the sky. I crawl to beyond its reach, floundering in the slimy mess, lose my footing and fall into a void.

I'm in the middle of a vast plain. Its long, wide expanse has nothing but trees, grass and some footpaths through the grass. No sign at all of human habitation, or humans.

Where the trees thin out, there are some fields. I can sense their smell. Fields have smelled like that since time immemorial. I know that somewhere, hiding among the lilacs, there are soldiers, and here's a barbed-wire fence covered in flowers, and that's the muted flapping of some large wings.

The air tastes like iron.

I turn round. I have to get back. This used to be a tram route. Somewhere there has to be the terminus. A tram shed. But everywhere is just grass, sand and desolation, and over there, in the open, behind some invisible lilacs, lies darkness.

I'm walking down an interminably long footpath between areas of grass. I'm brought up short by a waterworks. It's quite noisy. It hides the sky behind its grey concrete. It has a tall tower crowned with seven little turrets. Seven tiny windows.

A door set in the tower silently opens, melts away and turns into steam. Behind the door is another, and behind that a third and a narrow corridor with nothing but a forgotten coatstand and at the far end a glass door.

On the lonely coatstand hangs a brown coat.

The corridor, coatstand and coat exude a savage coldness like a washery in winter or filthy, ice-coated snow.

A black Alsatian is sniffing gruffly at my long men's trousers. Snaps at them. Growls. Bares its teeth. Lets out a throaty sound like a coarsely plaited rope. I run for it. But the distance between the doors is too short. The door handles have become interlocked and in every corner and behind every door there's a dog snarling and it feels as if everything about me that had once been white is now exhausted for good.

I go out into the early evening onto a footpath between areas of grass. The place seems familiar. It was here, at this very spot, that I used to wait, beneath a street lamp that hadn't come on yet, near a clock that used to chime out the time.

It's October, around seven in the evening, but the clock has dematerialized, stopped, doesn't show the time, doesn't chime, and my legs are growing limp, torpid, gasping for breath. I'm dragging them along behind me, step by step, one step, then another, and suddenly I see them. They're standing by the path in broken lines, like a Morse code. Each dot is the muzzle of a pistol. Each dash a tight-lipped grin. They move towards me. Surround me. The one who leads me away is wearing a brown coat.

Sometimes I feel like a drifter, a wanderer from one memory to the next, one image to the next, from nights to days, from one stage to the next in the unreal reality that constitutes almost the totality of Europe's twentieth century, "that dance across heads, that music of inverted words, perverted minds, topsy-turvy dreams" (Laco Novomeský). Many things distress me, many alarm me and many make me happy. My inner firmament has not been clouded over by even the worst of the whirlwinds of history.

In my present the past lives on. Words silenced. Explosions frozen. Movements arrested. Smoke blown away. Screams with memory loss. In it, time marches on: Left, right... Left, right... It crosses the boundaries of human existence, reaches back for shadows in the wind, says goodbye to battlefields, gallows and piles of rubble. But it does carry with it warnings to be on the lookout for signs of new catastrophes, explosions of totalitarianism, and the peril of hankerings after a totalitarian past.

And hope, too, lives on in me, the hope that I inherited from my young parents. Love and sorrow, pain and joy have all constructed a haven inside me. They carry the scent of straw, and the breath of all that lives closest blends into a luminous certainty.

Prague. Bridges over Vltava.

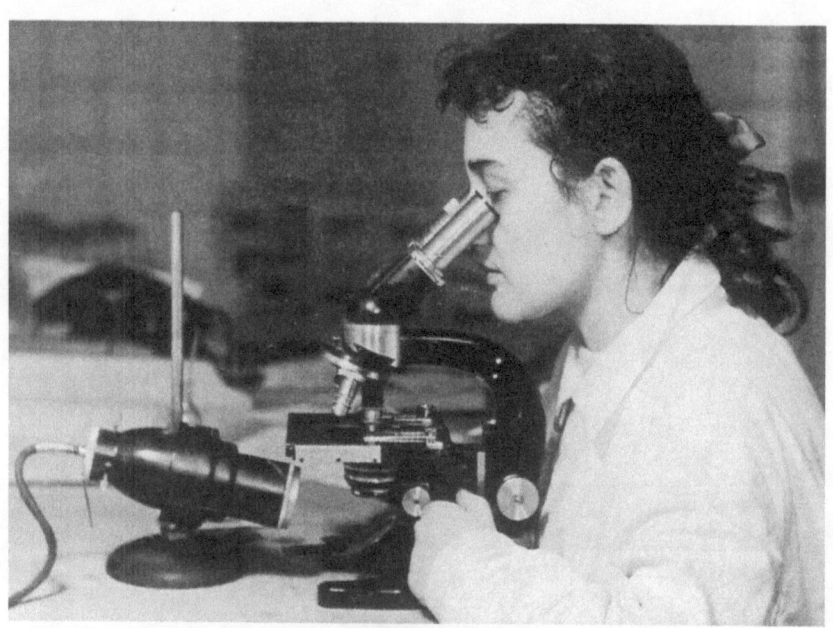

Lila.

With Danish architecture students: Søren, Dea, Grethe, Aage and Ida in Prague 1946.

A song for friends I should soon disappoint with my political stance.

In front of Magdeburg railway station on tour with the Danish Broadcasting Corporation. Older railway workers could still remember the cattle wagons with concentration camp prisoners standing on the railway tracks during one of the major air bombardments in the winter of 1945. From the left: Aage Pedersen, me, Benny Rasmussen and my husband Otto.

I had become a member of the Danish Author Society, 1965.

Kerteminde 1969. In the middle of life.

The three sisters.

NOTES

Once upon a time

1. Because of the name of the village, derived from the noun *vŕba* [willow].
2. This because the name of the town, which contains the morpheme *div*, coextensive with the noun meaning "wonder", "miracle" etc.
3. Today, more simply, Liptovský Mikuláš, often referred to herein as simply Mikuláš, a town in Northern Slovakia, in the 19th century a major centre of Slovak culture.
4. I.e. the synagogue.
5. She is speaking Czech here.
6. Usu. *Waag* in English. A major tributary of the Danube that flows round north-western and western Slovakia.
7. Built in 1842-46; it is now a concert hall.
8. The apple trees are just part of the young girl's imaginings. The song only mentions roses and parsley.
9. Title song used to promote the eponymous 1928 silent adventure film-romance.
10. A song written by Ray Henderson, Buddy De Sylva and Lew Brown and sung by Al Jolson in the 1928 part-talkie *The Singing Fool*.
11. In 1 Samuel 27.
12. A reference to the poem *Smrť Jánošikova* [The Death of Jánošík] from 1862 by Slovak Romantic poet Ján Botto.
13. Milan Rastislav Štefánik, Slovak politician and a leading member of the Czechoslovak National Council, founded by Czech and Slovak émigrés during World War I involved with the cause of Czechoslovak sovereignty.
14. Czech authors of books published in the "Library for Girls" edition.
15. *Braunbuch über Reichstagsbrand und Hitlerterror*, Paris, 1933.
16. Named after Michal Miloslav Hodža (1811-1870), a leading figure of Slovak national movement in the 1840s.
17. The opening words of many Central-European folk or fairy tales.
18. The militia maintained by the fascist Hlinka's Slovak People's Party.
19. Elsewhere described as hills, interpretable as the Tatra, Fatra and Matra ranges.

Flight

1. i.e. "Slovaks".
2. "kaiserlich und königlich", the pre-WWI attributes of the Austro-Hungarian Empire.

3. A variation of the material collected by the Grimm brothers as *Die drei Männlein im Walde*; instead of three men, it contains twelve men. They create a miracle to help a girl who is ordered by her wicked stepmother to go out into the forest in winter and bring back violets, and then strawberries.
4. Anita Lasker-Wallfisch, MBE (1925-), a German Jew from Breslau, survivor of Bergen-Belsen and founder of the English Chamber Orchestra.
5. "Seventh Heaven of Love" (Dancing Through The Skies), a song by Lilian Harvey from the film *Sieben Ohrfeigen* [Seven slaps in the face], composed by Friedrich Schröder, 1937.

Darkness. Pages from a retrospective diary

1. This is a reference to Jakubowska's drama *Ostatni etap* [*The Last Stage*], 1948.

A Long, Slow Dawning

1. In the Mecklenburg lake district.
2. Small towns in the centre of the area between Leipzig and Dresden.
3. On April 25, 1945.
4. As I translate this, there are exactly similar reports of the doings of criminal members of Vladimir Putin's army in Ukraine.
5. Juraj Jánošík, the legendary 17th-century Slovak outlaw who would become a symbol of resistance against oppression.
6. *Rohonczi* in the author's day.
7. The militia maintained by the fascist Slovak People's Party in the period 1938-45.
8. A few miles south-east of Mikuláš.
9. From *Pašovanou ceruzkou* [With a smuggled pencil] by Laco Novomeský (1904-1976), Slovak Communist author and politician.
10. The conventional salutation of Czechoslovak Communists, *Česť práci!*
11. Czech impressionist poet and an anarchist (1877-1952).
12. *Kupředu levá, zpátky ani krok*, one of the best-known Czech propaganda songs in the period of the "construction of socialism".

Interview with the Author

1. Published in the second Slovak edition of the book (2016) and authorized again in 2025.
2. Political show trial with high-ranking Czech Communist politician Rudolf Slánský (1901-1952), instigated by Stalin to ensure the loyalty of Czechoslovakia to the USSR. Slánský was one of fourteen leaders arrested in 1951, tortured into confessing their "crimes", and charged with high treason.
3. Olga Scheinpflugová (1902-1968), Czech actress and writer, wife of the writer Karel Čapek.

4. Now known as ČKD (Českomoravská Kolben-Daněk), this was and is one of the largest engineering companies in former Czechoslovakia and today's Czech Republic.
5. An agreement between Nazi Germany, the United Kingdom, France, and Italy signed on 30 September 1938 in Munich, which provided for the German annexation of part of Czechoslovakia called the Sudetenland, populated by more than three million people, mainly ethnic Germans.

INTERVIEW WITH THE AUTHOR

By Dobrota Pucherová (2025) and Ján Púček (2016)[1]

DP: You were born into a Slovak family, but you have a Hungarian first name. Why?

IWH: Both of my parents were born in Austria-Hungary. My mother in Piešťany. She had family in Budapest and she visited them as a young woman. There was this popular song at the time: "Ibolya, lila Ibolya, ez a bánom, semmi más" [Ibolya, violet Ibolya, this is my regret, nothing else.] My mother liked the song and she told herself: if I have a daughter, her name will be Iboja (i.e., Ibolya Slovakized). I remember the song and can sing it.

DP: This also explains why your sister is called Lila. Is there any particular reason why you have named your daughters Anne-Léna and Nina Eva?

IWH: No. They are universal names.

DP: You wrote your memoir many years after the events you describe happened. The first edition of *The Mulberry Tree* was

published in 1991. How were you able to remember so many details and names? Your narrative is also very coherent, in contrast to the confusing and absurd events you describe.

IWH: I wrote *The Mulberry Tree* in one go and I realized that I remembered everything in detail. My brain recorded everything, like a movie, so that later I could put it into my writing. In *The Mulberry Tree*, I write: "I register that despite my eternal fatigue, despite being relocated into a topsy-turvy world, I am still taking in everything going on around me with precision and lucidity. Later, all happenings were to spill out into a kind of patience-saturated twilight, where the horror of reality had become blurred and pain diluted. Misty ahead, misty behind. Yet without any conscious effort on my part, every impression passed through this benevolent mist to sink deep into my memory."

DP: How did you deal with describing things that elude language? Did you read other memoirs about Auschwitz before writing your own? Did it help you verbalize your experiences?

IWH: With poetic language, you can express everything. I am a poet. Poetry can express any feelings. I was born with a sense for language. I did not need to read about it. I was there. Writing the book helped me to heal. I could not forget Auschwitz, but I did not allow it to poison the rest of my life. And there is in the world so much to learn and experience.

DP: Did you read any Holocaust memoirs?

IWH: Yes. I read Imre Kertész and Primo Levi. They describe the same experiences, to which they react differently. They made a deep impression on me, but they did not influence my own memoir. The reason I wrote *The Mulberry Tree* was because I was asked to do it by the director of Gyldendal. While they were waiting for me to write it, they published a collection of my poems.

DP: Did you read the memoir by Rudolf Vrba, *I Escaped from Auschwitz*?

IWH: I met Rudo Vrba for the first time around 1939, he must have been about 16, at the Jewish School in Mikuláš, where my mother was a teacher and we lived across the school yard. The school building was large and two rooms were assigned to Jewish refugees, who were mainly young Czech and Polish girls from Silesia. Rudo came to Mikuláš to check out the girls and that is how we met.

The second time I met him was in Auschwitz. It was very brief, we happened to meet on the camp road and we exchanged a few sentences. Any longer talk was dangerous. The fact that Vrba and Wetzler then managed to trick the SS was an unbelievable miracle and for us, the other prisoners, it was extremely encouraging, almost like when the dead come to life, and suddenly we could hope to return home one day.

The last time I met him was in 1968 in Copenhagen. He came there to see his two daughters by his first wife Gerta, who had emigrated from Czechoslovakia and was staying temporarily in Copenhagen on her way to Britain. We met and talked for a long time.

I learned of Vrba's exceptional courage, integrity and intelligence from Lanzmann's documentary film *Shoah*, and later on when I read his testimony.

DP: How did you perceive the fact that the Allies did not bombard the gas chambers or even the railway tracks leading to the camp, even after Vrba and Wetzler escaped and were able to tell the world? Did you perceive it as a betrayal?

IWH: The Allies bombarded Auschwitz only after the Germans were almost defeated. Our explanation for this was that it was most important to defeat the Germans and that the bombs would have killed everyone. I remember how overjoyed we were when he heard about Stalingrad, but all of this was tempered by patience, which was most important for our survival, and the necessity of paying attention to every-day challenges. What was happening in Auschwitz was *ad absurdum* and could not be compared to anything normal.

DP: How was it possible for you to keep your humanity in this death factory?

IWH: As a child I read Slovak fairy tales where evil is always defeated by goodness. It was thanks to the ethical values I received from my parents, their love and interest in social injustice, literature and art of all kinds. What they had given me, Auschwitz could not undo.

JP: How do you reflect on the war's aftermath? You must have had very mixed feelings – on the one hand, you were grieving after your dead family members, on the other, you were happy that some survived...

IWH: When the war ended, my sister Lila and I returned to Mikuláš. That was in June 1945 – it was night, the moon was up and by its light we could see that the war had left its mark on the town. The tiny flat in Nižný Hušták, into which my parents, brother and sister had been moved as to a kind of ghetto – I'd learned its address in Žilina – and where there was no one waiting for us, was charged with a cold, burglarized emptiness. The moonlight was falling on the only piece of furniture left, an old divan. We sat down and, without speaking, just waited for what we felt had to come, the final stroke after the many that had gone before. When it came, it fell like a stone into a deep well. The backsplash didn't reach high. But the well remained. You see, when someone has been a fugitive in Hungary, survived the Auschwitz mass-murder factory behind the thick wall of an uncommunicative world, where each and every minute was an invisible boundary between life and death, and that person did survive only by chance, intuition and a kind of stagnant perseverance imposed by circumstances, that perseverance lives on, misting over mood swings, but sharpening observational skills. And mine were sharpened. My parents and siblings were no more, and no one could replace them. What there had been and remained was the town: the town of Liptovský Svätý Mikuláš, blighted by war, losses, and changes, but still *my* town in the same natural setting and beside the same river, and friends that survived the war, who helped us. Here, for too short a time, unfortunately, lived and worked my enlightened – I have no hesitation in calling them that – parents. Their approach was: never raise a hand to anyone, explain, read, learn, stand on your own two feet even as a woman, and never identify with the image of you held by people ill-disposed towards you. For eighteen years I lived in the democratic Czechoslovak Republic, at school, particularly the grammar school, they taught us tolerance and about our democratic rights, and about the world around us. The Hodža Grammar School made a European of me. To me it didn't matter in the slightest that I was Jewish, but there were people to whom it did matter. The town and the republic were both rich in spirit, culture, poets, literature, philosophy and scholarship. For any young person this was an amazing source of education and experience. After Hitler won in Germany and the subsequent occupation of our country, almost every poet, including my beloved Surrealists, were anti-fascists and Communists. They saw the Soviet Union as our only friend and I, already wrathful over the unjust distribution of wealth, fell under the spell of hope for a more just world and became a leftie. And I have to say that at the time this helped me to live.

JP: You started your new, post-war life in Prague, where you studied and worked for the radio. Did you believe in the

promises of bright future that was to come after the war? When did you start having doubts?

IWH: As a young woman in Prague, I believed that communism was going to save the world from wars, social injustice and everyone would have as much as they needed. I believed this even after Auschwitz. I read Marx, Engels, Lenin, everything about the French Revolution and the Encyclopaedists. In Marx I read that an ideology has to be verified by practice. However, I found that the opposite was the rule and that those kept in check were primarily those who went by Marx's teachings, so I began to watch closely how events unfolded.

I found the first political trials disturbing, and the Slánský trial[2] really opened my eyes and I started to ask questions. The only person to whom I confided my doubts was a Norwegian who worked in the Overseas Section of Czechoslovak Radio. He ratted on me to the boss, who then told me about it.

At university, where I was the only one who knew about dialectical materialism and would help out at seminars with Marxist analyses of texts, the working-class personnel officer, who knew that I knew he had worked the black market during the war, accused me of cosmopolitanism, Trotskyism and petty-bourgeois matrimony. My bourgeois leanings were allegedly expressed in how I dressed and how I'd been inspired by the West. I was threatened with prison for spying. Suddenly my friends stopped speaking to me and I became surrounded by the chill of cold shoulders. Only one classmate came to warn me about the plot. His name was Sergei and he was a Circassian from a White Guard family that had been living in Prague since 1919. I was thrown out of university on the grounds that I'd stopped attending lectures, which was, of course, a lie, as witnessed by my credit book, which showed A's everywhere. An old friend from the Central Committee of the Party, who was jailed two months later for humanistic deviancy, helped me get back to studying.

We studied the history of literature and philosophy through analyzing books – even those that were banned – in a spirit of dialectical materialism only. That struck me as evidence of some mistrust, which was why, one day, I asked Professor Štoll how I could produce an analysis of a book that I hadn't read. He looked at me with an inscrutable smile and said, "You've still got a lot to learn, lassie..." How right he was! By the door stood a young man who'd jotted my words down in a red notebook; he said, "You watch it, you're starting to have doubts..." That was my basic misdemeanour. To have doubts meant to be influenced by the West. The black mark of distrust of the party had stuck to me: "She's been in the West and it's had an effect on her."

After having finished my studies, I got the job in Czechoslovak Radio thanks to a friend who regretted his previous behaviour, though I may have also been taken on because of my extensive knowledge of languages.

The Communist Party of Czechoslovakia, from which the entire pre-war leadership had been removed, was, up until 1968, one of the most dogmatic. Obligatory informing on others and the psychological torture of confessing to ideological sins at meetings depressed me, and even at the Radio it was exploited for the purpose of getting higher-grade jobs, with tragic results.

JP: Your marriage had a fundamental impact on your life trajectory. You met your husband in Prague. How did it happen?

IWH: I met my future husband, Aage, in the summer of 1946 at the Roosevelt Hall of Residence in Prague, at a time when student life was a celebration of every day of freedom. Food was still rationed: we got one egg per week, though food for thought was plentiful. Day and night, over wine or without wine, we would hold vehement, unrestrained, sometimes quite aggressive discussions on the Republic's future regime.

This was the atmosphere that greeted a group of exchange students from Denmark. In Czechoslovakia, the only country in Central Europe to have remained a democracy after the war, they wanted to see for themselves how West and East were coming together. And when these relaxed, tolerant, Nordic students of Architecture, Slavonic Studies and Law discovered that our discussions were more than just petty squabbles, they enjoyed to the full the post-war high spirits of that Prague student summer.

JP: In 1947, you married a Dane and became a Danish citizen. Nine years later you left Czechoslovakia with your husband and settled permanently in Copenhagen. Was this a difficult decision?

IWH: My first husband worked in Prague as an architect. I worked at the Czechoslovak Radio. Working at the Radio was very interesting and in other circumstances I would have stayed there longer. But the atmosphere was awash with absurdity. I was being watched the whole time. They paid me 400 Crowns less than the other editors. The head of department had absolutely no qualms over making me correct articles written by my section head, a working-class woman, and he stamped firmly on any hint of protest on my part. When the dogmatic atmosphere eased somewhat after Stalin's death, they let me produce some items of my own. My last reportage from Czechoslovakia was a talk with Olga Scheinpflugová[3] about Karel Čapek. It was checked over by the female watchdog whose job was to ensure the ideological purity of literary texts; using her red pencil, she randomly crossed out a word here and there. One of my girlfriends was the daughter of the former managing director of Kolben-Daněk[4] who was subjected to a tough interrogation before being permitted to marry a Communist, a jet pilot, and she told me that from her interrogation she gathered that the secret police knew more about me than I knew myself! Finally, one day, we really had enough and left with our three-year-old daughter for Denmark. We left because we felt we had to.

DP: What was it like for you to start a new life in Denmark and start writing?

IWH: It was not difficult at all. I had a Danish husband and immediately became a Danish citizen and his friends became my friends. After some years I started writing. My first story was published in a magazine called *Dialog*, and I got letters from people who said: "Write! You know how to write, and if you write one page a day, you will have a book in a year." It gave me the courage to send my Danish poems, and later also my translations of Czech and Slovak poems into Danish, to the magazine *Hvedekorn* [Grain of Wheat]. The Arena publishing house suggested I publish a whole collection with them. After it came out, Torben Brostrøm, the foremost Danish literary critic at the time, praised my beautiful Danish language. It seems that I'd succeeded in carrying the spirit of melodious, lyrical Slovak over into the Danish language. And so it went on, poems, lyrical verse and songs, books for children, translations of poems and prose with other publishing houses, a lot of broadcasts for Danish Radio, and lectures all over the country. But what delighted me most was when the Danish critic Lilian Røsing wrote of my memoir that I was carrying twentieth-century humanism over into the twenty-first century, and suggested it as 2001's book of the year.

DP: What was it like to write your memoir in your adopted language, Danish? Was it even possible to write such deeply intimate memories in an adopted language?

IWH: Languages come to me easily. Danish is like Slovak. Or German. Or English. Or whatever language I have learned in the countries I have lived in. I switch easily from one language to another. My mother was a teacher and could speak Slovak,

Hungarian and German fluently, and a fairly decent French. At home we were bilingual, Slovak and German, then in grammar school I had French and Latin, and I was taught English privately. When I was a refugee in Hungary, I learned Hungarian. When I moved to Denmark, I learned to speak and write Danish in a year. When I lived in Iran with my husband, I learned Farsi. In Kenya, I learned Swahili.

DP: What was it like to then translate yourself into Slovak? What was the impulse for the Slovak edition?

IWH: Of course, I never forgot Slovak. Writing *The Mulberry Tree* first in Danish and then in Slovak felt natural to me. I have always been a cultural link between Denmark and Slovakia – for this reason I have received an award from the Slovak Embassy and was appointed an honorary citizen of Liptovský Mikuláš.

DP: Were you able to keep in touch with your sisters, Lila and Dalma, after you emigrated to Denmark?

IWH: Yes, we kept in touch, by phone and visits. Lila settled in Prague, where she studied medicine and specialized in tropical diseases. Dalma lived in Bratislava and became an actress. Together with her husband Juraj Spitzer she had been involved in the anti-fascist resistance in 1944. We three sisters were in contact throughout our lives, as much as was possible under socialism. Dalma visited me every summer for six weeks and from morning to evening everyone could hear us talk, laugh and sing in Slovak. I will always remember the last words of my father, when we were leaving illegally to go to Hungary: "You will make it!" And we did, all three of us. Unfortunately, I am the only one left behind.

DP: All over the world we see the rise of the extreme right and antisemitism, even in the oldest democracies such as France, Germany and the USA. Do you observe the same tendencies in

Denmark? Do you see patterns that resemble the rise of the extreme right in the Europe of the 1930s? Why is it happening again?

IWH: Unfortunately I see similar patterns, also in Denmark, yes, but not to the same extent. After all wars you say "never again". And here we are. Of course there are reasons, obvious and hidden, but mostly it is about striving for power. Disrespect for human lives, violence and lies as a political weapon are sadly on the rise again. And the future is unpredictable. Why is it happening? That is a very complicated question. But if you look at the world you see democracy fighting against dictatorship, hope against insecurity; nationalism and populism are spreading, extreme ideologies are growing, we still have social inequities, fake information and lack of diplomacy which are turning the world into an insecure place.

DP: Does the current war in Ukraine remind you of World War II?

IWH: The war in Ukraine, everything that has led to it and the current situation remind me of what happened to Czechoslovakia after the Munich Agreement.[5]

DP: When you compare contemporary young people – in their twenties – with you at that age, what are the differences?

IWH: Basically, the young people here in Denmark have the same feelings, ideas, dreams, fears, insecurities and determination that we had. They are also different from my generation – they have fewer taboos and more freedom, they can travel all over the world and have much more independence than we had at their age. Many of them are doing something to save the environment and are concerned about the future of the world. I have one granddaughter, Kathrine, out of four grandchildren. She is studying and composing film music at a film school in London.

We are very close and I believe that if the same happened to her, as happened to me, she would act in the same way.

DP: Do you see any reason for optimism today?

IWH: I was born an optimist. At the moment I am very concerned about the unpredictability of world events, but I am very happy about every attempt to save the environment, democracy and human rights on our beautiful blue planet.

ACKNOWLEDGEMENTS

First and foremost I would like to thank my late husband Otto Wandall-Holm, who never stopped believing in me and the importance of my work, and my daughters Lena and Nina for their love, support and patience with my absence, when I wrote, travelled abroad to report and gave lectures throughout Denmark.

Thank you to the Danish writer and poet, the former Director at the publishing house Gyldendal, Klaus Rifbjerg, who strongly urged me to write this book; I'm not sure I would have been written it otherwise.

Thank you to the late poet and editor Ivan Laučík for promoting the Slovak release of *Farewell to the Century* at the publishing house Kalligram and to poet, author and editor at the publishing house Absynt, Ján Púček, for promoting the Slovak release of *The Mulberry Tree*. Without the Slovak version the current English translation of *The Mulberry Tree* would not have become a reality.

Thank you to Dobrota Pucherová for her great effort and persistence in getting this book translated into English and published.

Thank you to translator and author David Short for the beautiful translation of the book from Slovak to English. The translator is eternally grateful to Dr Dobrota Pucherová of Bratislava for the great care which she took over preparation of the final typescript.

Thank you to Angus Blair for stepping in without notice when most needed.

Also thank you to the publisher, Liesbeth Heenk of Amsterdam Publishers, and to my daughter Nina Wandall-Holm for taking on all the work I was too tired to do during the process of getting this book published.

And last but not least, I extend my deepest gratitude for every good review and all the letters I have received from my readers throughout the years.

ABOUT THE AUTHOR AND TRANSLATOR

Iboja Wandall-Holm is a Danish writer and translator born in 1921 in Czechoslovakia, one of the few democracies arising after World War I from the dissolution of the three European empires: Russia, Germany and Austria-Hungary. In 1942, she fled with her younger sister Lila to Hungary to escape deportation to the Nazi death camps. She was caught, but then survived Auschwitz, Birkenau and Ravensbrück. After the war she studied Political Economics in Prague and worked for Czechoslovak Radio there. In 1947 she married a Dane and became a Danish citizen. In 1956 she moved to Copenhagen, where she still lives. As the wife of a United Nations ambassador, she has also lived in Africa, Iran, the USA and Austria.

She writes in both Danish and Slovak. In the early 1960s she began publishing poems, short stories, essays and translations from Czech and Slovak literature. Her first collection of verse, *Digte*, came out in 1965, to be followed by more collections. She joined the Union of Danish Writers and collaborated with Danish Radio. She has also written children's books and collections of songs, translated Slovak fairy tales, as well as Slovak, Czech, Polish, German and Hungarian prose fiction and poetry. In addition, she has written a series of lectures, chronicles and other productions for the Danish Broadcasting Corporation.

In 1991 she published her Holocaust memoir, *Morbærtræet* [The Mulberry Tree] in Danish. It went into a second, expanded edition in 2000 under the title *Farvel til århundredet* [Farewell to the Century]. In 2003, it was published in her own Slovak translation in Bratislava under the title *Zbohom, storočie* [Farewell, Century], reprinted in 2016 and 2021 under the original title *Moruša*.

In recognition of her work, Iboja Wandall-Holm is listed in the Blue Book, an encyclopaedia of people who have significantly enhanced the Kingdom of Denmark.

David Short (1943-) is a prize-winning translator from Czech and Slovak. He took a degree in Russian and French at the University of Birmingham, followed by a year of Slavonic Philology, after which, in 1966, he went to Prague to acquire Czech, remaining there until 1972. From 1973 to 2011 he taught Czech and Slovak at the University of London School of Slavonic and East European

Studies. His translations include works by such major Czech writers as Bohumil Hrabal, Karel Čapek and Vítězslav Nezval, as well as by the author of the first Slovak novel, Jozef Ignác Bajza, in addition to academic works in the fields of art, literature, linguistics and semantics.

AMSTERDAM PUBLISHERS HOLOCAUST LIBRARY

The series **Holocaust Survivor Memoirs World War II** consists of the following autobiographies of survivors:

Outcry. Holocaust Memoirs, by Manny Steinberg

Hank Brodt Holocaust Memoirs. A Candle and a Promise, by Deborah Donnelly

The Dead Years. Holocaust Memoirs, by Joseph Schupack

Rescued from the Ashes. The Diary of Leokadia Schmidt, Survivor of the Warsaw Ghetto, by Leokadia Schmidt

My Lvov. Holocaust Memoir of a twelve-year-old Girl, by Janina Hescheles

Remembering Ravensbrück. From Holocaust to Healing, by Natalie Hess

Wolf. A Story of Hate, by Zeev Scheinwald with Ella Scheinwald

Save my Children. An Astonishing Tale of Survival and its Unlikely Hero, by Leon Kleiner with Edwin Stepp

Holocaust Memoirs of a Bergen-Belsen Survivor & Classmate of Anne Frank, by Nanette Blitz Konig

Defiant German - Defiant Jew. A Holocaust Memoir from inside the Third Reich, by Walter Leopold with Les Leopold

In a Land of Forest and Darkness. The Holocaust Story of two Jewish Partisans, by Sara Lustigman Omelinski

Holocaust Memories. Annihilation and Survival in Slovakia, by Paul Davidovits

From Auschwitz with Love. The Inspiring Memoir of Two Sisters' Survival, Devotion and Triumph Told by Manci Grunberger Beran & Ruth Grunberger Mermelstein, by Daniel Seymour

Remetz. Resistance Fighter and Survivor of the Warsaw Ghetto, by Jan Yohay Remetz

My March Through Hell. A Young Girl's Terrifying Journey to Survival, by Halina Kleiner with Edwin Stepp

Roman's Journey, by Roman Halter

Beyond Borders. Escaping the Holocaust and Fighting the Nazis. 1938-1948, by Rudi Haymann

The Engineers. A memoir of survival through World War II in Poland and Hungary, by Henry Reiss

Spark of Hope. An Autobiography, by Luba Wrobel Goldberg

Footnote to History. From Hungary to America. The Memoir of a Holocaust Survivor, by Andrew Laszlo

Farewell Atlantis. Recollections, by Valentīna Freimane

The Courtyard. A memoir, by Benjamin Parket and Alexa Morris

The Mulberry Tree. The story of a life before and after the Holocaust, by Iboja Wandall-Holm

The Boy in the Back. A True Story of Survival in Auschwitz and Mauthausen, as told to Fern Lebo by Jan Blumenstein

Beneath the Lightless Sky. Surviving the Holocaust in the Sewers of Lvov, by Ignacy Chiger

Mendel Run, by Milton H. Schwartz

The series **Holocaust Survivor True Stories** consists of the following biographies:

Among the Reeds. The true story of how a family survived the Holocaust, by Tammy Bottner

A Holocaust Memoir of Love & Resilience. Mama's Survival from Lithuania to America, by Ettie Zilber

Living among the Dead. My Grandmother's Holocaust Survival Story of Love and Strength, by Adena Bernstein Astrowsky

Heart Songs. A Holocaust Memoir, by Barbara Gilford

Shoes of the Shoah. The Tomorrow of Yesterday, by Dorothy Pierce

Hidden in Berlin. A Holocaust Memoir, by Evelyn Joseph Grossman

Separated Together. The Incredible True WWII Story of Soulmates Stranded an Ocean Apart, by Kenneth P. Price, Ph.D.

The Man Across the River. The incredible story of one man's will to survive the Holocaust, by Zvi Wiesenfeld

If Anyone Calls, Tell Them I Died. A Memoir, by Emanuel (Manu) Rosen

The House on Thrömerstrasse. A Story of Rebirth and Renewal in the Wake of the Holocaust, by Ron Vincent

Dancing with my Father. His hidden past. Her quest for truth. How Nazi Vienna shaped a family's identity, by Jo Sorochinsky

The Story Keeper. Weaving the Threads of Time and Memory - A Memoir, by Fred Feldman

Krisia's Silence. The Girl who was not on Schindler's List, by Ronny Hein

Defying Death on the Danube. A Holocaust Survival Story, by Debbie J. Callahan with Henry Stern

A Doorway to Heroism. A decorated German-Jewish Soldier who became an American Hero, by W. Jack Romberg

The Shoemaker's Son. The Life of a Holocaust Resister, by Laura Beth Bakst

The Redhead of Auschwitz. A True Story, by Nechama Birnbaum

Land of Many Bridges. My Father's Story, by Bela Ruth Samuel Tenenholtz

Creating Beauty from the Abyss. The Amazing Story of Sam Herciger, Auschwitz Survivor and Artist, by Lesley Ann Richardson

On Sunny Days We Sang. A Holocaust Story of Survival and Resilience, by Jeannette Grunhaus de Gelman

Painful Joy. A Holocaust Family Memoir, by Max J. Friedman

I Give You My Heart. A True Story of Courage and Survival, by Wendy Holden

In the Time of Madmen, by Mark A. Prelas

Monsters and Miracles. Horror, Heroes and the Holocaust, by Ira Wesley Kitmacher

Flower of Vlora. Growing up Jewish in Communist Albania, by Anna Kohen

Aftermath: Coming of Age on Three Continents. A Memoir, by Annette Libeskind Berkovits

Not a real Enemy. The True Story of a Hungarian Jewish Man's Fight for Freedom, by Robert Wolf

Zaidy's War. Four Armies, Three Continents, Two Brothers. One Man's Impossible Story of Endurance, by Martin Bodek

The Glassmaker's Son. Looking for the World my Father left behind in Nazi Germany, by Peter Kupfer

The Apprentice of Buchenwald. The True Story of the Teenage Boy Who Sabotaged Hitler's War Machine, by Oren Schneider

Good for a Single Journey, by Helen Joyce

Burying the Ghosts. She escaped Nazi Germany only to have her life torn apart by the woman she saved from the camps: her mother, by Sonia Case

American Wolf. From Nazi Refugee to American Spy. A True Story, by Audrey Birnbaum

Bipolar Refugee. A Saga of Survival and Resilience, by Peter Wiesner

In the Wake of Madness. My Family's Escape from the Nazis, by Bettie Lennett Denny

Before the Beginning and After the End, by Hymie Anisman

I Will Give Them an Everlasting Name. Jacksonville's Stories of the Holocaust, by Samuel Cox

Hiding in Holland. A Resistance Memoir, by Shulamit Reinharz

The Ghosts on the Wall. A Grandson's Memoir of the Holocaust, by Kenneth D. Wald

Thirteen in Auschwitz. My grandmother's fight to stay human, by Lauren Meyerowitz Port

The Jewish Woman Who Fought the Nazis. Bep Schaap-Bedak's life during the Holocaust in Holland, by Eli Schaap

Voices of Resilience. An Anthology of Stories written by Children of Holocaust Survivors, Edited by Deborah (Devora) Ross-Grayman

Dreaming of the River, by Pauline Steinhorn

The series **Jewish Children in the Holocaust** consists of the following autobiographies of Jewish children
hidden during WWII in the Netherlands:

Searching for Home. The Impact of WWII on a Hidden Child,
by Joseph Gosler

Sounds from Silence. Reflections of a Child Holocaust Survivor,
Psychiatrist and Teacher, by Robert Krell

Sabine's Odyssey. A Hidden Child and her Dutch Rescuers,
by Agnes Schipper

The Journey of a Hidden Child,

by Harry Pila and Robin Black

The series **New Jewish Fiction** consists of the following novels, written by Jewish authors. All novels are set in the time during or after the Holocaust.

The Corset Maker. A Novel, by Annette Libeskind Berkovits

Escaping the Whale. The Holocaust is over. But is it ever over for the next generation? by Ruth Rotkowitz

When the Music Stopped. Willy Rosen's Holocaust, by Casey Hayes

Hands of Gold. One Man's Quest to Find the Silver Lining in Misfortune, by Roni Robbins

The Girl Who Counted Numbers. A Novel, by Roslyn Bernstein

There was a garden in Nuremberg. A Novel, by Navina Michal Clemerson

The Butterfly and the Axe, by Omer Bartov

To Live Another Day. A Novel, by Elizabeth Rosenberg

The Right to Happiness. After all they went through. Stories, by Helen Schary Motro

Five Amber Beads, by Richard Aronowitz

To Love Another Day. A Novel, by Elizabeth Rosenberg

Cursing the Darkness. A Novel about Loss and Recovery, by Joanna Rosenthall

The series **Holocaust Heritage** consists of the following memoirs by 2G:

The Cello Still Sings. A Generational Story of the Holocaust and of the Transformative Power of Music, by Janet Horvath

The Fire and the Bonfire. A Journey into Memory, by Ardyn Halter

The Silk Factory: Finding Threads of My Family's True Holocaust Story, by Michael Hickins

Winter Light. The Memoir of a Child of Holocaust Survivors, by Grace Feuerverger

Out from the Shadows. Growing up with Holocaust Survivor Parents, by Willie Handler

Hidden in Plain Sight. A Family Memoir and the Untold Story of the Holocaust in Serbia, by Julie Brill

The Unspeakable. Breaking my family's silence surrounding the Holocaust, by Nicola Hanefeld

Eighteen for Life. Surviving the Holocaust, by Helen Schamroth

Four Survivor Grandparents. Run. Rely. Rebuild, by Jonathan Schloss

Austrian Again. Reclaiming a Lost Legacy, by Anne Hand

The series **Holocaust Books for Young Adults** consists of the following novels, based on true stories:

The Boy behind the Door. How Salomon Kool Escaped the Nazis. Inspired by a True Story, by David Tabatsky

Running for Shelter. A True Story, by Suzette Sheft

The Precious Few. An Inspirational Saga of Courage based on True Stories, by David Twain with Art Twain

Dark Shadows Hover, by Jordan Steven Sher

The Sun will Shine Again, by Cynthia Goldstein Monsour

The Memory Place, by Monica van Rijn

The series **WWII Historical Fiction** consists of the following novels, some of which are based on true stories:

Mendelevski's Box. A Heartwarming and Heartbreaking Jewish Survivor's Story, by Roger Swindells

A Quiet Genocide. The Untold Holocaust of Disabled Children in WWII Germany, by Glenn Bryant

The Knife-Edge Path, by Patrick T. Leahy

Brave Face. The Inspiring WWII Memoir of a Dutch/German Child, by I. Caroline Crocker and Meta A. Evenbly

When We Had Wings. The Gripping Story of an Orphan in Janusz Korczak's Orphanage. A Historical Novel, by Tami Shem-Tov

Jacob's Courage. Romance and Survival amidst the Horrors of War, by Charles S. Weinblatt

A Semblance of Justice. Based on true Holocaust experiences, by Wolf Holles

Under the Pink Triangle. Where forbidden love meets unspeakable evil, by Katie Moore

Amsterdam Publishers Newsletter

Subscribe to our Newsletter by selecting the menu at the top (right) of **amsterdampublishers.com**

www.ingramcontent.com/pod-product-compliance
Lightning Source LLC
LaVergne TN
LVHW091548070526
838199LV00024B/582/J